AF361599

The Suffering Servant
in Aquinas

The Suffering Servant in Aquinas

Isaiah 53 and Thomas's Theology of Christ's Passion

DANIEL R. WALDOW

FOREWORD BY WILLIAM M. WRIGHT IV

The Catholic University of America Press

Washington, D.C.

Copyright © 2024
The Catholic University of America Press
All rights reserved
The paper used in this publication meets the minimum
requirements of American National Standards for Information
Science—Permanence of Paper for Printed Library Materials,
ANSI Z39.48-1992.
∞

Cataloging-in-Publication Data is available
from the Library of Congress

ISBN: 978-0-8132-3888-3
eISBN: 978-0-8132-3889-0

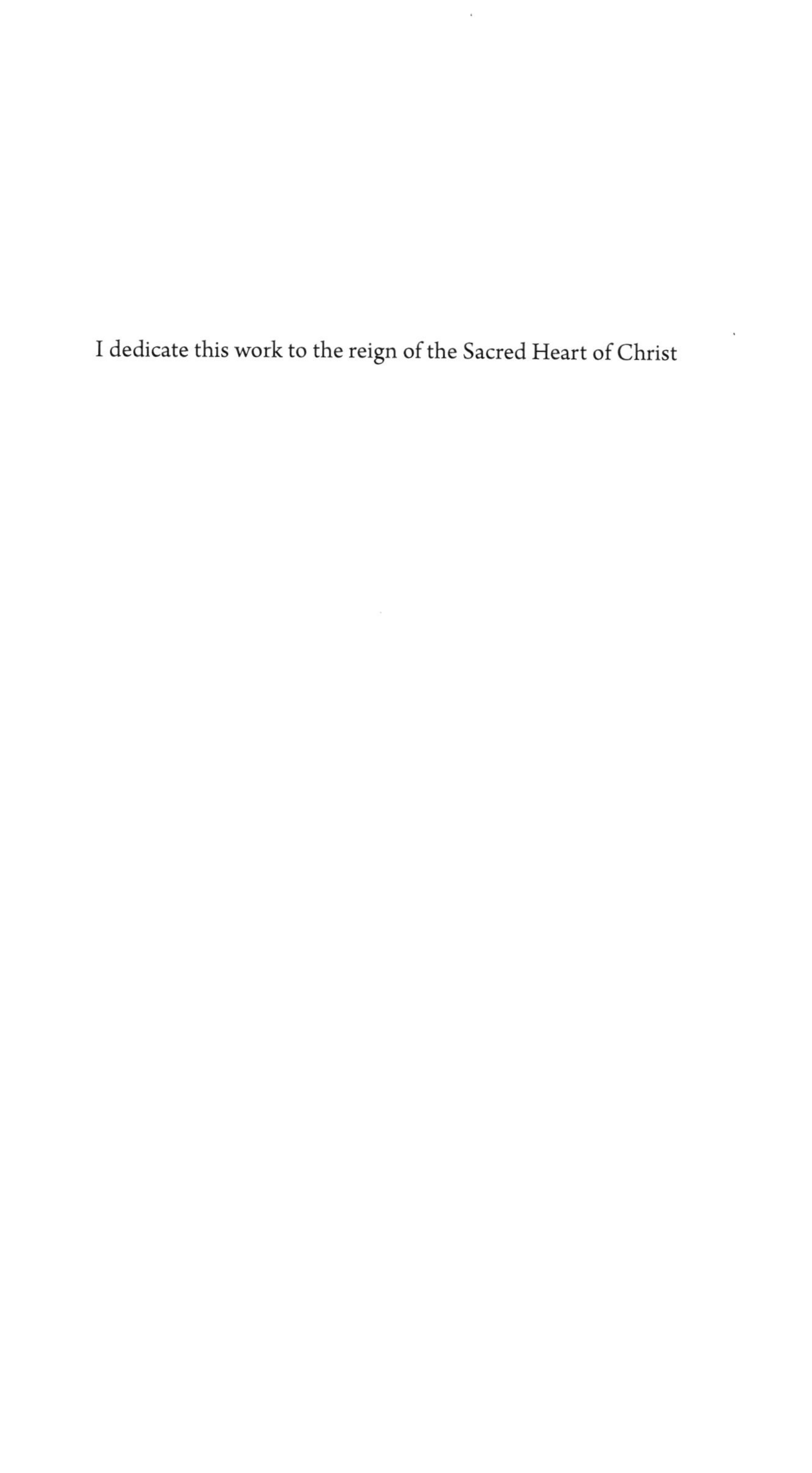

I dedicate this work to the reign of the Sacred Heart of Christ

Table of Contents

Acknowledgments

Because this is my first book, I would like to thank all those who assisted and supported the theological education and research that has led me to this point. Above all, I thank Jesus Christ for the gift of my faith in him and for calling me to serve him as a theologian; my parents, Steve and Kathy, for raising me in the faith and for supporting my theological studies; my siblings, Meghan, Stephen, and Patrick, for living the faith alongside of me in our youth and for encouraging my theological pursuits; my undergraduate professors and classmates at Saint Vincent College, especially John and Jordan; Jim Towey, for all of his help; my graduate professors and classmates at Ave Maria University for fostering my love for the works of St. Thomas Aquinas; the Aquinas Center for Theological Renewal at Ave Maria and the St. Paul Center for Biblical Theology for organizing the 2019 conference "Thomas Aquinas: Biblical Theologian," which sparked my interest in biblical Thomism; Dr. Bill Wright of Duquesne University for suggesting the idea of this book to me and for directing my research for it; Catharine Ryan, for funding my doctoral fellowship; my colleagues at St. Francis University for their encouragement throughout this project; John Martino and the staff at The Catholic University of America Press for their guidance; my in-laws, the Kennas, for their love and support throughout the years; the late Edward Kenna, for his example of *studiositas* and for portions of his Thomistic library; and my beloved children Peter Karol, Emma Therese, Leo Anselm, Magdalena Rose, and the baby, simply for being themselves. Finally, I am forever grateful to my beautiful wife, Mary Kate, for making countless sacrifices over the years to support my theological study and work. I offer this book to the holy Trinity as a small sacrifice on her behalf.

Foreword

WILLIAM M. WRIGHT IV

Scholarship in the twentieth and early twenty-first centuries has done much to increase awareness and appreciation of St. Thomas Aquinas as an interpreter of the Bible. Trends such as *ressourcement* and biblical Thomism have brought welcome attention to the scriptural shape of Aquinas's theological thinking, the content of his biblical commentaries, and the place of scripture in his career as a *magister in sacra pagina*. With *The Suffering Servant in Aquinas: Isaiah 53 and Thomas's Theology of Christ's Passion*, Daniel R. Waldow makes a fine contribution to biblical Thomism, and as such, it deserves attention from systematic and historical theologians, biblical scholars, and all students of the Angelic Doctor.

As suggested by the title, Waldow is concerned in this book with the ways in which Aquinas interprets the figure of the Suffering Servant in Isaiah 53 with respect to Christ's passion and death. Chapter 1 locates scripture within the context of Aquinas's life and thought. Waldow documents the role of scripture in Aquinas's life as a Dominican friar and university professor, his programmatic thinking about scripture as a theological reality, and features of his exegetical practice. Waldow pays careful attention to Aquinas's account of the literal sense and the ways in which he works with it. Such concern is especially significant for this project because Aquinas reads Isaiah 53 in its literal sense as a direct prophecy of Jesus's passion. That is, the suffering and death of Jesus is the *res* of which the *verba* of Isaiah 53 speak. Chapter 2 examines the contents of the fourth Servant song in Isaiah 53 (a text which begins in

Is 52:13). The purpose here is not to delve into the various critical issues which attend this text but rather to set forth the basic contents of this biblical passage as a composition.

Chapters 3 through 9 constitute the heart of this project. Following Valkenberg, Waldow undertakes an examination of Aquinas's use of the Isaianic text which is *quantitative* and *qualitiative* as well as chronological. That is, Waldow documents every single instance where Aquinas references Isaiah 53 in his theological writings (quantitative), examines the interpretive substance of each reference (qualitative), and does so in the order in which Aquinas likely composed these works over his career (chronological). Waldow thus begins with Aquinas's early lectures in the *Super Isaiam* and concludes with Aquinas's latest works on the *Tertia Pars* and *Commentary on the Psalms*. Waldow then summarizes his findings in a conclusion and includes an appendix which examines the few references to Isaiah 53 in Aquinas's *Opuscula*.

In his conclusion, Waldow observes that while Aquinas makes more extensive use of Isaiah 53 in his later works (i.e., the *Commentary on Matthew*, *Commentary on John*, and the *Tertia Pars*), his basic view of this text remains constant over the course of his career. As mentioned above, Aquinas reads Isaiah 53 as speaking directly of Jesus' suffering and death. Among the important theological topics or themes which Aquinas consistently discerns in this text are the freedom with which Jesus offered himself on the cross, the virtues with which he underwent his suffering (especially his charity), and the "what" and "why" of Christ's sufferings.

From the perspective of theologically-attuned biblical scholarship, Waldow's study also points to some ways in which biblical scholars might engage constructively with Aquinas's biblical exegesis. While many aspects could be cited, such as Aquinas's attention to the biblical language, the intertextual connections which he discerns, and his locating of scripture within the ambit of *sacra doctrina*, I wish to focus here on one specific example which illustrates both the challenges and constructive possibilities for working with Aquinas's exegesis.

Waldow shows that Aquinas cites Isaiah 53:7 more than any other part of this chapter: 40 of the 115 references in the major works are to this verse (20 to the first strophe and 20 to the second strophe). Aquinas frequently appeals to the first strophe, Isaiah 53:7a, which reads as follows in his text: "He was offered because he himself willed it." Aquinas capitalizes on the strophe's claim that the Servant, that is, Christ, voluntarily offered his life. From an exegetical perspective, a problem arises here because (as Waldow notes in chapter 2) the reading of Isaiah 53:7a in Aquinas's Vulgate text differs dramatically from both the Hebrew Masoretic Text and the Septuagint. Neither the Hebrew nor the Greek readings of Isaiah 53:7a make any mention about the Servant willingly offering his life. The ancient Hebrew and Greek texts do not offer a reading of this verse which support the meaning which Aquinas adduces from this particular verse. At the same time, Aquinas is perfectly correct in the theological conclusion about Christ's free self-offering on the cross. Not only does Jesus himself make this claim in the New Testament (e.g., Mk 10:45, Jn 10:17–18), but the fourth Servant song likewise makes this claim about the Servant in Isaiah 53:10. From the perspective of modern exegesis, Aquinas's reading of the literal sense of Isaiah 53:7a may be wanting. But the theological content which he discerns with respect to this verse (i.e., the free self-offering of the Servant) is sound.

This example, highlighted by Waldow, shows the value in making a soft distinction between Aquinas's interpretation of the biblical *verba* and the *res* of which they speak. Aquinas can often be a very illuminating reader of the literal sense of scripture. But his exegesis is also limited by the understanding of the biblical text and interpretive resources which were available in his day (in this case, a version of the Vulgate). Even though Aquinas's reading of the biblical letter may be deficient from the perspective of modern criticism, his treatment of the *res*, the content of which the text speaks, can be a separate matter. For Aquinas's theological exposition can provide much insight into the significance of the biblical *res*, even when his treatment of the biblical *verba* may not rise to the same level. Readers should therefore attend to what Aquinas says not only about a given biblical text but also about the reality of which the biblical text speaks.

With this study of Aquinas's exegesis of Isaiah 53, Daniel Waldow makes a valuable contribution to scholarship not only on Aquinas but also on scripture and its theological interpretation. He demonstrates well that we can all benefit from contemplating the mystery of our salvation through the cross of Jesus Christ when we contemplate it with St. Thomas Aquinas, our Angelic and Common Doctor.

List of Tables

List of Abbreviations

NRSV-CE   New Revised Standard Version Catholic Edition (Holy Bible)

SS   *Sentences Commentary* (Thomas Aquinas)

ST   *Summa Theologiae* (Thomas Aquinas)

The Suffering Servant
in Aquinas

Introduction

The Nature and Structure of This Work

This book is about the theological exegesis and biblical theology of Thomas Aquinas. This project has been generated by the conviction that "sustained engagement with scripture needs to be a distinguishing mark of contemporary Thomist theology."[1] Thomists must be attentive to scripture because, as this work will demonstrate, scripture was a foundational and essential feature of Aquinas's own theological method and works. To fully appreciate Aquinas's theology, one must recognize the omnipresent role of scripture within that theology. In this work I will cast a spotlight upon the place and function of the text of Isaiah 53 in the theology of Aquinas. Specifically, this work is about Aquinas's Christological exegesis of Isaiah 53 and the role of that biblical text in his speculative theological account of Christ's passion.

In this introductory chapter I provide a detailed overview of the nature and structure of this book. First, I explain the purpose, scope, and original contribution of this work. Second, I describe the methodology that I employ throughout this project. Third, I provide a basic overview of the number and place of Aquinas's references to the text of Isaiah 53 throughout his theological corpus. Finally, I conclude this introduction with a synopsis of the ensuing chapters of this work.

---

1. Matthew Levering, *Paul in the "Summa Theologiae"* (Washington, D.C.: The Catholic University of America Press, 2014), vii.

THE END, SCOPE, AND CONTRIBUTIONS
OF THIS WORK

This book explores Thomas Aquinas's reception of the text of Isaiah 53 throughout all of his theological works. In particular, I explore the role that Isaiah 53 plays in Aquinas's theological account of the nature and saving value of Christ's suffering and death. Hence, the principal end of this study is to provide an answer to the following central question: *how does Aquinas interpret and use the Suffering Servant text of Isaiah 53:1–12 in his theology of the cross?*[2] In order to answer this question and achieve my end, in this work I will examine every reference to Isaiah 53 that Aquinas makes in his theological corpus.[3] My conclusion is that Aquinas consistently identifies the literal sense of Isaiah 53 as a prophecy of the passion of Christ, and he frequently turns to Isaiah's text in order to interpret the Gospel narratives. Further, throughout his biblical commentaries and systematic works, Aquinas repeatedly draws upon the text of Isaiah 53 in order to shed light upon the origin and nature of Christ's suffering as well as upon the voluntary and virtuous manner in which Christ bore that suffering.

Given the nature of my end, this book is intended primarily as a contribution to the historical and systematic study of the theology of Thomas Aquinas. In particular, since my leading task throughout will be to examine the ways in which the biblical text of Isaiah 53 contributes to Aquinas's theological treatment of Christ's passion, this project can be specified as a work of "biblical Thomism."[4] This

2. Contemporary scholarship identifies Isaiah's Fourth Suffering Servant Song as consisting of Is 52:13–53:12. The overwhelming majority of Aquinas's engagement with that portion of Isaiah, however, consists of engagement with Is 53:1–12. Hence, those verses will constitute the primary scope of this work. Nonetheless, I will examine Aquinas's comments upon Is 52:13–15 in his lecture on Is 52 in the *Commentary on Isaiah*.

3. By investigating every occasion in which Aquinas quotes a particular scriptural text within a specific range of his works, I am following in the methodological footsteps of Wilhelmus G. B. M. Valkenberg and Matthew Levering. In his *Words of the Living God: Place and Function of Holy Scripture in the Theology of St. Thomas Aquinas* (Leuven: Peeters, 2000), Valkenberg analyzes Aquinas's use of scripture in his treatments of the resurrection of Christ in the *Sentences* commentary as well as in the *ST*. In *Paul in the Summa Theologiae*, Levering examines all of Aquinas's references to the epistles of Paul throughout the *ST*.

4. "Biblical Thomism" is a field of study "in which Aquinas's thought is being explored through his study of Scripture." See Piotr Roszak and Jorgen Vijgen (eds.), *Reading Sacred*

species within the genus of Thomism consists in the exploration of one or more of the following themes.

The first theme of biblical Thomism pertains to the general principles of Aquinas's biblical theology. It considers issues such as Aquinas's understanding of the nature of scripture, the role of scripture as a source in theology, and the methodological tools that Aquinas uses to exegete scripture and derive speculative theological conclusions from the sacred text.[5] The second theme considers Aquinas's verse by verse commentaries upon particular books of scripture. These biblical commentaries are studied both for their exegetical value as well as for their significance as unique sources of Aquinas's speculative theology.[6] The third theme analyzes the number, location, and purpose of references to scripture in Aquinas's works of speculative and systematic theology.[7]

Scripture with Thomas Aquinas: Hermeneutical Tools, Theological Questions and New Perspectives (Turnhout: Brepols, 2015), x.

5. For example, see the essays on "Hermeneutical Tools" in "Part 1" of *Reading Sacred Scripture With Thomas Aquinas* (ed. Roszak and Vijgen), 3–348; Michael Sirilla, "*Lectio Scripturae* at the Heart of Aquinas's Theology and Preaching"; and Jorgen Vijgen's "Scripture as a Guidepost for How Not to Read Scripture: Aquinas on the Apologetic Function of Scripture," in *Thomas Aquinas: Biblical Theologian*, ed. Roger Nutt and Michael Dauphinais (Steubenville, Ohio: Emmaus Academic, 2021); Christopher Baglow, "Rediscovering St. Thomas Aquinas as Biblical Theologian," *Letter and Spirit* 1 (2005): 137–46; Piotr Roszak, "Revelation and Scripture: Exploring the Scriptural Foundation of *sacra doctrina* in Aquinas," *Angelicum* 93 (2016): 191–218.

6. For example, see Thomas G. Weinandy, Daniel A. Keating, and John P. Yocum (eds.), *Aquinas on Scripture: An Introduction to His Biblical Commentaries* (London: T&T Clark International, 2005); Michael G. Sirilla, *The Ideal Bishop: Aquinas's Commentaries on the Pastoral Epistles* (Washington, D.C.: The Catholic University of America Press, 2017); Matthew Levering and Michael Dauphinais (eds.), *Reading John with St. Thomas Aquinas: Theological Exegesis and Speculative Theology* (Washington, D.C.: The Catholic University of America Press, 2005) and *Reading Romans with St. Thomas Aquinas* (Washington, D.C.: The Catholic University of America Press, 2012); Matthew Levering, Piotr Roszak, and Jorgen Vijgen (eds.), *Reading Job with St. Thomas Aquinas* (Washington, D.C.: The Catholic University of America Press, 2020); Thomas F. Ryan, *Thomas Aquinas as Reader of the Psalms* (Notre Dame, Ind.: University of Notre Dame Press, 2020).

7. E.g., see Valkenberg, *Words of the Living God*, esp. 54–140; Levering, *Paul in the "Summa Theologiae"*; A. Paretzky, "The Influence of Thomas the Exegete on Thomas the Theologian: The Tract on Law (I-II qq. 90–108) as a Test Case," *Angelicum* 71 (1994): 549–77; Michael Waldstein, "On Scripture in the *Summa Theologiae*," *Aquinas Review* 1 (1994): 73–94; Kevin E. O'Reilly, OP, "'The Light of Thy Countenance, O Lord, is signed Upon Us': Psalm 4:7 and the Christological Foundations of the Natural Law," *The Thomist* 86, no. 3 (July 2022): 335–72; Serge-Thomas Bonino, *Reading the Song of Songs with St. Thomas Aquinas*, trans. Andrew Levering (Washington, D.C.: The Catholic University of America Press, 2023).

This book involves inquiry into each of these themes, but my original contribution will come specifically in regards to the second and third themes. There have been many recent studies of Aquinas's theology of the cross.[8] Further, there have been recent works that explore the role of particular biblical texts in Aquinas's understanding of Christ's suffering and death.[9] However, none of these studies have explored the presence and influence of the text of Isaiah 53 in Aquinas's theological account of Christ's passion. Hence, this work will fill that lacuna. In doing so, this study of Aquinas's reception of Isaiah 53 will be of value not only to Thomists, but also to all those with an interest in the theological meaning of Isaiah 53. This book ensures that Aquinas has a seat at the contemporary table where many valuable discussions are taking place regarding the Christological and soteriological meaning of Isaiah's Suffering Servant texts.[10]

8. For example, see Eleonore Stump, *Atonement* (Oxford: Oxford University Press, 2018); Thomas Joseph White, *The Incarnate Lord: A Thomistic Study in Christology* (Washington, D.C.: The Catholic University of America Press, 2017), 277–380; Romanus Cessario, *The Godly Image: Christian Satisfaction in Aquinas* (Washington, D.C.: The Catholic University of America Press, 2020); William P. Loewe, *Lex Crucis: Soteriology and the Stages of Meaning* (Minneapolis, Minn.: Fortress Press, 2016), 103–56; Rik Van Nieuwenhove, "'Bearing the Marks of Christ's Passion': Aquinas's Soteriology," in *The Theology of Thomas Aquinas*, ed. Rik Van Nieuwenhove and Joseph Wawrykow (South Bend, Ind.: University of Notre Dame Press, 2010), 277–302; Niewenhove, "St. Thomas Aquinas on Salvation, Making Satisfaction, and Restoration of Friendship with God," *The Thomist* 83, no. 4 (2019): 521–45; Daniel Waldow, "Aquinas on the Nature of Christ's Punishment and Its Role in His Work of Satisfaction," *New Blackfriars* 103, no. 1103 (January 2022): 7–28.

9. For example, see Roger Nutt, "'Obedient unto Death': The Function of Philippians 2 in St. Thomas's Theology of the Cross," in *Thomas Aquinas: Biblical Theologian* (ed. Nutt and Dauphinais); in addition to his *Paul in the "Summa Theologiae,"* 49–75 and 267–82, see Matthew Levering's *Christ's Fulfillment of Torah and Temple: Salvation according to Thomas Aquinas* (Notre Dame, Ind.: University of Notre Dame Press, 2002); Joel Matthew Wallace, "Chapter 5: Charity: Source of Christ's Voluntary Action in the Biblical Commentaries," in *"Inspiravit ei voluntatem patiendi pro nobis, infundendo ei caritatem": Charity, the Source of Christ's Action according to Thomas Aquinas* (Siena: Edizioni Cantagalli, 2013); Piotr Roszak, "The Earnest of Our Inheritance (Eph 1:5): The Biblical Foundations of Thomas Aquinas's Soteriology," *Przeglad Tomistyczny* 23 (2017): 213–33, and "Aquinas on Christ's Will to Die and Our Salvation," *Nova et Vetera* (English edition) 19, no. 1 (2021): 199–216.

10. For example, Fleming Rutledge, *The Crucifixion: Understanding the Death of Jesus Christ* (Grand Rapids, Mich.: Eerdmans, 2015), 53, 76, 81, 83, 90, 146, 209, 220, 257, 414, 462, 469, 474–76, 479, 481, 493, 504, 517, 528, 610; "Isaiah's Servant of the Lord," in William Lane Craig, *Atonement and the Death of Christ: An Exegetical, Historical, and Philosophical Exploration* (Waco, Tex.: Baylor University Press, 2020); Steve Jeffery, Michael Overy, and Andrew Sach (eds.), *Pierced for Our Transgressions: Rediscovering the Glory of Penal Substitution* (Wheaton, Ill.: Crossway Books, 2007), esp. 52–66 and 208–17; Simon Gathercole, *Defending Substitution: An Essay on Atonement in Paul* (Grand Rapids, Mich.: Baker Academic, 2015),

THE METHODOLOGY OF THIS STUDY

In this work I use the following methods as I investigate Aquinas's references to the text of Isaiah 53. First, I undertake a "quantitative analysis" of the "place" of the text of Isaiah 53 in Aquinas's theological works.[11] As Wilhelmus Valkenberg explains, a quantitative analysis of Aquinas's references to scripture "provides an answer to the question: does Scripture play a part in this theological text?"[12] Put simply, quantitative analysis identifies the number and location of scriptural citations within Aquinas's theological corpus. Such quantitative analysis can give an indication of the significance of particular biblical texts to Aquinas's theological projects. With that being said, as Roger Nutt has pointed out, merely "noting the quantity of biblical references in Aquinas's work … does little to establish him as a biblical theologian of any merit."[13] Simply counting the sheer number of biblical citations within Aquinas's works does not show that he is interpreting those biblical texts in an exegetical and theologically coherent way. Nor does such quantitative analysis on its own adequately indicate the degree to which Aquinas's theology is informed by particular biblical texts. Quantitative analysis, while foundational, must be complemented by what Valkenberg calls "qualitative analysis."[14]

Hence, after quantifying Aquinas's references to the text of Isaiah 53, my second methodological step is to conduct a qualitative analysis of these biblical references within his corpus. Such an analysis answers the question, "what part does Scripture play in this theological text?"[15] To examine the quality of Aquinas's references to Isaiah 53 is to analyze how Aquinas is reading that biblical text in each particular context and to explain the role or "function" that Isaiah 53 plays in the service of Aquinas's greater theological task in that specific

---

esp. 61–73; Gerald O'Collins, *Jesus Our Redeemer: A Christian Approach to Salvation* (Oxford: Oxford University Press, 2007), 148–52.

11. These labels were first employed by Valkenberg, *Words of the Living God*, 2.

12. Ibid., 8.

13. Nutt, "'Obedient unto Death,'" in *Thomas Aquinas: Biblical Theologian* (ed. Nutt and Dauphinais), 232.

14. Valkenberg, *Words of the Living God*, 8.

15. Ibid.

context.[16] In particular, I focus upon the functions that Isaiah 53 performs in Aquinas's biblical and systematic accounts of Christ's passion. I explain how Isaiah 53 is directing, clarifying, supporting, or even challenging what Aquinas wants to say about Christ's suffering and death in a specific setting. For the sake of brevity, as I undertake this qualitative analysis I do not employ Valkenberg's practice of labeling any particular scriptural citation by Aquinas as serving a function that is "theologically primary" or "theologically secondary" in relation to Aquinas's greater theological argument in that context.[17] Rather, following Matthew Levering's approach in his *Paul in the "Summa Theologiae,"* I simply describe what Aquinas is doing with the text of Isaiah 53 in each particular context.[18]

Third, I am attentive to the historical context of Aquinas's life and works. In Chapter 1, I provide a brief overview of the defining features of Aquinas's life and theological career. There I introduce readers to the central aspects of his understanding of scripture as well as to his major principles of biblical exegesis. Throughout this book, before probing Aquinas's references to Isaiah 53 in a particular text, I first provide a brief overview of the origin, style and purpose of the text in question. I also engage Aquinas's individual works in their historical, chronological order. This historical sensitivity and chronological approach has two advantages.

First, it enables the reader to recognize how Aquinas's interpretations of Isaiah 53 do not occur in a vacuum. Rather, Aquinas's approach to Isaiah 53 was informed by the medieval, religious, scholarly environment of which he was a part. Keeping this context in mind enables us to better understand and evaluate his reception of

---

16. Ibid., 2.

17. Ibid., 51–53. For Valkenberg, Aquinas uses scripture for a "theologically primary function" in his theological writing when he cites a biblical text in order "to indicate the revelation of God as the incontestable source of theology" and to specify "the domain within which theology has to proceed" (51). Aquinas uses the Bible in a merely "theologically secondary function" when he cites scripture "in the same manner as any other source of human wisdom and knowledge," such as "to give examples and illustrations" (51).

18. Levering, *Paul in the "Summa Theologiae,"* xvii–xviii: "Rather than burdening the reader with theoretical apparatus, I simply move through the citations of Paul and discuss each one in relation to the topic that Aquinas is addressing in the article ... I purposefully keep the interpretative framework quite spare, in hopes of focusing attention on the work that the Pauline quotations do."

Isaiah 53. Second, exploring Aquinas's works in chronological order helps the reader to identify interpretative changes and shifts in emphasis that Aquinas makes over the years in regards to his engagement with Isaiah 53. For, as James Weisheipl observes, "Even though the thought of Thomas has a transcendent significance, it is wrong to read his works as though they were written in one sitting and devoid of all intellectual development. Thomas, like everyone else, developed intellectually and spiritually."[19] This attention to the development of Aquinas's thought is not only of historical value, but also theological. Being aware of the various ways Aquinas interpreted Isaiah 53 over the years enables us to dialectically weigh and evaluate the different exegetical moves that he made toward that biblical text throughout the course of his theological career.

My fourth methodological step in this book is to observe how Aquinas's interpretations of Isaiah 53 are grounded in his Latin versions of the Bible. Acknowledging Aquinas's reliance upon a Latin version of Isaiah 53 is necessary to properly evaluate the merit of his interpretations. Aquinas's exegesis is unique and insightful, but also limited by the fact that he did not have access to the Hebrew or Greek texts of the Old Testament that we have today. Throughout my qualitative analysis of Aquinas's references to Isaiah 53, I point out when and how his theological exegesis of Isaiah 53 is based on precise words and phrases from the Latin biblical text(s) at his disposal.

---

19. James A. Weisheipl, *Friar Thomas D'Aquino: His Life, Thought, and Work* (Garden City, N.Y.: Doubleday, 1974), x. After acknowledging that Aquinas's theological positions developed over the course of his career, Weisheipl then comments: "The amazing fact is, however, that early in life Thomas grasped certain fundamental philosophical principles that never changed. Always there was development, deeper understanding, and even rejection of earlier views. But there was never a metamorphosis in his approach to reality. There was never a 'conversion' or violent rejection of earlier thought, but only corrections and modifications that led to a fuller, more human, and more divine appreciation of the basic problems of life" (x). Similarly, in *Toward Understanding Saint Thomas* (Chicago: Henry Regnery Company, 1964), M. D. Chenu comments, "It will be quickly discovered that, from his very first extensive work, Saint Thomas had established his basic positions and that his master intuitions already held sway. Yet, satisfaction will also be found in observing the progress, at times in quality, at times in technique, that the *Disputed Questions* and then the organic purviews of the *Summa* have provided for his genial mind" (272–73).

BASIC QUANTITATIVE ANALYSIS OF AQUINAS'S
ENGAGEMENT WITH ISAIAH 53

In this section I identify the number and place of references to Isaiah 53 in Aquinas's theological works. I identify the individual works of Aquinas that feature references to Isaiah 53 as well as the number of references within those works. This basic quantitative analysis sets the stage for the ensuing qualitative analysis that will constitute the majority of this book.

In addition to the chapter on Isaiah 53 in his *Commentary on Isaiah*, Aquinas explicitly refers to the text of Isaiah 53 a total of 121 times throughout his theological corpus.[20] Five of those cases are found in other chapters of the *Commentary on Isaiah*, while 110 cases are found in Aquinas's other biblical commentaries as well as in the systematic *Commentary on the Sentences* and the *Summa Theologiae* (hereafter *ST*). The final six cases are spread across five small works which are numbered among the *Opuscula*, or 'little works,' of Aquinas.[21] Hence, the overwhelming majority of Aquinas's references to Isaiah 53 are found in his major theological works of biblical commentary and systematic analysis. Consequently, the body of this book will consist of an examination of Aquinas's engagement with the text of Isaiah 53 in those major theological works, namely, the biblical commentaries, the *Sentences* commentary, and the *Summa Theologiae*. I use an appendix at the conclusion of the book to examine the remaining six cases that are found in the *Opuscula*. Having

---

20. The ensuing statistics were compiled using the following online index of Aquinas's work: "Index Thomisticus," Corpus Thomisticum, available at corpusthomisticum.org/it/index.age.

21. The Index Thomisticus identifies several additional references to Is 53 that Aquinas himself makes in Latin, but he is mistaken; the verses he is quoting are not from Is 53. For specifics, see the quantitative analysis provided in chapters 3–9. Further, it is worth noting that these 121 references do not include possible references to Is 53 that Aquinas may have made without citing the chapter number. For instance, it is possible that there are times in Aquinas's corpus where he cites a text from Is 53 but does not specify (nor does the editor) that the text he is citing is from Is 53. This is generally not Aquinas's nor modern editors' practice, but it bears stating that any such references fall outside of the scope of this book. Nonetheless, there are two such references in *ST* III, q. 47, a. 3, co., which I managed to spot, and so I have included them in the total. The Index Thomisticus does not catch these references. See my analysis in chapter 9 on *ST*. Further, the Index Thomisticus mistakenly identifies an additional case of Is 53 in the *Super Psalmos*, but the text Aquinas quotes is actually from Is 52. See chapter 10.

established this focus and plan, I will now detail how the references to Isaiah 53 that constitute the focus of this study are distributed throughout Aquinas's works.

Several of Aquinas's biblical commentaries do not contain any explicit references to Isaiah 53. The commentaries that lack cases of Isaiah 53 are on the following biblical books: Job, Philippians, Colossians, 1 Thessalonians, 1 Timothy, Titus, and Philemon. The most surprising member of this list is Aquinas's *Commentary on Job*, given that Job's experience of suffering while innocent could easily be linked to Isaiah's Suffering Servant. In any event, this means that seven of Aquinas's twenty biblical commentaries (excluding the *Commentary on Isaiah*) lack an explicit reference to the text of Isaiah 53.

In addition to the *Commentary on Isaiah*, the following thirteen biblical commentaries contain cases of Isaiah 53. In what follows I first give the title of the biblical book upon which Aquinas wrote the commentary and then provide the number of explicit references to Isaiah 53 that are contained in that commentary. This list is organized numerically beginning with the commentary that contains the least number of cases: Lamentations[22] (one case), 2 Corinthians (x1), Galatians (x1), 2 Thessalonians (x1), 2 Timothy (x1), Romans (x2), Jeremiah (x3), Ephesians (x4), Hebrews (x5), 1 Corinthians (x6), the Psalms (x12), the Gospel of John (x15), and the Gospel of Matthew (x24). Added together, there are seventy-six total cases of Isaiah 53 throughout these thirteen biblical commentaries. Just over half (thirty-nine) of these cases are contained in the commentaries on Matthew and John alone.

Hence, in terms of sheer numbers, the text of Isaiah 53 figures most prominently in Aquinas's exegesis of the Gospels. When we add the twelve cases contained in the *Commentary on the Psalms* to the thirty-nine cases in the commentaries on the Gospels, we see

---

22. In the most recent edition of his biography of Thomas (*Saint Thomas Aquinas*), Jean-Pierre Torrell asserts that "the Commentary on the Lamentations is probably not authentic" (398). Nonetheless, I have chosen to examine this commentary's lone reference to Is 53 given the commentary's traditional inclusion within Aquinas's corpus and its contemporary publication in English alongside Aquinas's *Commentary on Jeremiah*. See Thomas Aquinas, *Commentary on Jeremiah and Lamentations*, trans. Ben Martin and Mark Foudy (Steubenville, Ohio: Emmaus Academic, 2022).

that these three commentaries account for just over two-thirds (fifty-one) of the seventy-six total cases in the biblical commentaries. Of the remaining twenty-five cases, there are eighteen cases (almost one-quarter of the seventy-six total cases) spread almost evenly across four commentaries: 1 Corinthians, Hebrews, Ephesians, and Jeremiah. The following table summarizes the quantitative analysis provided above by identifying the place and number of Aquinas's references to Isaiah 53 in his major theological works, beginning with Aquinas's earliest work and proceeding chronologically.

We can now quantify Aquinas's references to Isaiah 53 in his two major works of systematic theology. The *Commentary on the Sentences* of Peter Lombard contains seven cases of Isaiah 53. The entire *Summa Theologiae* contains twenty-seven cases, and twenty-five

TABLE 1-1. CASES OF ISAIAH 53 IN AQUINAS'S MAJOR THEOLOGICAL WORKS

Name of Work	Number of Cases of Isaiah 53
Commentary on Isaiah	5 (outside of the lecture on Isaiah 53)
Commentary on Jeremiah	3
Commentary on Lamentations	1
Commentary on the Sentences	7
Commentary on the Gospel of Matthew	24
Commentary on the Gospel of John	15
Commentary on Romans	2
Commentary on 1 Corinthians	6
Commentary on 2 Corinthians	1
Commentary on Galatians	1
Commentary on Ephesians	4
Commentary on 2 Thessalonians	1
Commentary on 2 Timothy	1
Commentary on Hebrews	5
Summa Theologiae	27
Commentary on the Psalms	12

of those cases are found in the *Tertia Pars*. So, the *Tertia Pars* and the *ST* as a whole have more cases of Isaiah 53 than any of Aquinas's other major biblical and systematic works. Of the 110 cases of Isaiah 53 outside of the *Commentary on Isaiah* that I will be examining throughout Aquinas's corpus, almost one-fourth (24.5%) of those cases occur in the *ST*. Again, the table above summarizes the distribution of cases of Isaiah 53 across Aquinas's major theological works.

The quantitative analysis that I have provided in this section gives a basic indication of how my qualitative analysis will be distributed throughout this book. I begin with a thorough treatment of the lecture on Isaiah 53 and the five cases of Isaiah 53 that are contained in Aquinas's *Commentary on Isaiah*. Following this foundational analysis, I then briefly examine the eleven cases of Isaiah 53 that are spread throughout the commentaries on Jeremiah, Lamentations, and the *Sentences*. The majority of this book is concerned with the ninety-nine cases of Isaiah 53 that are spread throughout the *ST* and the biblical commentaries on Matthew, John, the Pauline epistles, and the Psalms.

STRUCTURE AND CHAPTER SYNOPSIS

I now conclude this introduction with a description of the structure of this work and with a synopsis of each ensuing chapter. Chapters 1 and 2 will establish the historical, theological, and biblical context that is needed in order to properly understand and evaluate Aquinas's reception of Isaiah 53. Chapters 3 through 8 are the core of this work and contain its original scholarly contribution to the field of biblical Thomism. In those chapters I conduct the quantitative and qualitative analysis of Aquinas's reception of Isaiah 53 throughout the biblical commentaries and systematic works mentioned above. The final concluding chapter provides a quantitative and qualitative synthesis of the findings from chapters 3 through 8. In the Conclusion, I highlight the central quantitative and qualitative features of Aquinas's engagement with Isaiah 53, and I provide a synthetic exposition of the theology of the cross that Aquinas draws out from Isaiah's text.

Chapter 1 provides a historical and theological overview of Aquinas's life, scholarly career, and understanding of scripture. I describe the various religious and scholarly ways in which he engaged scripture throughout his life and explicate his understanding of the theological nature of the Bible. I also present the primary features of his exegetical methodology as well as of his account of the relationship between scripture and theology. With this foundation in place, the reader will be better equipped to understand the various ways that Aquinas reads Isaiah 53 throughout his corpus.

Chapter 2 is an overview of the content and manuscripts of the text of Isaiah 53. I first conduct a basic description of the main features and contours of the text of Isaiah 53. I then compare Aquinas's Latin version of Isaiah 53 to the best contemporary Hebrew and Greek editions of that biblical text that we possess today. With these basic observations regarding the content and diverse texts of Isaiah 53 in place, the reader will be better equipped to appreciate the peculiarities of Aquinas's own exegesis of Isaiah 53.

Chapter 3 is the beginning of my analysis of Aquinas's interpretations and uses of Isaiah 53. This chapter explores Aquinas's engagement with Isaiah 53 in his earliest theological works, namely, the biblical commentaries on Isaiah, Jeremiah, and Lamentations.[23] The structure of chapter 3 will be mirrored in each ensuing chapter up through chapter 8. Chapter 3 begins by historically situating the *Commentary on Isaiah* and then proceeds to examine the references to Isaiah 53 that Aquinas makes in that commentary outside of his lecture on the fifty-third chapter itself. The majority of this chapter consists of a detailed explication and analysis of the lecture on Isaiah 53. Then, I proceed to examine the historical context and cases of Isaiah 53 in the *Commentary on Jeremiah* and the *Commentary on Lamentations*. This chapter, like the ensuing chapters through chapter 8, concludes with a theological synthesis of

---

23. Details regarding the dating of Aquinas's biblical and systematic works will be put forth in ensuing chapters when each work is considered. The chronology employed here is based primarily on the historical analysis provided by Jean-Pierre Torrell, *Saint Thomas Aquinas, vol. 1: The Person and His Work* (3rd ed.), trans. Robert Royal and Matthew K. Minerd (Washington, D.C.: The Catholic University of America Press, 2023). For a summary of the dates of all Aquinas's works and the arguments put forth in support of those dates, see "Brief Catalogue of the Works of Saint Thomas Aquinas," 383–436.

Aquinas's interpretations of Isaiah 53 throughout the various works considered. This synthesis highlights how the text of Isaiah 53 contributes to Aquinas's theological account of Christ's passion.

Chapter 4 focuses upon Aquinas's references to Isaiah 53 in his systematic *Commentary on the Sentences.* This work of systematic theology was produced at the beginning of Aquinas's teaching career. It provides an early look at the way in which Aquinas uses Isaiah 53 in order to answer speculative theological questions about the origin, nature, and effects of Christ's suffering and death. Many of Aquinas's interpretations of Isaiah 53 in this work will return, but with more depth and clarity, in the *ST*, written at the end of his academic career.

The bulk of this book unfolds in chapters 5 through 8. These chapters examine Aquinas's references to Isaiah 53 in his commentaries on Matthew, John, the Pauline epistles, and in the *ST*, respectively. Chapters 5 and 6 show how Aquinas draws extensively upon Isaiah 53 in order to exegete the Gospel's passion narratives and their other references to Christ's suffering and death. Chapter 7 examines the cases of Isaiah 53 in the Pauline commentaries in the canonical order of those biblical texts, namely, Romans, 1 and 2 Corinthians, Ephesians, Galatians, 2 Thessalonians, 2 Timothy, and Hebrews. Chapter 8 investigates the *ST*, especially the *Tertia Pars*, and demonstrates the significant role that Isaiah 53 plays in Aquinas's mature, speculative exposition of the mystery of Christ's suffering and death.

My chronological investigation of Aquinas's references to Isaiah 53 in his major theological works concludes with chapter 9. This chapter explores the cases of Isaiah 53 in Aquinas's final work, namely, the *Commentary on the Psalms.* Despite only containing analysis of Psalms 1–54, this biblical commentary nonetheless contains a significant number of references to Isaiah 53 and manifests Aquinas's final, mature Christological engagement with that biblical text. In the final chapter, I summarize the quantitative and qualitative data that was presented in chapters 3 through 8. I identify the overall number of times that Aquinas quoted particular verses from Isaiah 53 as well as the places in which those quotes occurred. Finally, I explicate the major features of the theology of the cross that Aquinas draws out from the text of Isaiah 53.

1

Contextualizing Aquinas's Biblical Theology

The goal of this chapter is to give readers historical and theological context that will help them to see why Aquinas used and interpreted the text of Isaiah 53 in the ways that he did. Aquinas's interpretations of Isaiah 53 are consistently informed by certain basic principles that he affirmed regarding the nature and exegesis of scripture. Hence, awareness of these principles is essential to a proper understanding of Aquinas's approach to Isaiah 53. In this chapter, therefore, I introduce readers to these basic principles of Thomistic exegesis and biblical theology.[1]

This chapter is divided into four parts. The first part provides a brief chronology of Aquinas's life and works and describes the role of scripture throughout his religious and scholarly life. The second part concerns Aquinas's understanding of the theological nature of scripture. It explains Aquinas's views on the literal and spiritual senses of scripture. The third part focuses on the exegetical methods

1. In setting forth Aquinas's principles of biblical exegesis, my intention is descriptive, not evaluative. For contemporary, positive assessments of Aquinas's exegetical methodology, see William Wright IV and Francis Martin, *Encountering the Living God in Scripture: Theological and Philosophical Principles for Interpretation* (Grand Rapids, Mich.: Baker Academic, 2019), esp. 109–216; Matthew Ramage, *Dark Passages of the Bible: Engaging Scripture with Benedict XVI and Thomas Aquinas* (Washington, D.C.: The Catholic University of America Press, 2013), esp. 17–154; Matthew Levering, *Participatory Biblical Exegesis* (Notre Dame, Ind.: University of Notre Dame Press, 2008).

that Aquinas used to discover the literal sense of scripture. The fourth part shows how Aquinas situated biblical exegesis in relation to the larger enterprise of theology. This section explains how scripture functions in Aquinas's systematic works as well as how his biblical commentaries generate systematic theological reflections.

THE ROLE OF SCRIPTURE IN AQUINAS'S

RELIGIOUS AND SCHOLARLY LIFE

I begin this overview of Thomas Aquinas's religious and scholarly engagement with scripture with a brief chronology of the major moments in his life and work.[2] Thomas died on March 7, 1274, at which point he was somewhere between the age of forty-eight and fifty years old. Consequently, he would have been born as early as 1224 or as late as 1226. When he was a child, Thomas's parents desired that he would one day become the abbot of the ancient and influential Benedictine abbey of Montecassino. And so they sent him there to live as an oblate from 1230 to 1239. After this Thomas went to study at the University of Naples, and while in Naples he entered the Dominican order in 1244. The Dominicans sent Thomas to Paris to receive further education from 1245 to 1248, and during this time he studied under Albert the Great. From 1248 to 1251 or 1252, Thomas was stationed with Albert at the newly established Dominican *studium* in Cologne, and there his job was to record notes of the lectures that Albert gave. While in Cologne, Thomas was ordained to the priesthood around 1250 or 1251.[3]

Having studied and worked under Albert, Thomas was prepared to begin his first assignment as a lecturer in theology. He was sent to the University of Paris, and there he lectured as a bachelor of the Bible and of the *Sentences* from 1251 or 1252 to 1256. Thomas earned the title of *magister in sacra pagina* in 1256, and he continued to teach in Paris until 1259. His next assignment was to give lectures at the Dominican house in Orvieto. He began this post

2. Unless otherwise noted, the ensuing chronological data provided in the present and following paragraph is taken from Torrell, *Saint Thomas Aquinas*, 379–83.

3. Weisheipl, *Friar Thomas D'Aquino*, 351.

somewhere between 1259 to 1261 and remained there until 1265. From 1265 to 1268, Thomas was the founding lecturer and leader of a new Dominican *studium* in Rome. At the conclusion of this assignment, he returned to the University of Paris and taught there once more as a *magister* from 1268 to 1272. Thomas's final teaching post was in Naples, where he once more oversaw a new Dominican theological *studium* from 1272 to 1273. While saying Mass on December 6, 1273, he had a mysterious experience that took away his scholarly drive. He ceased all teaching and writing and became physically ill.[4] He died a few months later, in March 1274.

Having established this basic outline of the major events and periods of Thomas's life, we can now examine the ways in which he encountered and worked with scripture. Thomas's first significant exposure to the Bible occurred when he was a child at the abbey of Montecassino. As Jean-Pierre Torrell explains, Thomas began to live at the abbey when he was "five or six," and "he there received elementary training in reading and writing" as well as "an introduction to the Benedictine religious life."[5] As an oblate, Thomas "had the value of a true monastic profession, though it was conditional and temporary."[6] At the age of "fourteen or fifteen" Thomas left the abbey and went to Naples for more advanced studies, but even there he likely "spent some time at the monastery of San Demetrio," which was "a lodging place for the Cassinese monks in the city."[7] Hence, prior to his entrance into the Dominican order in 1244, Thomas was for all intents and purposes a Benedictine monk.[8] As James Weisheipl explains, Thomas "was at that time a 'Benedictine' in the same sense that, when he became a novice in the order of preachers, he was a 'Dominican' waiting to profess solemn vows."[9]

Consequently, for roughly a decade of his life, at the very least,

4. On the nature and effects of Thomas's experience during that Mass of December 6, 1273, see Simon Tugwell, "Thomas Aquinas: Introduction," in *Albert and Thomas: Selected Writings*, trans. and ed. Simon Tugwell (New York: Paulist Press, 2008), 233–34 and 265–67.

5. Torrell, *Saint Thomas Aquinas*, 6.

6. Ibid., 7.

7. Ibid., 6–7.

8. For a thorough overview of Aquinas's relationship to the Benedictines throughout his life, and especially on the influence of St. Benedict upon Thomas's theology, see Andrew Hofer, "St. Thomas Aquinas on St. Benedict," *The American Benedictine Review* 71, no. 4 (2020): 412–34.

9. Weisheipl, *Friar Thomas D'Aquino*, 11.

Thomas received instruction "in the ways of the spiritual life according to the Benedictine rule."[10] During that period he would have been exposed to and participated in the Benedictine practices of praying with the scriptures through *lectio divina* and the liturgical praying of the Psalms. Thomas O'Meara speculates that "the impact of the monastic life in that great and ancient institution [Montecassino]—communal order in graced tranquility, education joined to liturgy—must have impressed the young Thomas."[11] Weisheipl claims that "the Psalms were undoubtedly learned by heart" by Thomas while he was at Montecassino as a result of his "daily choral recitation of the Divine Office."[12] Torrell remarks, "Thomas would all his life retain a deep esteem for the Benedictine ideal."[13] For our purposes, the key point is that Thomas's intellectual and spiritual life was deeply grounded in Benedictine approaches to scripture long before he began to study the Church Fathers and pagan philosophers. From the Benedictines he would have learned to appreciate scripture as a source of revelation and prayer, and during those formative years of his youth he developed habits of biblical prayer and study.[14] Consequently, we should not be surprised that the Bible would come to occupy a central place in Thomas's theological teaching and writing, nor should we be startled by the fact that Thomas did not reduce biblical interpretation to the application of merely natural historical and literary hermeneutical principles.

Thomas's next significant encounters with scripture took place in the context of his Dominican religious life. Almost immediately after he joined the Dominicans, Thomas's parents forced him to leave the order and return to the family castle. During this period of house arrest, Thomas supposedly "read the entire Bible."[15] Then, upon rejoining his brother friars, Thomas's life became further imbued with scripture. The principal and unique mission of the Dominicans

10. Ibid.

11. Thomas Franklin O'Meara, *Thomas Aquinas: Theologian* (Notre Dame, Ind.: The University of Notre Dame Press, 1997), 4.

12. Weisheipl, *Friar Thomas D'Aquino*, 11.

13. Torrell, *Saint Thomas Aquinas*, 17.

14. For more on the influence of Benedictine spirituality and the Psalms in particular upon the life of Thomas, see David Berger, *Thomas Aquinas and the Liturgy*, trans. Christopher Grosz (Naples, Fla.: Sapientia Press of Ave Maria University, 2005), 12–15.

15. Torrell, *Saint Thomas Aquinas*, 13.

was to engage in evangelical preaching. As a means to the end of effective preaching, all Dominicans were obligated to "the choral recitation of the Divine Office" as well as to the "assiduous study of divine truth."[16] Hence, not only as a Benedictine, but also as a Dominican, Thomas's daily life would have involved frequent prayer of the Psalms and other biblical texts. Further, the study to which Dominicans were obligated focused upon the Bible. As Weisheipl explains, "every Dominican priory had to have a lector whose obligation was to give theological lectures on the Sacred Scriptures to all the brethren," and "not even the prior was exempt from attendance at these lectures."[17] As the order grew, the number of biblical lectors in a particular priory grew, and eventually some of these Dominican teachers and their students conducted their biblical courses at major universities such as the one in Paris. In sum, the Dominican devotion to the biblical prayer of the divine office as well as the scholarly study of scripture was all meant to give the friars the ability "to contemplate and to give to others the fruits of [their] contemplation."[18]

In addition to the divine office and scholarly study, Thomas encountered scripture on a daily basis in the liturgy of the Eucharist. As a priest, Thomas himself said Mass once per day, and every day he also "heard a second one by his companion or someone else, in which he very often served at the altar."[19] Now, the Catholic Mass contains readings from scripture, biblically inspired prayers and chants, as well as a central ritual (the reenactment of Jesus' words and actions over the bread and wine at the Last Supper) that is drawn directly from scripture. Consequently, Thomas did not engage the Bible merely in classrooms as a text to be analyzed with historical and literary tools. Rather, he read and heard scripture everyday in the context of liturgical prayer. Hence, for him scripture was a means of communication with God.

As a Dominican and university teacher, Thomas was consistently tasked with giving courses upon different books of the Bible.

16. Weisheipl, *Friar Thomas D'Aquino*, 23.

17. Ibid., 24.

18. Ibid., 25.

19. David Berger, *Thomas Aquinas and the Liturgy*, 15, quoting Aquinas's medieval biographer, William of Tocco. Berger adds that Thomas's daily practice of attending multiple Masses shows that the Eucharist was "the undisputed center" of his life.

Michael Sirilla remarks, "Thomas Aquinas was, by profession, a biblical commentator," and "lecturing on Scripture was the chief occupation of his academic life."[20] For instance, at the University of Paris, Thomas had to help teach the following six-year curriculum for theology students: years 1–2 consisted of cursory courses on individual books of scripture; years 3–4 were on Peter Lombard's *Sentences*; years 5–6 consisted of more in-depth courses on additional books of scripture.[21] From 1252 to 1256 Thomas taught the first four years of the curriculum as a *"cursor biblicus* (cursory reader of the Bible)" and as a master of the *Sentences*.[22] Then, from 1256 to 1259 and again from 1268 to 1272, Thomas was a *magister in sacra pagina*.[23] In this position, his responsibility was to teach the fifth- and sixth-year courses on scripture, and these courses involved "a minute and prolonged exegesis" of a particular biblical book.[24] In addition to his duties at Paris, Thomas continued to give courses on individual books of the Bible during his teaching assignments in Orvieto, Rome, and Naples. In fact, though Thomas wrote the *Summa contra Gentiles*, the *Summa Theologiae*, and numerous commentaries on Aristotle, he did not teach those texts in the classroom. Rather, "what Thomas taught in his classroom as a master of theology was Scripture."[25] Hence, teaching courses on scripture was a constant and major component of Thomas's scholarly career.

Further, Thomas's courses on scripture served as the foundation for the two other duties for which he was responsible as a master of theology at the University of Paris. M.-D. Chenu describes these three "closely linked functions" of the *magister* as follows: "*legere* or to explain the text, *disputare* or to solve by discussion the questions it raises, *praedicare* or to preach it to the faithful."[26] So, in addition to lecturing (*legere*) on the text of scripture, Thomas's consequent duty

---

20. Michael G. Sirilla, "*Lectio Scripturae* at the Heart of Aquinas's Theology and Preaching," in *Thomas Aquinas: Biblical Theologian* (ed. Nutt and Dauphinais), 64.

21. Chenu, *Toward Understanding Saint Thomas*, 242.

22. Ibid.

23. Sirilla, "*Lectio Scripturae* at the Heart of Aquinas's Theology and Preaching," 64.

24. Chenu, *Toward Understanding Saint Thomas*, 242.

25. John F. Boyle, *The Order and Division of Divine Truth: St. Thomas Aquinas as Scholastic Master of the Sacred Page* (Steubenville, Ohio: Emmaus Academic, 2021), 8.

26. Chenu, *Toward Understanding Saint Thomas*, 237–38.

would have been to participate in academic debates (*disputatio*) that relied heavily upon scripture. The purpose of these debates was to scrutinize logically the theological content of scripture and to answer the speculative, systematic theological questions that the biblical text generated. Sirilla explains: "Raising and responding to the difficulties elicited by the text itself, the disputations frequently developed argumentation with scriptural premises and theological conclusions."[27] Finally, the master's biblical lectures and consequent systematic disputes gave birth to his ability to engage in biblically grounded and systematically erudite preaching. Hence, the "theological end" of lecturing and disputing was ultimately ordered toward the "pastoral one" of "communicating what has been understood to others by preaching and teaching."[28] In sum, even Thomas's intense scholarly engagement with scripture was not undertaken for secular or purely academic ends. Rather, Thomas taught and disputed scripture so that he would be able to share the theological truths of the faith with his students and congregations.

AQUINAS'S UNDERSTANDING OF THE THEOLOGICAL NATURE OF SCRIPTURE

Having identified the primary contexts in which Aquinas encountered scripture as a religious and scholar, we are now in a position to examine his understanding of the literal and spiritual senses of scripture. Aquinas describes the difference between these two senses of scripture at the outset of the *ST*. He begins by establishing that "the author of sacred Scripture is God, in whose power it is to signify his meaning, not by words only (as man also can do), but also by things themselves."[29] As William Wright and Francis Martin point out, Aquinas is working here with a distinction between words

27. Sirilla, "*Lectio Scripturae* at the Heart of Aquinas's Theology and Preaching," 72.

28. Ibid., 71. For more on the historical development of and relationship between these three functions, and the role of scripture within them, see Beryl Smalley, *The Study of the Bible In The Middle Ages* (Notre Dame, Ind.: University of Notre Dame Press, 1964), 208–13; Weisheipl, *Friar Thomas D'Aquino*, 110–11, 116–17, 123–28; Torrell, *Saint Thomas Aquinas*, 54–55, 59–63, 69–74.

29. Thomas Aquinas, *ST* I, q. 1, a. 10. All references to the *Summa* are based on the Leonine edition of the Latin text and the English translation by Lawrence Shapcote, edited and revised by the Aquinas Institute, available at aquinas.cc/la/en/~ST.I.

(*verba*) and the things or realities (*res*) to which the words refer.[30]
For Aquinas, the "historical or literal" sense is "that first signification whereby words signify things."[31] So, as John Boyle remarks, for
Aquinas "to know the literal sense is to know the reality intended by
the author and signified by those words."[32] Aquinas says that scripture also has a "spiritual sense" when "the things signified by words
themselves signify other things."[33] The spiritual sense is thus "based
on the literal, and presupposes it."[34] So, for Aquinas, scripture consists of (1) words which point to things (the literal sense), and
(2) additional things (the spiritual sense) that are signified by the
former things.

We can better understand the distinct nature of and relationship between the literal and spiritual senses of scripture by using the
Book of Leviticus as an example. The words of Leviticus are about
the realities of the Jewish priesthood and the ritual sacrifices that
they offered. Those are the literal senses of Leviticus. But the realities of the Jewish priesthood and their sacrifices are themselves signs
of additional realities, namely, the priesthood and sacrifice of Jesus.
These additional, Christological realities are the spiritual senses of
Leviticus. Now, Aquinas further distinguishes between three kinds
of spiritual senses. The "allegorical sense" occurs when something in
the Old Testament is a sign of something in the New Testament.[35]
The "moral sense" is when something pertaining to Christ is a sign of
what Christians should do, and the "anagogical sense" is found when
something about Christ points to the eternal destiny of the saints.[36]

Having established these basic points about the literal and spiritual senses of scripture, Aquinas proceeds in the body of *ST* I, q. 1,
a. 10, to add depth to his account of the literal sense. He says, "Since
the literal sense is that which the author intends [*intendit*], and since
the author of sacred Scripture is God, Who by one act comprehends

30. Wright and Martin, *Encountering the Living God in Scripture*, 196.

31. *ST* I, q. 1, a. 10.

32. Boyle, *The Order and Division of Divine Truth*, 10.

33. *ST* I, q. 1, a. 10. Author's translation: "Illa vero significatio qua res significatae per
voces, iterum res alias significant, dicitur sensus spiritualis."

34. *ST* I, q. 1, a. 10.

35. Ibid.

36. Ibid.

all things by His intellect, it is not unfitting, as Augustine says (*Confess.* xii), if, even according to the literal sense, one word in Holy Writ should have several senses." Two things are worth noting here. First, Aquinas explicitly equates the literal sense with the intention of God. In talking about God's "intention" for the words of scripture, Aquinas is saying that there are particular things that God wants the words to "'point to' or 'refer to.'"[37] Second, precisely because God is the author of scripture, he can intend a single word or series of words to refer to multiple realities at once.

Aquinas's above teaching raises questions regarding the relationship between the intentions of the human author and the literal sense of scripture. He addresses this issue in *De Potentia*, q. 4, a. 1. He does so in the context of a discussion regarding the proper interpretation of the creation account in Genesis 1. He explains:

It is not inconceivable that Moses and the other authors of the sacred Scriptures were given to know the various truths that men would discover in the text, and that they expressed them *under one series of letters*, so that each truth is the sense intended by the author. And then, even if commentators adapt certain truths to the sacred text that were not understood by the [human] author, without doubt the Holy Spirit understood them, since he is the principal author of Holy Scripture.[38]

Aquinas is saying that Moses may have written the creation account of Genesis 1 with the intent to signify a variety of distinct realities. That is, he may have known of each and every reality that God intended his words to refer to. Yet, even if Moses or some other human author of scripture did not "mean all of those meanings, it does not matter. And it does not matter for one simple reason: the primary author of Scripture is God."[39] That is, "God could mean all

37. Mary Healy, "Aquinas's Use of the Old Testament in His Commentary on Romans," in *Reading Romans with St. Thomas Aquinas* (ed. Levering and Dauphinais), 186–87. She thus specifies that the 'literal sense' refers to "the *objective realities referred to by the text*, whether historical facts or atemporal truths." On the meaning of "intention" for Aquinas see also Boyle, *The Order and Division of Divine Truth*, 42.

38. Thomas Aquinas, *De Potentia*, q. 4, a. 1. The italicized text is the author's translation of "et ea sub una serie litterae designarent." All references to *De Potentia* are from the 1953 Marietti edition of the Latin text, which was transcribed by Roberto Busa and revised by the Aquinas Institute, and the English translation by the English Dominican Fathers, edited and revised by the Aquinas Institute. Both are available online at aquinas.cc/la/en/~QDePot.Q4.A1.C.2.

39. Boyle, *The Order and Division of Divine Truth*, 41.

of the literal meanings, and thus one would have multiple literal meanings, but without any such meanings on the part of the human author."[40] Consequently, for Aquinas, the attempt to discover the literal sense or literal senses of scripture is ultimately the attempt to discover those things that *God intended* to signify through the words of the human authors.[41]

One further clarification is in order regarding Aquinas's understanding of the nature of the literal sense, and that is that 'the literal sense' does not refer exclusively to *literalistic* statements. Rather, the literal sense employs words which signify things either "properly or figuratively."[42] When the figurative signification is used, then "the literal sense is not the surface meaning of the words but *that which is signified by the literary figure*."[43] Aquinas uses the following example: "When Scripture speaks of 'God's arm,' the literal sense is not that God has such a member, but only what is signified by this member, namely, operative power."[44] Hence, whereas today the word 'literal' tends to be used colloquially in contrast with 'fictional' or 'metaphorical,' Aquinas allows that the 'literal sense' of scripture can signify things through diverse literary genres such as narrative, parable, poetry, or metaphor.[45] Thus, to know the literal sense the reader must recognize the particular *way by which* words signify things. The way the words of the Gospel of Mark signify things is very different from the way the words of the Song of Songs signify things. The

40. Ibid. For arguments that Aquinas did not embrace a pluriform view of the literal sense of scripture, see Paul Synave, "La Doctrine de saint Thomas d'Aquin sue le sens littéral des Ecritures," *Revue Biblique* 35, no. 1 (1926): 40–65; Seraphinus M. Zarb, "Utrum S. Thomas unitatem an vero pluralitatem sensus litteralis in sacra Scriptura docuerit?," *Divus Thomas* 33 (1930): 337–59; Paul Synave and Pierre Benoit, *Prophecy and Inspiration: A Commentary on the "Summa Theologica" II-II, Questions 171–78*, trans. Avery R. Dulles and Thomas L. Sheridan (New York: Desclee Company, 1961), 147–55; Thomas Prugl, "Thomas Aquinas as Interpreter of Scripture," in *The Theology of Thomas Aquinas*, ed. Rik Van Nieuwenhove and Joseph Wawrykow (Notre Dame, Ind.: University of Notre Dame Press, 2005), 395–96.

41. That being said, at times Aquinas does explicitly identify the intention of the human author of scripture. See the analysis in Boyle, *The Order and Division of Divine Truth*, 42–44.

42. *ST* I, q. 1, a. 10, ad 3.

43. Healy, "Aquinas's Use of the Old Testament in His Commentary on Romans," 186.

44. *ST* I, q. 1, a. 10, ad 3.

45. See Gilbert Dahan, "Thomas Aquinas: Exegesis and Hermeneutics," in *Reading Sacred Scripture with Thomas Aquinas* (ed. Roszak and Vijgen), 58 and 60–71; Nicholas Healy, "Introduction," in *Aquinas on Scripture* (ed. Weinandy et al.), 16.

former signifies things in a 'proper' way, while the latter signifies things in a 'figurative' way. Yet both ways pertain to the literal sense of scripture.[46]

HOW TO DISCOVER THE LITERAL SENSE

The first thing to realize about Aquinas's approach to interpreting scripture is that he did not use many of the textual, historical, and linguistic resources that most contemporary biblical scholars use today. For instance, as Eleonore Stump observes, Aquinas "apparently knew very little Greek and virtually no Hebrew, and he does not seem to have been interested in acquiring these languages."[47] Consequently, Aquinas was limited to reading scripture in Latin, and "he shows no sign of a concern to try to recover the text in its original [Greek and Hebrew] form either through his own work or through the efforts of others."[48] Further, the Latin Vulgate "existed in several versions, and Aquinas apparently used more than one of them."[49] Yet "he rarely records any concern over the fact that he has differing [Latin] manuscripts of a biblical text; and sometimes, rather than choosing one of the alternatives as the more accurate or genuine reading, he simply incorporates an exegesis of each alternative into his commentary."[50] In sum, Aquinas's exegesis of scripture did not rely upon (1) the identification of Greek and Hebrew manuscripts that most accurately reflected the original texts of scripture,

46. Aquinas grants that there are instances where the exact mode of signification at work in a given scriptural passage may be unclear, and yet nonetheless one can know the reality that the words are intended to signify. For instance, he claims that the Book of Job is about God's providence, and that this is the case regardless of whether the book is a historical narrative or a parable. See "Prologue" in *Commentary on the Book of Job* (Lander, Wyo.: The Aquinas Institute for the Study of Sacred Doctrine, 2016), 8.

47. Eleonore Stump, "Biblical Commentary and Philosophy," in *The Cambridge Companion to Aquinas*, ed. Norman Kretzmann and Eleonore Stump (Cambridge: Cambridge University Press, 1993), 256.

48. Stump, "Biblical Commentary and Philosophy," 256.

49. Ibid., 255. Stump notes: "In some cases it is not clear what particular version of the Vulgate Aquinas was using; in other cases we can determine it with some confidence. For example, in commenting on the Psalms, Aquinas uses the Vulgate's 'Gallican Psalter,' although he sometimes also uses the 'Roman Psalter.'"

50. Ibid. Stump remarks: "In view of these facts, it is not at all clear that Aquinas would have welcomed contemporary historical biblical scholarship if he had known of it" (256).

(2) the ability to read any Greek and Hebrew versions of scripture, and (3) the identification and use of a Latin manuscript that most accurately reflected the best Greek and Hebrew manuscripts.

Therefore, the quality of Aquinas's exegesis is dependent upon the quality of the Latin translations of scripture that were at his disposal. For many, perhaps, this observation effectively renders Aquinas's biblical exegesis as unworthy of consideration. For my part, rather than *a priori* rejecting Aquinas's Latin exegesis, in this book I engage his biblical texts and interpretations with an analytical lens. In the next chapter I show how Aquinas's Latin version of Isaiah 53 is in substantial agreement with the best editions of scripture that we possess today. Even so, as I examine Aquinas's references to his Latin version of Isaiah 53, I make note of occasions in which his exegetical and theological conclusions are informed by uniquely Latin words and phrases. Hence, readers will be able to observe the ways in which Aquinas's Latin biblical manuscripts influence his interpretations, and they will consequently be able to judge the value of those interpretations for themselves.

With that context in mind, we can now examine the exegetical methods that Aquinas actually did employ to discern the literal sense of scripture. The foundation of Aquinas's exegetical tools were "two negative principles" that he used consistently when interpreting scripture.[51] The first of these principles is simply that, as Aquinas says in *ST* I, q. 1, "nothing false can ever underlie the literal sense of sacred Scripture."[52] Similarly, in *De Potentia*, Aquinas explains that it would be incorrect "to give to the words of Scripture an interpretation manifestly false."[53] For "falsehood cannot underlie the divine Scriptures which we have received from the Holy Spirit."[54] It is especially important to avoid any interpretation which views scripture as asserting things that are "contrary to the truth of faith [*veritati fidei*]."[55] The God who is truth did not inspire the biblical words in order to trick and deceive humanity; rather, scripture only asserts

---

51. Boyle, *The Order and Division of Divine Truth*, 38.
52. *ST* I, q. 1, a. 10, ad 3.
53. *De Potentia*, q. 4, a. 1.
54. Ibid.
55. Ibid. Author's translation of *veritati fidei*.

what is true. This means that exegetes must reject any interpretation of scripture that would serve to justify heresy, theological error, or blatantly false claims about philosophical and natural truths.

By embracing this exegetical principle, Aquinas situates himself in continuity with the ancient practice of reading scripture in light of ecclesial tradition. For Aquinas, the apostolic tradition of the Church is the first criterion by which one distinguishes true from false interpretations of scripture. As Elisabeth Reinhardt explains, this method of reading the Bible "*in Ecclesia*" means "the ultimate judgment about the canon of books and the interpretation of a particular text belong to the authority of the Church."[56] Further, Aquinas "not only consults the Magisterium, but also considers other sources present in the life of the Church as criteria of exegesis, such as the decretal collections of Canon Law, liturgical norms, and the life of the saints."[57] Aquinas was aware that scripture contained passages that could seem to oppose the revealed faith of the Church as well as even obvious natural truths. Nicholas Healy explains how Aquinas dealt with such passages: "when Scripture appears to be claiming something clearly untrue, its divine author must intend a meaning other than the apparent, one that can be true. The interpreter's responsibility is to find that meaning."[58] Aquinas is confident, therefore, that even scripture's challenging passages contain a divinely given meaning that is consistent with the rule of faith and with natural truths.

Aquinas's second negative principle of exegesis manifests his sensitivity to the meaning of the words on the page as well as his willingness to embrace a variety of interpretive possibilities. In *De Potentia* Aquinas states that "every truth that can be adapted to the sacred text without prejudice to the circumstance of the letter [*litterae circumstantia*] is the sense of Holy Scripture."[59] Later he specifies that scriptural interpretations are authentic as long as they

---

56. Elisabeth Reinhardt, "Thomas Aquinas as Interpreter of Scripture in the Light of His Inauguration Lectures," in *Reading Sacred Scripture with Thomas Aquinas* (ed. Roszak and Vijgen), 88.

57. Ibid., 89.

58. Healy, "Introduction," 17.

59. *De Potentia*, q. 4, a. 1; emphasis added. Author's translation of *litterae circumstantia*.

are "compatible [*patitur*] with the sense of the circumstance of the letter."[60] An interpretation is compatible with the circumstances of the letter when it "more or less fits the words and their context."[61] Exegesis must thus be attentive to the basic meaning of the words on the page and to the literary mode that those words employ. In this sense, Aquinas takes seriously the linguistic and rhetorical content of scripture.

Yet even sufficient attention to the rule of faith and to the linguistic intricacies of scripture does not always enable the reader to isolate one legitimate interpretation to the exclusion of all others. This is because, as we have already seen, a single series of letters in scripture can possess numerous literal senses. Given this reality, Aquinas says that readers of scripture must not "force" their own interpretation of scripture in such a way "as to exclude any other interpretations that are actually or possibly true according to the circumstance of the letter [*salva circumstantia litterae*]."[62] As Boyle explains, when Aquinas sees two different ways of interpreting the literal sense of scripture, he often "does not judge one to be correct, the other not," for "by his own criteria no such judgment can be made."[63] For example, Aquinas thinks that the Genesis creation account can legitimately be interpreted as saying either that God created all things at once or that he created all things gradually, little by little.[64] Neither interpretation violates the truth of faith or the circumstance of the letter, and so either can be held.

Yet this does not mean that both interpretations of Genesis are true. For, as Mark Johnson points out, "two mutually exclusive attributes cannot have occurred simultaneously," and "neither of these two modes of creation admits of the other."[65] The words of Genesis are not indicating that creation occurred both gradually and all at once, for this would mean that the words are signifying two incompatible things. Rather, Johnson says, "unless the context of the text of

---

60. Ibid.; emphasis added.

61. Boyle, *The Order and Division of Divine Truth*, 38.

62. *De Potentia*, q. 4, a. 1. Author's translation of *salva circumstantia litterae*.

63. Boyle, *The Order and Division of Divine Truth*, 40.

64. *De Potentia*, q. 4, a. 1.

65. Mark Johnson, "Another Look at the Plurality of the Literal Sense," *Medieval Philosophy and Theology* 2 (1992): 132.

Genesis, its *circumstantia litterae*, indicates to us clearly the modality of the creation of things, we shall not know that modality for certain. Thomas contends that the context allows for both accounts."[66] That is, in reality creation either occurred all at once or it occurred over time, but either view is consistent with the words of scripture and the truth of the faith. Neither the articles of the faith nor the words of scripture sufficiently specify the duration of God's creative activity, and so exegetes are justified in claiming that Genesis supports either view. In sum, Aquinas interprets scripture by being attentive to the meaning and mode of the words on the page, and he does so in light of the faith of the Church and truths that are knowable by human reason. Read in this way, scripture can convey a variety of true literal senses. Further, there are times when the content of the words can be legitimately interpreted in competing ways, but this does not mean that an individual word or series of words in scripture are intended to signify multiple, incompatible claims.

The third major exegetical method that Aquinas used to interpret scripture is what Reinhardt calls "explaining the Bible by the Bible."[67] For Aquinas, "a secure and connatural tool for explaining the Bible is the Bible itself, by using cross references which confirm or shed new light on a certain text."[68] One part of the Bible can interpret another part of the Bible given scripture's "uniformity of teaching," which refers to the notion that "all transmitters of revelation have taught the same doctrine unanimously."[69] There is a "profound harmony existing in the biblical texts, so that they illustrate and enlighten each other."[70] Given this harmony, as Piotr Roszak explains, Aquinas reads scripture "as a unity and not as a conglomerate of selected books read in isolation."[71] Scripture's unity of doctrine "results from the fact that God is the *auctor principalis* of the Holy Scripture and He leads the history of mankind."[72] Since salvation history is

---

66. Johnson, "Another Look at the Plurality of the Literal Sense," 132.

67. Reinhardt, "Thomas Aquinas as Interpreter of Scripture," 84.

68. Ibid.

69. Ibid., 78.

70. Ibid.

71. Piotr Roszak, "The Place and Function of Biblical Citations in Thomas Aquinas's Exegesis," in *Reading Sacred Scripture with Thomas Aquinas* (ed. Roszak and Vijgen), 119.

72. Roszak, "The Place and Function of Biblical Citations," 121.

directed by God, and since God inspired all of scripture, this means that "in the Old Testament the New is concealed," and "in the New the Old is revealed."[73] Consequently, interpreting the parts of the Bible in light of other parts and of the whole is not only helpful, but is in fact "necessary."[74]

As this book will show, Aquinas frequently quotes Isaiah 53 in order to shed light upon related biblical passages, such as the passion narratives of the Gospels. Conversely, he repeatedly draws upon other biblical texts in order to illuminate the meaning of Isaiah 53. He puts these various biblical texts into dialogue with one another on the basis of linguistic or thematic similarities that exist between them. In either event, though, Aquinas is putting the variously located *verba* of scripture into contact with one another in order to help him to discover the *res* that are signified by the main biblical text in question. Aquinas's method of interpreting the Bible in light of the Bible may seem like a strange method to contemporary readers who are accustomed to methods of exegesis that isolate the individual books of scripture, and even the various parts within a particular book, from one another. It thus bears repeating that the legitimacy of this practice, for Aquinas, is grounded in the legitimacy of the presuppositions that inform it. Those presuppositions are that God is the principal author of the entirety of scripture, and that all of scripture is about Christ, who is "the centre and summit of Sacred Scripture and ultimately the reason for its unity."[75]

Aquinas's fourth exegetical method was to interpret scripture with the help of the exegetical tradition of the Church. In accord with the custom of his age, Aquinas's exegesis drew heavily upon quotations from the Church Fathers. Leo Elders explains that for Aquinas "the proximity of the Fathers with the apostolic period" makes them "stand in a direct connection with Holy Scripture."[76] While "the authority of the Fathers is not absolute," nonetheless they

---

73. Ibid.

74. Ibid. On the various ways in which Aquinas uses a biblical citation in order to illuminate the meaning of another biblical text, see ibid., 131–38.

75. Reinhardt, "Thomas Aquinas as Interpreter of Scripture," 88.

76. Leo J. Elders, "The Presence of the Church Fathers in Aquinas's Commentaries on the Gospel of Matthew and the Gospel of John," in *Reading Sacred Scripture with Thomas Aquinas* (ed. Roszak and Vijgen), 257.

are a generally reliable "source of Christian doctrine insofar as they present and explain what is contained in the Bible and their teachings have been received by the Church."[77] In the *Summa Theologiae*, Aquinas specifies that the exegetical and theological arguments of the Church Fathers "may properly be used, yet merely as probable."[78] At times Aquinas presents diverse patristic interpretations of a particular passage of scripture because each of these interpretations help to draw out the numerous realities that a particular series of scriptural words signify. Yet, as Reinhardt explains, Aquinas's use of the Fathers "is not only reverential, but also critical and, when necessary, he resolves discrepancies and apparent contradictions between the different patristic sources."[79] While willing to disagree with particular patristic readings, often Aquinas does not think it is necessary to choose one patristic interpretation over another. For example, as Bruce Marshall points out, in *De Potentia*, q. 4, a. 1, Aquinas says that both Augustine's and the Cappadocians' interpretations of the creation account in Genesis are in accord with the truth of faith and the circumstances of the letter.[80] Hence, despite the tension between the two accounts, either can be held.[81] In sum, Aquinas uses the exegetical views of the Fathers frequently, reverently, and yet critically.

The fifth and final major exegetical method of Aquinas that we will consider here is the *divisio textus*, or, division of the text. Aquinas's commentaries on individual books of the Bible always included "an analysis of the [biblical] text into its component parts in order to elucidate their interrelationship and unity," and "Thomas often divides the text down to the level of the individual words themselves."[82] Many modern readers find Aquinas's divisions of the text to be unhelpful and at times even arbitrary.[83] Conversely, Boyle views

77. Ibid., 271 and 257, respectively. Aquinas's reverence for the exegesis of the Fathers is displayed with particular force in his *Catena Aurea* upon the four Gospels, which he composed at the request of Pope Urban IV. See Elders, "The Presence," 258.

78. *ST* I, q. 1, a. 8, ad 2.

79. Reinhardt, "Thomas Aquinas as Interpreter of Scripture," 85.

80. See Bruce Marshall, "Absorbing the Word: Christianity and the Universe of Truths," in *Theology and Dialogue: Essays in Conversation with George Lindbeck*, ed. Bruce Marshall (Notre Dame, Ind.: University of Notre Dame Press, 1990), 90–95.

81. Marshall, "Absorbing the Word," 93.

82. Sirilla, "Lectio Scripturae at the Heart of Aquinas's Theology and Preaching," 75.

83. For example, see the reservations expressed in Healy, "Introduction," 9–10.

the *divisio* as an example of the "genius" of Scholastic biblical commentaries.[84] For through the *divisio* "a commentator states some
theme that serves as an interpretive key for his commentary," with
the result that "no verse stands in isolation" from that main theme.[85]
The *divisio* is thus a way of identifying how the various parts of a
biblical text serve as means which are ordered toward the end of
the book as a whole.[86] The meaning and purpose of words, phrases,
sentences, verses and chapters can all be understood in relation to
the ultimate intent of the divine author for a particular book. "This
method," Sirilla explains, "evidently presupposes a theory of scriptural inspiration that discerns meaning in every part of the text."[87]
For Aquinas there are no superfluous portions of scripture; while
certain words and sections may not be as critical as others in terms
of their substance or rhetoric, nonetheless every word of scripture is
in some way ordered toward the end of the text in question. We will
see Aquinas's emphasis on the significance of particular words and
sentences of Isaiah 53 and other biblical texts throughout this book.
Further, in the chapter on the *Commentary on Isaiah,* we will see how
Aquinas divides the text of Isaiah 53 and relates it to the book of
Isaiah as a whole.

To summarize, Aquinas deployed five major methods in his exegesis of the literal sense: first, he presumed that scripture only asserts what is true, and therefore the literal sense of scripture can
never contradict the supernatural truths of the faith or truths that
can be known by the natural light of human reason; second, an individual passage may have multiple literal senses as long as each of
those meanings is in accord with the basic content of the words on
the page; third, since God is the principal author of the entirety of
scripture, and since Christ is the unifying theme of scripture, particular biblical texts function as keys which unlock and confirm the
meaning of other biblical texts; fourth, the Church Fathers are an
important witness to the meaning of the literal sense given their
proximity to the biblical era and the reception of their teachings

<hr>

84. Boyle, *The Order and Division of Divine Truth,* 17.
85. Ibid., 42–43.
86. Ibid.
87. Sirilla, "Lectio Scripturae at the Heart of Aquinas's Theology and Preaching," 75.

within the Church; fifth, Aquinas always divided and organized biblical books in a way that enabled him to identify the meaning of particular words, verses and chapters in light of the purpose of the book
as a whole. Having examined these five major methods, I now proceed in the final section of this chapter to explain how the reality of
the literal sense fits into the practice of theology.

AQUINAS'S UNDERSTANDING OF THE RELATIONSHIP BETWEEN SCRIPTURE AND THEOLOGY

Scripture is foundational to Aquinas's understanding of theology.
At the outset of the *Summa Theologiae*, Aquinas describes theology
as a science, which means that it is a particular kind of intellectual
discipline that has its own first principles, methods of discovery, and
scope. The first principles of theology are the contents of divine revelation. Using reason and all of the insights of the natural sciences,
the theologian strives to understand all that God has revealed about
himself and creation. The truths of divine revelation are preserved
and handed down in the Catholic Church's articles of faith as well as
in sacred scripture.[88] Hence, as Thomas O'Meara states, for Aquinas
"the scriptural text and the reality to which the text witnessed gave
theology's first foundation and inspiration."[89] Since scripture contains the divinely revealed truths that function as the first principles of the science of theology, this means that the first task of the
theologian is to clarify the literal sense of scripture. Then, the literal sense of scripture enables the theologian to perform two additional tasks. Wilhelmus Valkenburg explains, "in the second place,
theology uses Scripture as a proper and cogent element in its scholarly argumentation; in the third place, the theological truth found
in this argumentation is confronted with Scripture in order to check

88. *ST* I, q. 1, aa. 1–8. On Aquinas's understanding of the relationship between revelation,
scripture, and theology, see Francis Martin, *Sacred Scripture: The Disclosure of the Word*
(Naples, Fla.: Sapientia Press of Ave Maria University, 2006), 1–19; on the Christocentric
and biblical character of revelation, see Michael Dauphinais, "The Place of Christ and the
Biblical Narrative in Aquinas's Theology of Revelation," in *Thomas Aquinas: Biblical Theologian*
(ed. Nutt and Dauphinais), 1–34.

89. O'Meara, *Thomas Aquinas: Theologian*, 68.

whether it is in accordance with divine revelation."[90] In sum, for Aquinas the literal sense of scripture serves as the "basis and norm for any theological argument."[91]

Aquinas exercises these three theological tasks in his academic biblical commentaries. There he frequently moves from identifying the literal sense of a particular verse to a consideration of the speculative theological questions that are raised by the text in question. In order to answer these questions, he utilizes analytical philosophical reasoning. But he also attempts to answer these speculative questions by appealing to the authority of other biblical texts. These additional passages of scripture function as proofs which contribute to his philosophical arguments.[92] Hence, in Aquinas's biblical commentaries there is an inseparable and mutually enriching relationship between exegesis of the literal sense and speculative theology.[93]

A similar dynamic is on display in Aquinas's systematic works, and especially in the *Summa Theologiae*. There, as O'Meara points out, scripture's "words are on every page."[94] Biblical texts are frequently present in the *sed contra*, where they provide a basic answer to the question posed by the article and serve as the foundation for the speculative exposition of the answer that will unfold in the body of the article. In this sense, the body of the articles in the *Summa* are often like short, dense speculative commentaries upon the literal sense of the biblical text contained in the *sed contra*. Further, the body of the article itself often contains biblical passages that serve to provide further support and clarification to the answer that is being explicated. Biblical passages are also frequently present in the

90. Valkenburg, *Words of the Living God*, 16.

91. Healy, "Introduction," 16. See also 4–9, where Healy points out that Aquinas's insistence on the fundamental necessity of the literal sense to theological arguments was in response to heretics who tried to justify their false teachings on the basis of so-called spiritual senses.

92. Sirilla, "Lectio Scripturae at the Heart of Aquinas's Theology and Preaching," 66 and 71–73, and Chenu, *Toward Understanding Saint Thomas*, 253.

93. See "Introduction," in *Reading John with St. Thomas Aquinas* (ed. Dauphinais and Levering), xiii: "speculative thinking about divine realities emerges from within biblical exegesis itself," and there is a "circular movement from biblical exegesis to speculative theology and back again." Hence, "biblical exegesis depends upon the exegete's gifts as a speculative theologian, which in turn depends upon the exegete's acquaintance with not merely the particular text at hand but indeed the whole Scriptures."

94. O'Meara, *Thomas Aquinas: Theologian*, 69.

objections and replies within each article, showing that the attempt to answer the question posed by the article must be attentive to the witness of the inspired text. Hence, the *Summa* is "necessarily authorized and informed by exegesis."[95] While scripture is omnipresent in the *Summa*, O'Meara makes an important clarification: "the subject matter of Aquinas's [systematic] theology, however, is not so much biblical phrases as the realities to which they point: God active in history, covenant and incarnation, grace and life."[96] Aquinas's systematic works are imbued with scripture precisely because in those works he seeks to speculatively explore the realities that are signified by the biblical words.

CONCLUSION

Scripture was a foundational and central feature of Thomas Aquinas's religious and scholarly life. His personal and prayerful encounters with scripture began during his childhood years as a Benedictine oblate and continued on a daily basis throughout his adult life as a Dominican priest. As a university scholar, his primary tasks were to lecture on, dispute, and preach the scriptures. His biblical commentaries focus on expounding the literal sense and engaging the speculative theological questions that are raised by that sense. His systematic works, on the other hand, focus on speculative theological reflection and argument, and yet the foundation, framework, and often even the material for those speculative arguments are the scriptures themselves.[97] Hence, as M. D. Chenu puts it, Aquinas's biblical commentaries were an exercise in "*theological* exegesis" and his systematic works were forms of "biblical theology."[98] And throughout all of these works, Aquinas attempted to interpret scripture with due deference to natural truths, the faith of the Church, and the entirety of the biblical canon.

---

95. Healy, "Introduction," 12–13.

96. O'Meara, *Thomas Aquinas: Theologian*, 69.

97. See Scott Hahn, "Foreword," in *Thomas Aquinas: Biblical Theologian* (ed. Nutt and Dauphinais), x: "The centrality of Scripture for Aquinas is evident in the two Summas, which contain around twenty-five thousand explicit biblical citations."

98. Chenu, *Toward Understanding Saint Thomas*, 253 and 259, respectively.

With this historical and theological context in mind, we are now better equipped to understand how and why Aquinas uses and interprets the text of Isaiah 53 in the various ways that he does throughout his biblical commentaries and systematic works. The various functions of scripture in Aquinas's theology that were described in this chapter apply to his engagements with Isaiah 53. As we will see, he reads Isaiah's prophecy as a normative source of divine revelation; as a foundation for speculative and deductive theological reasoning; and as a proof in theological argumentation, both in objections and in replies to objections. At all times, Aquinas analyzes the words of Isaiah 53 in order to pass through them to the divine realities that they signify. Having concluded this historical overview of Aquinas's engagement with and understanding of scripture, we are now in a position to complete one more contextualizing step before proceeding to the original contribution of this book. In the next chapter, our task is to examine the basic content of the text of Isaiah 53 and to compare Aquinas's edition of that text with our own.

2

—— ⦂ ——

Contextualizing Isaiah 53

In the previous chapter, I presented the central features of Aquinas's engagement with and understanding of scripture as manifested throughout his religious and scholarly career. In this chapter, I will continue to establish context which will enable us to better understand and appreciate Aquinas's Christological interpretations of Isaiah 53. Specifically, I will survey the basic literary and theological features of the text of Isaiah 53. This exegetical presentation will introduce the major contours and themes of Isaiah's text. With this basic understanding of the text of Isaiah 53 in place, the reader will be better equipped to understand and evaluate Aquinas's particular reception of that text. Then I will build upon this exegetical survey of Isaiah 53 by looking specifically at Aquinas's Latin version of the text of Isaiah 53. I will provide a basic comparison of Aquinas's edition to contemporary translations of critical editions (Hebrew and Greek) of Isaiah 53. The textual and exegetical analysis of this chapter will give the reader a framework to critically examine Aquinas's various interpretations of Isaiah 53 that I will analyze in the remainder of this work.

BASIC FEATURES AND THEMES OF
THE TEXT OF ISAIAH 53

Isaiah 53 is the major portion of a text that contemporary exegetes call the "fourth Servant song," and this text consists of Isaiah 52:13–53:12.[1] There is debate regarding whether or not the Servant of Isaiah's four Servant songs is an individual, a group, or both. Further, among those who agree that the Servant is an individual, many still disagree regarding the identity of that individual.[2] Richard Clifford states that the fourth Servant song "remains especially controverted. Who is the Servant, ideal Israel or a historical individual? Whose sins has he borne—the nations' or Israel's? What is meant by his vicarious suffering, otherwise unattested in the OT?"[3] Hence, Clifford concludes that there is no "consensus" regarding these issues.[4] Despite the obscurities of these elements of the fourth Servant song, we can nonetheless make some observations regarding the basic content of the text.

The fourth Servant song consists of three principal parts. Hans-Jurgen Hermission states that the "clear structure" of the song becomes evident when one pays attention to the "changing speakers" of the text.[5] God is the one speaking in Isaiah 52:13–15 as well as in 53:11b–12.[6] These "two Yahweh speeches" constitute "the beginning and end" of the song, and "in between [them] stands 53:1–11a."[7] This latter, "central section" is divided "into verses 1–6 and verses 8–11a," while "verse 7 takes up a special position between the two parts of the text."[8] The uniqueness of v. 7 lies in the fact that it alone speaks of

1. Richard J. Clifford, "Second Isaiah," in *The Anchor Bible Dictionary, vol. 3: H–J*, ed. David Noel Freedman (New York: Doubleday, 1992), 500. The first three Servant songs are Is 42:1–4, 49:1–6, and 50:4–9, respectively (see ibid., 499).

2. Clifford, "Second Isaiah," 499.

3. Ibid., 500.

4. Ibid.

5. Hans-Jurgen Hermisson, "The Fourth Servant Song in the Context of Second Isaiah," in *The Suffering Servant: Isaiah 53 in Jewish and Christian Sources*, ed. Bernd Janowski and Peter Stuhlmacher (Grand Rapids, Mich.: Eerdmans, 2004), 31.

6. Is 53:11b begins with "my Servant ..." Unless otherwise noted, all quotations from Isaiah 53 in this chapter are taken from NRSV-CE.

7. Hermisson, "The Fourth Servant Song in the Context of Second Isaiah," 31.

8. Ibid.

"the Servant's own independent behavior in response to the suffering inflicted upon him," whereas all of the surrounding verses in the central section "speak only of the fate the Servant must suffer."[9] In sum, the fourth Servant song begins and ends with two speeches by God (52:13–15 and 53:11b–12) that summarize the fate of the Servant, and the central portion of the song is a dramatic description of the Servant's suffering, his reaction to that suffering, and the attitude of his peers toward him (53:1–11a).

The three major parts of the fourth Servant song each have their own subdivisions and thematic emphases. In the first part (52:13–15), God "announces the triumph of the Servant" and "the amazement of the nations" at the Servant's victory.[10] In these verses, God is speaking about the "humiliation" of the Servant in the "past" and proclaiming the Servant's "future destiny" of "exaltation."[11] The second part (53:1–11a) focuses primarily upon the suffering of the Servant. Carroll Stuhlmueller subdivides this part into four sections: the "narrative of sorrows" (vv. 1–3), "sorrow as part of the Servant's ministry" (vv. 4–6), "sorrow, silently accepted" (vv. 7–9), and "good results" (vv. 10–11a).[12] The third part (53:11b–12) features God once again as the speaker, and once again God describes the Servant's past suffering as well as his future exaltation or "the compensation for his previous fate."[13] Further, this final part is "about the good effects of the Servant's ministry."[14] The *Navarre Bible* nicely summarizes the major themes of the fourth Servant song: "In terms of content, the song is unusual in that it shows the Servant triumphing through his humiliation and suffering. Even more than that—he makes the pains and sins of others his own, in order to heal them and set them free."[15]

---

9. Ibid. Is 53:7 states: "He was oppressed, and he was afflicted, yet he did not open his mouth; like a lamb that is led to the slaughter, and like a sheep that before its shearers is silent, so he did not open his mouth."

10. Carroll Stuhlmueller, "Deutero-Isaiah and Trito-Isaiah," in *The New Jerome Biblical Commentary*, ed. Raymond E. Brown, Joseph A. Fitzmyer, and Roland E. Murphy (Englewood Cliffs, N.J.: Prentice Hall, 1990), 342.

11. Hermisson, "The Fourth Servant Song in the Context of Second Isaiah," 31.

12. Stuhlmueller, "Deutero-Isaiah and Trito-Isaiah," 342.

13. Hermisson, "The Fourth Servant Song in the Context of Second Isaiah," 31.

14. Stuhlmueller, "Deutero-Isaiah and Trito-Isaiah," 342.

15. *The Navarre Bible: Major Prophets—Isaiah, Jeremiah, Ezekiel, Daniel* (New York: Scepter, 2005), 233.

Having established this outline of the major sections and themes of the fourth Servant song, we can now take a brief look at each of its verses, with a special focus upon Isaiah 53:1–12. My purpose here is not to provide an in-depth, critical analysis of these verses. Rather, my goal here is simply to set forth the basic sense of the words and to give the reader a sense of the logical flow of the song as a whole.[16] The first part of the song (52:13–15) begins in v. 13 with God proclaiming the future exaltation of the Servant. Then, in 53:14, he acknowledges how in the past the Servant endured intense suffering, such that "many were astonished at him." In 52:15, God states that the exaltation of the Servant, after his previous, public suffering, will "startle many nations" and silence kings, for they shall recognize the newfound glory of the Servant. Hence, Isaiah 52:13–15 summarizes the salvific activity of the Servant: he has suffered and been rejected, and yet God is going to exalt him. When God does so, nations and kings will be amazed.

The second part (53:1–11a) begins in 53:1, where the discourse shifts from God to a different, unspecified speaker. The speaker indicates that no one has believed the proclamation of God about the exaltation of the Suffering Servant that was conveyed in 52:13–15. The reason for this unbelief regarding the exaltation of the Servant is precisely because of the great suffering and misery that the Servant underwent publicly. This suffering begins to be presented in 53:2, which describes the miserable origin and appearance of the Servant before the world. Because of this misery, 53:3 explains, the Servant was "despised and rejected by others." In 53:4, the speaker states how the Servant suffered with the pains that are due to sinners. Hence his peers interpreted his suffering as a punishment which was imposed upon him by God as a consequence for his sins. But 53:5 offers a corrective to the view of the Servant's peers: the Servant is not suffering

16. For further contemporary literary and theological commentary on Is 52:13–53:12, see Charles E. Shepherd, *Theological Interpretation and Isaiah 53: A Critical Comparison of Bernhard Duhm, Brevard Childs, and Alec Motyer* (London: Bloomsbury, 2014); Brevard S. Childs, *Isaiah* (Louisville, Ky.: Westminster John Knox Press, 2001), 407–23; Joseph Blenkinsopp, *The Anchor Bible: Isaiah 40–55: A New Translation with Introduction and Commentary* (New York: Doubleday, 2002), 344–57; Hermission, "The Fourth Servant Song in the Context of Second Isaiah," in *The Suffering Servant: Isaiah 53 in Jewish and Christian Sources*, 16–47; John L. McKenzie, *The Anchor Bible: Second Isaiah—Introduction, Translation, and Notes* (Garden City, N.Y.: Doubleday, 1968), 132–35.

due to his own sins, but rather for the sins of others. Further, his suffering is a source of healing for sinners. In 53:6, the reason for the Servant's suffering is further explained: "all we like sheep have gone astray." The people have turned away from God through sin, and so for this reason God places the "iniquity" (53:6) of all those sinners upon the Servant, and 53:7 explains how the Servant handles his suffering, namely, with silence and passive resignation, "like a lamb that is led to the slaughter." Despite the fact that he was "oppressed" and "afflicted" (53:7), the Servant does not even offer a verbal defense of his innocence.

In 53:8, the speaker states that the Servant is killed, that his death was unjust, and once again that he died as a consequence of the people's sins. Given that the Servant was rejected even to the point of being put to death, his future exaltation is inconceivable: "who could have imagined his future?" (53:8). Next, 53:9 reiterates that the Servant was killed as if he was a criminal, and yet the truth is that the Servant was completely innocent. In 53:10, the speaker clarifies the role of divine providence in the Servant's suffering and death. God willed that the Servant endure suffering, and the Servant's very endurance of that pain was "an offering for sin" (53:10). As a result of his sacrificial, atoning offering of self, the Servant will be personally rewarded by God with offspring and prolonged life. Further, "the will of the LORD shall prosper" (53:10) amidst the people as a result of the Servant's humiliation and exaltation, while 53:11 reiterates that the Servant will be rewarded for his suffering and that his suffering will produce salvific effects for the people.

Part III of the Servant song (53:11b–12) begins in 53:11b ("my Servant shall make many righteous"), where God once again becomes the speaker and proclaims that the Servant will justify the people precisely because he bore "their iniquities." The song ends with the proclamation of God in 53:12. There, God once more states that he will exalt the Servant precisely because he "poured himself out to death and was numbered with the transgressors." Further, God clarifies, the Servant suffered precisely for the salvation of the "many" from their sins, and he gave of himself as "intercession" for them (53:12). Hence, the song ends with God's declaration that the

Servant's suffering was ordered toward the salvation of sinners, and further with the promise that God himself will reward the Servant for his saving sacrifice.

Having examined the basic structure, content, and meaning of Isaiah 53 within the context of the fourth Servant song, we can now proceed to examine Aquinas's specifically Latin version of the text of Isaiah 53.

AQUINAS'S LATIN VERSION OF ISAIAH 53

I begin here with a few general observations regarding Aquinas's Latin text. Aquinas used the same Latin version of Isaiah 53 in all of the works that I examine in this book. There are a few occasions when he paraphrased that text or, quoting from memory, errantly combined phrases from distinct verses into one, original formulation. Hence, in those latter instances his wording departs from the Latin text of Isaiah 53 that he typically works with. But, in the overwhelming majority of cases, Aquinas's quotations of Isaiah 53 are accurately taken from a Latin version of that biblical text that he used as normative throughout his theological career, beginning with his *Commentary on Isaiah* and ending with his *Commentary on the Psalms*. In table 2-1 I present this Latin text of Isaiah 53 along with an English translation of that text.[17] With the exception of a few instances that I will note, throughout this book I use this English translation.

Having established Aquinas's Latin version of Isaiah 53, we can now compare his edition of this biblical text to other significant editions of that text that are in use today. In table 2-2, I place the English translation of Aquinas's text of Isaiah 53 alongside contemporary English versions of Isaiah 53 that are translated from Hebrew and Greek editions. The English translation from Hebrew is the version of Isaiah 53 that is contained in the *New Revised Standard Version Catholic Edition* (hereafter NRSV-CE). This translation is based

---

17. This complete Latin version of Is 53, as well as the English translation, is contained in chap. 53 of Aquinas's *Commentary on Isaiah*, trans. Louis St. Hilaire, edited and published by the Aquinas Institute and available at aquinas.cc/la/en/~Isaiah.C53. The Latin text is from the 1974 Leonine edition of Aquinas's work.

TABLE 2-1. AQUINAS'S LATIN VERSION OF ISAIAH 53

1. Quis credidit auditui nostro? Et brachium Domini cui revelatum est?	1. Who has believed our report? and to whom is the arm of the Lord revealed?
2. Et ascendet sicut virgultum coram eo et sicut radix de terra sitienti. Et non est species ei neque decor; et vidimus eum, et non erat aspectus. Et desideravimus eum	2. And he shall rise up as a tender plant before him, and as a root out of a thirsty ground: there is no form in him, nor comeliness: and we have seen him, and there was no sightliness, that we should be desirous of him:
3. despectum et novissimum virorum, virum dolorum et scientem infirmitatem; et quasi absconditus vultus ejus et despectus: unde nec reputavimus eum.	3. Despised, and the most abject of men, a man of sorrows, and acquainted with infirmity: and his look was as it were hidden and despised, whereupon we esteemed him not.
4. Vere languores nostros ipse tulit et dolores nostros ipse portavit; et nos reputavimus eum quasi leprosum et percussum a Deo et humiliatum.	4. Truly he has borne our infirmities and carried our sorrows: and we have thought him as it were a leper, and as one struck by God and afflicted.
5. Ipse autem vulneratus est propter iniquitates nostras, attritus est propter scelera nostra; disciplina pacis nostræ super eum, et livore ejus sanati sumus.	5. But he was wounded for our iniquities, he was bruised for our sins: the chastisement of our peace was upon him, and by his bruises we are healed.
6. Omnes nos quasi oves erravimus, unusquisque in viam suam declinavit, et Dominus posuit in eo iniquitatem omnium nostrum.	6. All we like sheep have gone astray, every one has turned aside into his own way: and the Lord has laid on him the iniquity of us all.
7. Oblatus est quia ipse voluit, et non aperuit os suum. Sicut ovis ad occisionem ducetur, et quasi agnus coram tondente se obmutescet, et non aperiet os suum.	7. He was offered because he himself willed it,[1] and he opened not his mouth: he shall be led as a sheep to the slaughter, and shall be dumb as a lamb before his shearer, and he shall not open his mouth.
8. De angustia et de judicio sublatus est. Generationem ejus quis enarrabit? Quia abscissus est de terra viventium. Propter scelus populi mei percussi eum.	8. He was taken away from distress, and from judgment: who shall declare his generation? because he is cut off out of the land of the living: for the wickedness of my people have I struck him.
9. Et dabit impios pro sepultura et divites pro morte sua, eo quod iniquitatem non fecerit neque dolus fuerit in ore ejus;	9. And he shall give the ungodly for his burial, and the rich for his death: because he has done no iniquity, neither was there deceit in his mouth.
10. et Dominus voluit conterere eum in infirmitate. Si posuerit pro peccato animam suam, videbit semen longævum et voluntas Domini in manu ejus dirigetur;	10. And the Lord was pleased to bruise him in infirmity: if he shall lay down his life for sin, he shall see a long-lived seed, and the will of the Lord shall be directed in his hand.
11. pro eo quod laboravit anima ejus, videbit et saturabitur: in scientia sua justificabit ipse justus servus meus multos et iniquitates eorum ipse portabit.	11. Because his soul has labored, he shall see and be filled: by his knowledge shall this my just servant justify many, and he shall bear their iniquities.
12. Ideo dispertiam ei plurimos, et fortium dividet spolia, pro eo quod tradidit in mortem animam suam, et cum sceleratis reputatus est. Et ipse peccatum multorum tulit et pro transgressoribus rogavit.	12. Therefore will I distribute to him very many, and he shall divide the spoils of the strong, because he has delivered his soul unto death, and was reputed with the wicked: and he has borne the sins of many, and has prayed for the transgressors.

1. Author's translation of "Oblatus est quia ipse voluit." Unless otherwise noted, throughout this chapter and book I consistently translate Aquinas's Latin version of Is 53:7a in this way.

primarily on the Hebrew *Biblia Hebraica Stuttgartensia* of 1983, which is itself based on the "Codex Leningradensis" of 1008.[18] As John Bergsma and Brant Pitre explain, *Leningradensis* is "the oldest complete manuscript of the Hebrew books of the Old Testament" and it "is a complete copy of the Masoretic Text written in Galilee around A.D. 1000."[19] The English translation from Greek is the version that is contained in the 2007 *New English Translation of the Septuagint.*[20] This translation is of a contemporary critical edition Greek text that is based on the fourth-century Egyptian *Codex Alexandrinus,* which is "our best available witness" to the ancient, Greek version of the text of Isaiah.[21]

Table 2-2 shows the basic similarities and differences between Aquinas's Latin version of Isaiah 53 and our contemporary translations of Hebrew and Greek versions of that biblical text. A comparison of these three versions shows that a substantial similarity exists between them on two levels. First, in terms of the overall message, and second, in terms of the language that is used to convey that message. All three versions are clearly referring to the same central *res,* and they do so in their respective ways by using very similar *verba.* That is, the Latin, Hebrew, and Greek versions of Isaiah 53 that are represented above can all be accurately rendered into English in very similar, and often even identical, ways. In light of this, the fact that Aquinas's interpretations of Isaiah 53 are dependent upon a Latin version of that text should not cause us to immediately discount his

18. See Bruce M. Metzger, "To the Reader," in NRSV-CE, xi; "The Biblia Hebraica Stuttgartensia," German Bible Society, available at academic-bible.com/en/bible-society-and-biblical-studies/scholarly-editions/hebrew-bible/bhs/.

19. John Bergsma and Brant Pitre, *A Catholic Introduction to the Bible, vol. 1: The Old Testament* (San Francisco, Calif.: Ignatius Press, 2018), 34. They explain: "*Leningradensis* is almost universally regarded as the oldest and best copy of the Masoretic Text," and so "when translating or studying the Old Testament today, scholars typically begin from the Hebrew of the Masoretic Text" as contained in an "edition of *Leningradensis*" (35).

20. "Esaias 53," trans. Moises Silva, in *A New English Translation of the Septuagint,* ed. Albert Pietersma and Benjamin G. Wright (Oxford: Oxford University Press, 2007), 865–66.

21. Silva, "Esaias: To the Reader," in *A New English Translation of the Septuagint,* 823. As Bergsma and Pitre point out in *A Catholic Introduction to the Bible,* the Septuagint translation was begun around 250 B.C. Further, "the majority of the Old Testament quotations in the New Testament are taken from the Greek Septuagint," and "our oldest more-or-less complete manuscripts of the entire Bible come from" the fourth century A.D. "and consist of the Septuagint plus the New Testament in Greek" (36).

TABLE 2-2. LATIN, HEBREW, AND GREEK VERSIONS OF ISAIAH 53

From the Latin:	From the Hebrew:	From the Greek:
1. Who has believed our report? and to whom is the arm of the Lord revealed?	1. Who has believed what we have heard? And to whom has the arm of the Lord been revealed?	1. Lord, who has believed our report? And to whom has the arm of the Lord been revealed?
2. And he shall rise up as a tender plant before him, and as a root out of a thirsty ground: there is no form in him, nor comeliness: and we have seen him, and there was no sightliness, that we should be desirous of him:	2. For he grew up before him like a young plant, and like a root out of dry ground; he had no form or majesty that we should look at him, nothing in his appearance that we should desire him.	2. He grew up before him like a child, like a root in a thirsty land; he has no form or glory, and we saw him, and he had no form or beauty.
3. Despised, and the most abject of men, a man of sorrows, and acquainted with infirmity: and his look was as it were hidden and despised, whereupon we esteemed him not.	3. He was despised and rejected by others; a man of suffering and acquainted with infirmity; and as one from whom others hide their faces he was despised, and we held him of no account.	3. But his form was without honor, failing beyond all men, a man being in calamity and knowing how to bear sickness; because his face is turned away, he was dishonored and not esteemed.
4. Truly he has borne our infirmities and carried our sorrows: and we have thought him as it were a leper, and as one struck by God and afflicted.	4. Surely he has borne our infirmities and carried our diseases; yet we accounted him stricken, struck down by God, and afflicted.	4. This one bears our sins and suffers pain for us, and we accounted him to be in trouble and calamity and ill-treatment.
5. But he was wounded for our iniquities, he was bruised for our sins: the chastisement of our peace was upon him, and by his bruises we are healed.	5. But he was wounded for our transgressions, crushed for our iniquities; upon him was the punishment that made us whole, and by his bruises we are healed.	5. But he was wounded because of our acts of lawlessness and has been weakened because of our sins; upon him was the discipline of our peace; by his bruise we were healed.
6. All we like sheep have gone astray, every one has turned aside into his own way: and the Lord has laid on him the iniquity of us all.	6. All we like sheep have gone astray; we have turned to our own way, and the Lord has laid on him the iniquity of us all.	6. All we like sheep have gone astray; a man has strayed in his own way, and the Lord gave him over to our sins.
7. He was offered because he himself willed it, and he opened not his mouth: he shall be led as a sheep to the slaughter, and shall be dumb as a lamb before his shearer, and he shall not open his mouth.	7. He was oppressed, and he was afflicted, yet he did not open his mouth; like a lamb that is led to the slaughter, and like a sheep that before its shearers is silent, so he did not open his mouth.	7. And he, because he has been ill-treated, does not open his mouth; like a sheep he was led to the slaughter, and as a lamb is silent before the one shearing it, so he does not open his mouth.
8. He was taken away from distress, and from judgment: who shall declare his generation? Because he is cut off out of the land of the living: for the wickedness of my people have I struck him.	8. By a perversion of justice he was taken away. Who could have imagined his future? For he was cut off from the land of the living, stricken for the transgression of my people.	8. In his humiliation his judgment was taken away. Who will describe his generation? Because his life is being taken from the earth, he was led to death on account of the acts of lawlessness of my people.

(table continues)

**TABLE 2-2. LATIN, HEBREW, AND GREEK
VERSIONS OF ISAIAH 53** *(continued)*

From the Latin:	From the Hebrew:	From the Greek:
10. And the Lord was pleased to bruise him in infirmity: if he shall lay down his life for sin, he shall see a long-lived seed, and the will of the Lord shall be directed in his hand.	10. Yet it was the will of the Lord to crush him with pain When you make his life an offering for sin, he shall see his offspring, and shall prolong his days; through him the will of the Lord shall prosper.	10. And the Lord desires to cleanse him from his blow. If you offer for sin, your soul shall see a long-lived offspring. And the Lord wishes to take away
11. Because his soul has labored, he shall see and be filled: by his knowledge shall this my just servant justify many, and he shall bear their iniquities.	11. Out of his anguish he shall see light; he shall find satisfaction through his knowledge. The righteous one, my servant, shall make many righteous, and he shall bear their iniquities.	11. from the pain of his soul, to show him light and fill him with understanding, to justify a righteous one who is well subject to many, and he himself shall bear their sins.
12. Therefore will I distribute to him very many, and he shall divide the spoils of the strong, because he has delivered his soul unto death, and was reputed with the wicked: and he has borne the sins of many, and has prayed for the transgressors.	12. Therefore I will allot him a portion with the great, and he shall divide the spoil with the strong; because he poured out himself to death, and was numbered with the transgressors; yet he bore the sin of many, and made intercession for the transgressors.	12. Therefore he shall inherit many, and he shall divide the spoils of the strong, because his soul was given over to death, and he was reckoned among the lawless, and he bore the sins of many, and because of their sins he was given over.

exegesis on the assumption that his texts are substantially different from the Hebrew and Greek texts that scholars often privilege today.

On the other hand, there are some differences between the three versions of Isaiah 53 that are worth noting. The Greek version of 53:4 does not indicate that the Servant's peers considered him to be struck by God. Whereas the Latin and Hebrew of 53:6 say that God has laid the iniquity of sinners onto the Servant, the Greek version says that God "gave him over to our sins." Perhaps most significantly, only Aquinas's Latin version of 53:7 begins with the statement that the Servant "was offered because he himself willed it." Neither the Hebrew nor the Greek versions have anything remotely similar to this statement in their seventh verses. Similarly, only in the Latin of 53:8 does it say that God is the one who "struck" the Servant, while the Hebrew and Greek merely indicate that the Servant is indeed stricken and killed. Also in 53:8, the Hebrew uses "his future" instead of "his generation." In 53:10, the Latin and Hebrew state that the Lord "was pleased" and "will[ed]" to strike the Servant, respectively. Conversely, the Greek version instead says that God "desires to cleanse him from his blow." Finally, unlike the Latin and Hebrew editions, only the Greek edition of 53:11 fails to explicitly indicate that the Servant's suffering will justify sinners.

Of all these differences, the most significant for our purposes are those that pertain to 53:7–8. Regarding the latter, Aquinas frequently interprets the 'generation' of the Servant in a Christological way, and this Christological reading would likely be lost if he had to use the Hebrew version, which employs 'future' instead of 'generation.' The most significant, unique feature of Aquinas's Latin text is the opening clause of 53:7. The reason is that, as we will see throughout this book, Aquinas refers to these words ("he was offered because he himself willed it") more times than he does to any other passages of Isaiah 53, with the exception of the latter portion of 53:7 ("he shall be led as a sheep to the slaughter"), which he quotes an equal number of times. Further, Aquinas's numerous references to the opening clause of 53:7 are often employed in the service of significant, systematic explanations regarding the voluntary nature of Christ's passion. It is beyond the scope of this book to identify why exactly Aquinas's Latin version of Isaiah 53:7 has this clause.[22] Nor is it my task at the moment to determine whether the inclusion of this clause is justified from a textual criticism standpoint.[23] My purpose here is simply to point out that Aquinas makes frequent and substantial theological use of a passage from Isaiah 53 that is not present in contemporary Hebrew and Greek editions of Isaiah 53.

22. This portion of 53:7 is not referred to in the comments of the medieval *Glossa Ordinaria* on Is 53, but it is present in Jerome's *Commentary on Isaiah*. Hence, Aquinas's possession and use of this version of 53:7 is by no means unique or new for his time. See Jerome, *Commentary on Isaiah: Including St. Jerome's Translation of Origen's Homilies 1–9 On Isaiah*, trans. Thomas P. Scheck (Mahwah, N.J.: Newman Press, 2015), 668–69 (book 14, no. 23).

23. This portion of 53:7 is included in the contemporary critical edition of the Vulgate published by the German Bible society. See *Biblia Sacra Vulgata: Editio quinta* (Stuttgart: Deutsche Bibelgesellschaft, 2007).

CONCLUSION

The goal of this chapter in relation to this book as a whole has been to establish context which will enable the reader to better understand and evaluate Aquinas's Christological reception of Isaiah 53. In this chapter we have examined the basic structure, features, and theological meaning of the text of Isaiah 53. By becoming aware of the basic form and content of Isaiah 53, we are now in a better position to appreciate the particular ways in which Aquinas reads that biblical text. This chapter has also acknowledged the basic, unique features of Aquinas's specifically Latin version of Isaiah 53 in relation to contemporary Hebrew and Greek versions of that same biblical text. This comparative analysis will enable the reader, in ensuing chapters, to recognize and assess those occasions in which Aquinas's exegesis of Isaiah 53 is based on his specific, Latin version of that text. Now that this contextualizing foundation has been laid, in the next chapter the original contribution of this work begins to unfold.

3

The Cursory Lectures on Isaiah, Jeremiah, and Lamentations

In the previous two chapters, I examined the historical, theological, and textual context that is necessary to understand and assess Aquinas's interpretations of Isaiah 53. With that foundational work in place, we can now proceed in this chapter to investigate the number, place, and quality of Aquinas's references to Isaiah 53. Thus, this chapter marks the beginning of the primary project and original contribution of this work, a contribution that will unfold up through chapter 9 as well as in a final concluding chapter.

The purpose of this chapter is to examine Aquinas's interpretations of Isaiah 53 in his three earliest biblical commentaries: the commentaries on Isaiah, Jeremiah, and Lamentations, respectively. The structure of this chapter is as follows. First, I will place the *Commentary on Isaiah* (hereafter *Super Isaiam*) in context and describe the distinctive literary style of that commentary. In the second and third sections of this chapter, I will examine the references to Isaiah 53 that Aquinas makes throughout the *Super Isaiam* and I provide a detailed explication of his lecture on Isaiah 53 itself. Fourth, I will briefly historically situate the commentaries on Jeremiah and Lamentations and then I examine their few references to Isaiah 53. This chapter then concludes with a synthesis of the various theological, Christological points that Aquinas draws out from the text of Isaiah 53 through his commentaries on Isaiah, Jeremiah and Lamentations.

THE DATE AND NATURE OF AQUINAS'S
SUPER ISAIAM

The *Super Isaiam* consists of Aquinas's lecture notes for a course that he gave on Isaiah at the outset of his academic teaching career. Torrell notes that "all contemporary specialists on St. Thomas" maintain, in accord with the Leonine commission, that Aquinas taught this course on Isaiah at the University of Paris, "likely in 1251–52 or 1252–53."[1] Aquinas delivered this course as a series of "cursory lectures" at some point during his "first two years" in Paris, during which time he was considered a "biblical bachelor."[2] The *Super Isaiam* was likely "'the first theological work of St. Thomas.'"[3]

The 'cursory' nature of Aquinas's lectures on Isaiah meant that they were typically brief and to the point. As Joseph Wawrykow explains, the treatment of Isaiah 53 that Aquinas provides in this work "typically 'run[s] over' quickly the biblical text, noting its principles of organization and pausing only to gloss obscure or especially significant terms."[4] For, "the goal of the bachelor is not to plumb to its full extent the riches of the biblical text, or to relate a given text to others that address cognate issues, but to offer his hearers a greater familiarity with the text."[5] Further, Torrell explains, in light of the portion of the manuscript of the *Super Isaiam* that survives in Aquinas's own handwriting, we can make some inferences regarding the manner of its composition:

---

1. Torrell, *Saint Thomas Aquinas*, 35. See also A. Oliva, *Les Débuts de l'enseignement de Thomas d'Aquin et sa conception de la Sacra Doctrina: Avec l'édition du prologue de son Commentaire des Sentences* (Paris: Vrin, 2006), 207–24, referenced in Pasquale Porro, *Thomas Aquinas: A Historical and Philosophical Profile*, trans. Joseph G. Trabbic and Roger W. Nutt (Washington, D.C.: The Catholic University of America Press, 2016), 5 and 440. See also Weisheipl, *Friar Thomas D'Aquino*, 45 and 369–70.

2. Torrell, *Saint Thomas Aquinas*, 36.

3. Ibid., quoting Leonine edition 28:20.

4. Joseph Wawrykow, "Aquinas on Isaiah," in *Aquinas on Scripture* (ed. Weinandy et al.), 44.

5. Ibid., 44.

The [lecture] notes for the *Super Isaiam* were quickly written down on parchment, day after day, by the young bachelor. He did this with an eye to the lectures that he had to give a few hours thereafter. Thus, they bear all the marks of hasty work. This should explain, at least in part, the choppy style, which seems to become even more pronounced after the first few chapters. Although he had a little time to prepare the first lectures, their frequency quickly drained these reserves, forcing him to speak using texts that were not fully drafted.[6]

Thus, in light of the manner and the purpose for which Aquinas composed his lectures on Isaiah, we need to approach his treatment of the Suffering Servant text in Isaiah 53, as well as other references to that text throughout the commentary, with modest expectations regarding their exegetical and theological depth. We will nonetheless find, as Torrell states, that Aquinas's "exposition of Isaiah, even if it sometimes leaves the reader a little hungry for more, possesses great riches on certain points."[7] Aquinas's cursory commentary on Isaiah provides us with both a valuable historical look into the young friar's understanding of the text of Isaiah 53 and a theologically significant exposition of the saving love of Christ enacted on the cross.

CASES OF ISAIAH 53 THROUGHOUT THE *SUPER ISAIAM*

In addition to his lecture on Isaiah 53 itself, in the *Super Isaiam* Aquinas also makes five theologically significant references to the text of Isaiah 53 in his lectures on Isaiah 1–52.[8] The first of these references occurs in his analysis of Jerome's preface to Isaiah. Jerome claimed that Isaiah was an "evangelist" who "describes all the mysteries of Christ and the Church" with clarity, as if he were talking about events that had already occurred.[9] Building on this remark, Aquinas

---

6. Torrell, *Saint Thomas Aquinas*, 37–38.

7. Ibid., 36.

8. There is a sixth reference in his lecture on Is 50, in no. 909, but it is too brief to be considered in depth. Here, Aquinas states that Is 50–52 are about impediments to union with God, and then he makes a partial reference to Is 53:1 in order to indicate simply that that future chapter will discuss the "remedies" to the impediments presently being discussed (see no. 955).

9. "Preface of St. Jerome," in Thomas Aquinas, *Literal Commentary on the Prophet Isaiah.*

identifies the passion of Christ as one among the many Christian "mysteries" that Isaiah will prophesy about in an "open and explicit manner."[10] He then demonstrates this by quoting Isaiah 53:7: "'he shall be led as a sheep to the slaughter, and shall be dumb as a lamb before his shearer.'"[11] Hence, right at the outset of the *Super Isaiam,* Aquinas identifies Isaiah 53 as an explicit prophecy of Christ's passion. Christ himself is the immediate *res* to which the *verba* of Isaiah 53 refer, and they do so plainly, without employing figures or symbols.

Aquinas's second citation of Isaiah 53 comes in his treatment of Isaiah 8:1–3. Here the text speaks of a son whom Isaiah will have, and Aquinas observes that there are some exegetes in his day who think the child that is being spoken of is Christ. These exegetes claim that the name that is given to the child ("Take away the spoils [*spolia*] with speed") is a "circumlocution" for the name of Christ.[12] They argue this on the basis of Isaiah 53:12, which states that God will do the following for the Suffering Servant: "'therefore will I distribute to him very many, and he shall divide the spoils [*spolia*] of the strong.'"[13] That is, both Isaiah 8 and Isaiah 53 speak of the Christ as one who will take spoils (*spolia*) from his enemies. While Aquinas is hesitant to embrace this Christological interpretation of the identity of the child spoken of in Isaiah 8, he nevertheless explains the Christological meaning of the line from Isaiah 53.[14] "Jesus is savior," he says, "in that he took away spoils [*spoilia*], that is, sinners, from the power of the devil, and plundered hell."[15] As a result of his passion, Christ the savior rescued sinners from the reign of the evil one; he entered the strong man's house and plundered his goods.[16] Aquinas will return to this theme in his lecture on chapter 53.

All future references to Aquinas's *Literal Commentary on the Prophet Isaiah* will be referred to as *Super Isaiam* and will feature the paragraph number of the text being cited. All citations and paragraph numbers are from the 1974 Latin Leonine edition and, unless otherwise noted, the English translation by Louis St. Hilaire, both of which are published online by the Aquinas Institute at aquinas.cc/la/en/~Isaiah.C53.v53.12.

10. Aquinas, "Exposition on Saint Jerome's Preface to Isaiah," in *Super Isaiam,* 14.

11. Ibid., quoting Is 53:7.

12. *Super Isaiam,* 269, quoting Is 8:1.

13. Ibid., quoting Is 53:12.

14. Ibid., 270.

15. Ibid., 269.

16. Mt 12:29; see Mk 3:27 and Lk 11:21–22.

Aquinas's third use of Isaiah 53 is found in his second lecture on Isaiah 9. Here, he makes a "note" (*item notandum*) about the meaning of the phrase "'upon his shoulder'" (*super humerum ejus*) that is written in Isaiah 9:6 concerning the child who is to be a "Prince of Peace."[17] Aquinas says that these words are about that which "God laid 'upon the shoulder' of Christ."[18] The first thing that God places upon Christ's shoulder are "sins, as upon one who makes satisfaction."[19] Aquinas immediately follows this statement with a quotation from Isaiah 53:6: "'the Lord has laid upon him [*posuit super eum*] the iniquity of us all.'"[20] Both Isaiah 9:6 and 53:6 speak of that which is 'laid upon' the Christ, and Isaiah 53 specifies that at least one aspect of the weight that is laid upon Christ and which he must carry is the responsibility to make satisfaction for the sins of humanity. At this point, Aquinas offers no further explanation of what exactly 'satisfaction' is or how Christ's passion enacts such satisfaction. In fact, even in his lecture on Isaiah 53 Aquinas does not use the term 'satisfaction' in reference to Christ's passion, though he will refer to Christ's suffering as a 'penance' for sins. At the very least, we can see that here Aquinas interprets Isaiah 53:6's remarks about God 'laying the iniquity of all' upon the Suffering Servant merely as a reference to Christ's task of offering salvific satisfaction for sins, and nothing more.

The fourth instance in which Aquinas refers to the text of Isaiah 53 is found in his lecture on Isaiah 16. This chapter of Isaiah begins with the words "Send forth, O Lord, the lamb, the ruler of the earth, from the rock of the desert, to the mount of the daughter of Zion" (Is 16:1). In a "note" on the phrase "send forth the lamb" (*Emitte agnum*), Aquinas identifies this lamb as Christ and connects

17. *Super Isaiam*, 310, quoting Is 9:6. Such "notes" appear throughout the *Super Isaiam* as we have it today. They were originally written by Aquinas in the margins of his written lectures on Isaiah. In the thirteenth century Jacobino d'Asti produced a copy of Aquinas's lectures and moved these marginal notes (which he called *collationes*) into the main body of the text. See Joseph Wawrykow, "Aquinas on Isaiah," in *Aquinas on Scripture* (ed. Weinandy et al.), 50; see Chenu, *Toward Understanding Saint Thomas*, who claims that the *collationes* are probably the original work of Jacobinus, not Aquinas (245). For a theological commentary on these *collationes* see Jean-Pierre Torrell and Denise Bouthillier, "Quand saint Thomas méditait sur le prophète Isaïe," *Revue Thomiste* 90 (1990): 5–47.

18. *Super Isaiam*, 310.

19. Ibid.

20. Ibid.

Isaiah 16:1 to three other scriptural texts that speak of Christ as a lamb.[21] Christ is a lamb on account of his "purity of life" (Ex 12:5) and the fact that his death was an "expiation of sin" (Jn 1:29).[22] Further, Aquinas says Christ can be compared to a lamb "because of the meekness of his death," and he then quotes Isaiah 53:7 in order to illustrate this point: "as a lamb before his shearer, he shall open not his mouth."[23] Here Aquinas employs Isaiah 53 simply in order to highlight the passivity of Christ in response to the attacks of his enemies, as well as to link Isaiah 53's description of Christ as a lamb with the lamb terminology used in Isaiah 16:1, Exodus 12:5, and John 1:29. In his lecture on Isaiah 53 Aquinas will delve deeper into the notion of Christ's 'meekness' amidst his passion.

Aquinas's fifth and final significant reference to the text of Isaiah 53 in the lectures on Isaiah 1–52 occurs in his treatment of Isaiah 49. He interprets Isaiah 49:7–8 as a prophecy of the exaltation of a king who will liberate the people of Israel from oppression. After saying that this prophecy could be referring to King Cyrus, he goes on to state that it could be interpreted as a reference to Christ. For Christ "was despised [*contemptus*] in his passion and was judged like a Servant: 'we have seen him despised' [*despectum*] (Is 53:2–3), but afterward he was literally adored by kings: 'all kings of the earth shall adore him' (Ps 72:11)."[24] Aquinas has linked Isaiah 49:7's description of the exiled people as "despised" (*contemptibilem*) with Isaiah 53's portrait of Christ as the one who is "despised" (*despectum*).[25] Both were initially despised by their peers prior to being exalted by God. Christ was despised in his passion, and yet was exalted in his resurrection. In his lecture on Isaiah 53 Aquinas identifies the exaltation of Christ as one of the chapters' primary themes. It is to that lecture that we can now turn.

21. Ibid., 450.
22. Ibid.
23. Ibid.
24. Ibid., 901, paraphrasing Is 53:2–3.
25. Ibid.

THE LECTURE ON ISAIAH 53 IN THE *SUPER ISAIAM*

Aquinas's Exegesis of Isaiah 52:13–15

In order to better contextualize our examination of Aquinas's lecture on Isaiah 53, it will be helpful to begin this section with a brief analysis of Aquinas's comments upon Isaiah 52:13–15. This portion of Isaiah is the beginning of what contemporary exegetes identify as the Fourth Servant Song (Is 52:13–53:12). Further, since Isaiah 52 concludes with vv. 13–15, this passage constitutes the transition from Isaiah 52 to Isaiah 53.

Aquinas's treatment of Isaiah 52:13–15 is brief but noteworthy. He says that beginning with v. 13, Isaiah "foretells the liberation of the gentiles from slavery to sin," and this liberation is "carried out by the Son of God."[26] This verse is about the "eminence of grace" that Christ the "liberator" possesses,[27] and it identifies four aspects of the eminence of Christ: first, his wisdom; second, the human nature that he assumed and in which he served; third, his power; and fourth, his ascension into heaven and enthronement at the right hand of the Father.[28] Aquinas then proceeds to v. 14, which is about "the ignominy of his [Christ's] Passion."[29] Christ's appearance will be rendered "inglorious" by the suffering that he undergoes.[30] Finally, v. 15 is specifically about the "liberation" of the gentiles that Christ brings about through "the remission of sins."[31] Commenting upon v. 15's statement that the Servant "shall sprinkle many nations," Aquinas remarks: "'he shall sprinkle,' with the sprinkling of his blood, per 1 Pt 1:2, and the water of baptism, per Heb 10:22: 'having our hearts sprinkled,' etc."[32] Since Aquinas interprets Isaiah 52:15 in light of 1 Peter 1:2 and Hebrews 10:22, it will be helpful for us to take a closer look at these texts.

---

26. Ibid., 953.

27. Ibid.

28. Ibid.

29. Ibid. Interestingly, Aquinas interprets the people's "'astonishment'" (Is 52:14) toward the Servant as a reference to the astonishment that people will experience in reaction to Christ's "example, miracles, and teachings," and he references Mt 12:23 to justify this.

30. *Super Isaiam,* 953, quoting Is 52:14.

31. Ibid., 954.

32. Ibid., quoting Is 52:15 and Heb 10:22, respectively.

The text of 1 Peter 1:2 states that Christians have been chosen "by God the Father and sanctified by the Spirit to be obedient to Jesus Christ and to be sprinkled with his blood."[33] By quoting this text in connection with Isaiah 52:15, Aquinas's point is that the sprinkling of the Servant's blood upon believers results in their sanctification by the Holy Spirit. Further, this language of sprinkling blood appears to be reminiscent of sacrificial practice. This cultic interpretation is confirmed by Aquinas's reference to Hebrews 10:22, which in its broader context states:

Therefore, my friends, since we have confidence to enter the sanctuary by the blood of Jesus, by the new and living way that he opened for us through the curtain (that is, through his flesh), and since we have a great priest over the house of God, let us approach with a true heart in full assurance of faith, with our hearts sprinkled clean from an evil conscience and our bodies washed with pure water.[34]

Hebrews 10:19–22 clearly depicts Christ as a priest and sacrificial victim whose blood enables sinners to confidently enter into the sacred presence of God. Further, v. 22 connects the interiorly purifying and sanctifying power of Christ's blood with the external purification that is brought about by water. For our purposes, the point is this: by interpreting Isaiah 52:15 in light of 1 Peter 1:2 and Hebrews 10:22, Aquinas reads Isaiah 52:15 as a prophecy of Christ's priestly, sacrificial, purifying, and sanctifying action on our behalf.

We can now conclude our analysis of Aquinas's treatment of Isaiah 52:13–15 and explain how this sets the stage for his engagement with Isaiah 53. For Aquinas, Isaiah 52:13 is about Christ, God incarnate, who is coming to liberate the gentiles. Isaiah 52:14 indicates that, despite his unmatched eminence in grace, Christ will undergo horrible suffering as a human being. Then, Isaiah 52:15 shows that this suffering will be a sacrifice that Christ himself, as a priest, offers for the sake of humanity's liberation from sin and entrance into the presence of God. With this context in place, we can now turn explicitly to Aquinas's lecture on Isaiah 53.

33. 1 Pt 1:2 (NRSV-CE)
34. Heb 10:19–22 (NRSV-CE).

Aquinas's *divisio textus* of Isaiah 53:1–12
and His Interpretation of v. 1

Aquinas begins his lecture on Isaiah 53 with a detailed division of the text. I have outlined this division in Table 3-1, below. As this table indicates, Aquinas claims that the primary purpose of Isaiah 53 is to describe the passion of Christ as a remedy against the sins of humanity.[35] Consequently, Isaiah 53 builds on the closing verses of Isaiah 52. Isaiah 52:13–15 describes the personal glory of Christ, his suffering as a man, and the saving fruits of that suffering, respectively. For Aquinas, Isaiah 53 presupposes and expands upon each of these themes, for Isaiah 53 describes how (1) Christ, as true God and true man, (2) will undergo suffering (3) in order to save humanity from sin. Isaiah 53 begins in v. 1 by establishing that the ensuing report about the Suffering Servant is a great "mystery" which "is not easily believed" and "nor is it easily seen."[36] This mystery regards the "'arm of the Lord,'" namely, Christ, "the Son of God [and] the power of God."[37] The remainder of Isaiah 53, namely, vv. 2–12, consists of a description of "the order of the deed," that is, of the actual salvific work of the Servant of the Lord.[38] This description of the "order of the deed" begins in the first part of v. 2 with a "similitude" of the Servant's activity, and it proceeds in the latter portion of v. 2 through to v. 12 with a detailed exposition of the meaning of that similitude.[39] The detailed exposition of vv. 2–12 focuses upon two central themes, namely, Christ's humiliation (vv. 2–7) and his exaltation (vv. 8–12). Within these two themes there are further, diverse subpoints.[40]

---

35. *Super Isaiam*, 955.

36. Ibid.

37. Ibid., quoting Is 53:1. Aquinas interprets Isaiah's reference to the arm (*brachium*) of the Lord with the help of a quotation from Job 40:4 ("and have you an arm like God?").

38. *Super Isaiam*, 956.

39. Ibid., 956–57. The "similitude" is "and he shall rise up as a tender plant before him, and as a root out of a thirsty ground" (Is 53:2) and the exposition of the meaning of that similitude begins with "there is no form in him, nor comeliness" (Is 53:2).

40. *Super Isaiam*, 956–57. See table 3-1.

TABLE 3-1. AQUINAS'S *DIVISIO TEXTUS* OF ISAIAH 53:1–12

1) **Major Elements and Divisions:**
   1. **Primary theme:** The passion of Christ as the remedy for sin.
   2. **Two major components of the primary theme:**
      - v. 1: "the height of the mystery, for the report [about Christ's passion] is not easily believed"
      - vv. 2–12: "The order of the deed" (vv. 2–12), i.e., a description of Christ's passion
        - v. 2: "A similitude as to his exaltation"
        - vv. 2–12: "Explanation of the similitude"
          - vv. 2–7: Christ's humiliation
          - vv. 8–12: Christ's exaltation

2) **Further Subdivisions within the Two Major Components:**
   1. **Christ's humiliation (vv. 2–7):**
      a. **Christ's "humility" (vv. 2–6):**
         i. **"the office of his humility" (v. 2)**
            1. humility in "the hiding of his majesty" (v. 2: "there is no form in him, nor comeliness")
            2. Humility in "the exposing of his infirmity" (v. 2: "that we should be desirous of him … [v. 3] acquainted with infirmity").
               a. "A sign of his infirmity" (v. 4: "truly ..")
         ii. **"the contempt of him in humiliation" (v. 3)**
            1. "Majesty hidden in the removal of honor" (latter half of v. 3: "as it were hidden")
         iii. **"the fruit of his humiliation" (v. 5)**
            1. "The moving reason" (v. 5: "but he was wounded")
            2. "The consequent usefulness in the reconciliation of peace" (v. 5: "the chastisement of our peace")
            3. "The imminent necessity on our part, for all are sick" (v. 6: "all we like sheep")
      b. **Christ's "meekness in humiliation" (v. 7)**
         i. **"He sets out the meekness itself" (v. 7)**
            1. "As to his voluntary offering of himself" (v. 7: "he was offered")
            2. "As to his patient suffering" (v. 7: "and he opened not his mouth")
         ii. **"He sets out a similitude" (v. 7: "as a sheep to the slaughter")**
   2. **Christ's exaltation (vv. 8–12)**
      a. **"His escape from dangers" (v. 8)**
         i. "The reward" (v. 8: "he was taken away")
         ii. "His merit," "the worthiness of the sufferer" (v. 8: "his generation")
      b. **"Vengeance ["vindication"] against his enemies" (v. 9)**
         i. His enemies' "reward" (v. 9: "and he shall give the ungodly")
         ii. "His merit as to the innocence of his life" (v. 9: "because he has done no iniquity") and "as to the obedience of his death" (v. 10: "and the Lord was pleased to bruise him")
      c. **"The justification of men" (v. 10)**
         i. "The reward for the sorrow of his death" (v. 10: "if he shall lay down his life") and "the reward for the labor of his teaching" (v. 11: "because his soul has labored")
         ii. "His merit as to the exercise of his preaching" (v. 11: "by his knowledge") and "as to the torment of his death" (v. 11: "he shall bear their iniquities"), that is, "the punishments for their iniquities"
      d. **"His victory over the rebellious" (v. 12)**
         i. "The subjection of the enemies" (v. 12: "therefore will I distribute to him")
         ii. "The reason for their subjection," namely, "his death" (v. 12: "because he has delivered his soul unto death")
         ii. "The salvation of those made subject to him" (v. 12: "and he has borne")

Aquinas's Exegesis of Isaiah 53:2–12

Having established that Isaiah 53:1 identifies Christ as the "arm of the Lord" whose suffering will be described in vv. 2–12, Aquinas turns his attention to the latter verses and begins his exegesis with an analysis of the "similitude" provided in the first portion of v. 2.[41] This similitude ("And he shall rise up as a tender plant before him, and as a root out of a thirsty ground") is a symbol of Christ's "exaltation."[42] Christ, Aquinas says, "'Shall rise up,' in being born from the womb of his mother, in rising from the dead, in ascending from the earth into heaven, and into the faith of the gentiles."[43] This 'rising' (*ascendet*) is like that of "'a tender plant,' which increases in height and is multiplied in width."[44] Further, that Christ rises "as a root out of a thirsty ground" (53:2) points to the fact of his miraculous conception in the virginal womb of Mary. For Christ "arose from his mother without the moisture of man," just as a root "out of ground without moisture" rises up.[45] Aquinas thus reads the first part of Isaiah 53:2 as a figurative prophecy of the conception, death, resurrection, and ascension of Christ, as well as the rising up of the gentile nations through their embrace of faith in Christ. The 'rising up' of Christ indicated in this verse further specifies the prophecy given earlier in Isaiah 11:1: "and there shall come forth a rod out of the root of Jesse, and a flower shall rise up [*ascendet*] out of his root."[46]

Aquinas views the remainder of Isaiah 53's description of the activity of the Suffering Servant as an "explanation of the similitude" detailed above.[47] This explanation begins with a treatment of the "humiliation" that Christ endured in his passion (Is 53:2–7).[48] This treatment first draws attention to the humility of Christ, which is discussed in the latter part of 53:2 and extends into v. 3. The first way in which Christ's "humility is shown" is in "the hiding of his majesty," a hiding of which Isaiah speaks when he says that "there

41. Ibid.
42. Ibid., 956.
43. Ibid.
44. Ibid.
45. Ibid.
46. Ibid.
47. Ibid., 957.
48. Ibid.

is no form ... nor comeliness" in Christ.[49] Aquinas explains that in fact Christ does have form (an "abundance of interior goods") and comeliness (an "abundance of exterior goods"), but that they were "hidden" from the understanding of unbelievers who saw Christ due to "the infirmity he assumed" and "the poverty he observed."[50] Aquinas thus reads Isaiah as saying that Christ's humility consisted in his willingness to endure the ignorance of his neighbors in regards to the riches of his majesty. He is willing to endure the pain that results from being misunderstood.

The second way in which Isaiah 53:2–3 speaks of Christ's humility being shown is in "the exposing of his infirmity."[51] Aquinas cites Haggai 2:8 to indicate that the chosen people were "expecting with desire that he [the Christ] should come as a great redeemer" who would be great "in dignity" (*dignitate*), "in prosperity" (*prosperitate*), and "in power" (*potestate*).[52] But, contrary to their expectations, Isaiah shows how the Christ would not come in dignity, prosperity, or power. Isaiah foretells how Christ, rather than being seen as having great dignity, will be viewed as "'despised,' inglorious, 'and the most abject of men,' because he suffered the most shameful kind of death."[53] Neither does the Christ come in prosperity, but rather when he comes he is seen as "'a man of pain,' as though poor and full of pain."[54] Aquinas emphasizes the great pain (*dolor*) with which Christ suffered when he came by citing Lamentations 1:12: "'O all ye that pass by the way, attend, and see if there be any pain [*dolor*] like to my pain.'"[55] Both Isaiah 53:3 and Lamentations 1:12 speak of the great pain (*dolor*) of the suffering Christ. Finally, Christ comes not in power, but rather as someone who is "'acquainted with infirmity,' through experience."[56] That is, the weakness and infirmity of Christ

---

49. Ibid., 958.

50. Ibid.

51. Ibid., 959.

52. Ibid. Aquinas's version of Hg 2:8 reads: "Ecce veniet desideratus cunctis gentibus" (Behold, the desired of all nations shall come).

53. *Super Isaiam*, 959, quoting Is 53:3.

54. Ibid. Throughout this paragraph I translate *dolor* as "pain," whereas St. Hilaire prefers "sorrow."

55. *Super Isaiam*, 959, quoting Lm 1:12.

56. Ibid., quoting Is 53:3.

rendered it such that he could be crucified by his enemies.[57] In sum, Christ shows his humility through the manifestation of his infirmity. His infirmity consisted in the fact that he was weak enough to be put to death in a shameful way, he was despised by his enemies as if he were a criminal, and he endured numerous and taxing pains.

Beginning with the latter half of Isaiah 53:3 ("'And his look was at it were hidden'"), Aquinas sees Isaiah as moving to an exposition of the "contempt" that Christ endured "in his humiliation."[58] Two points are made here. First, the divine majesty of Christ is "hidden" ("'as it were hidden [*absconditus*]'") in his humiliation, causing those who view him in this state to withhold from him the "honor that was due him" as God ("'whereupon we esteemed him not'").[59] Here Aquinas sees a connection to Isaiah 45:15, which states that "'truly you are a hidden [*absconditus*] God.'"[60] By seeing the linguistic connection between the Latin texts of Isaiah 45:15 and 53:3, Aquinas can interpret the latter as speaking of the hiding (*absconditus*) of Christ's divinity in the humiliation of his passion. The suffering of Christ hides his Godhead from the view of some.

The second aspect of the contempt that Christ endures in his humiliation is indicated in 53:4.[61] Here, Aquinas discusses "the sign of his infirmity," that is, the nature of Christ's suffering and the visible manifestations of that suffering.[62] Interspersing citations from Isaiah 53:4 with his own commentary, Aquinas explains:

Truly, as true man, **he has borne**, suffered, **our infirmities**, infirmities, such as hunger and thirst, **and carried our pains** [*dolores*] in the sensible passions and in sadness [*tristitiam*]; or, **our infirmities**, our sins, he has taken from us; or in our place, he has suffered punishments: *he bore our sins in his body upon the tree* (1 Pt 2:24). And he sets out the contempt: **and we have thought him as it were a leper**, unclean and a sinner, and therefore, **struck by God**, for his sins, as to the punishments he suffered, **and afflicted**, as to

<hr>

57. To illustrate this point Aquinas quotes 2 Cor 15:4, which states that Christ was "crucified through infirmity" (*nam si crucifixus est ex infirmitate*). See *Super Isaiam*, 959.

58. *Super Isaiam*, 960.

59. Ibid., quoting Is 53:3.

60. Ibid., quoting Is 45:15.

61. Is 53:4 states: "Truly he has borne our infirmities and carried our sorrows: and we have thought him as it were a leper, and as one struck by God and afflicted."

62. *Super Isaiam*, 960.

the ignominies he endured: *for your manifold wickedness and your infinite iniquities* (Job 22:5); *they abhor me* (Job 30:10).[63]

As a true man, Christ has experienced the pain of hunger and thirst, the pain of yearning for sensible goods, and the pain of sadness in the face of evil and privation. Most intriguing here is Aquinas's statement that Christ has experienced the "punishments" (*poenas*) that are due to sinners.[64] Since this is a cursory lecture on scripture, he does not provide us with a thorough explanation of the precise meaning of these *poenas*. But the context and the citation from 1 Peter indicates that the *poenas* that Christ experienced "in our place" (*vel loco nostri*) are simply his various forms of suffering and ultimately his death by crucifixion.[65] Aquinas does not specify here whether or not and to what degree God wills or is the cause of these 'punishments.' Instead, he merely states the material nature of these *poenas*.[66] What Aquinas does make clear here is that Christ endured his suffering in order to take away our sins. Yet, ironically and tragically, those who see him in his infirmity view him as a sinner whose *poenas* are inflicted upon him by God as a consequence for his own sins. Hence, despite his great humility and love for sinners, Christ is misunderstood and taken to be a sinner who is suffering on account of the evil he has done.

At this point in his cursory reading of Isaiah 53, Aquinas briefly steps aside from his chronological exegesis in order to offer a Christological "note" (*nota*) on 53:1–2.[67] Regarding the reference in 53:1 to the "arm [*brachium*] of the Lord," Aquinas identifies three

63. Ibid. In this passage I have made slight modifications to the English translation by St. Hilaire. The Latin text is as follows, with scripture citations in single quotation marks: "Secundo quantum ad infirmitatem ostensam, ponens infirmitatis signum: 'Vere,' sicut verus homo, 'languores,' infirmitates sicut famem, sitim, 'tulit,' sustinuit, 'dolores' sensibiles in passione et tristitiam; vel 'languores,' peccata abstulit a nobis; vel loco nostri poenas sustinuit, I Petri II 24 Peccata nostra pertulit super lignum. Ponens etiam contemptum: 'et nos reputavimus quasi leprosum,' immundum et peccatorem, et ideo 'percussum a Deo' pro peccatis suis, quantum ad poenas, 'et humiliatum,' quantum ad ignominias, Job XXII 5 Propter malitiam tuam plurimam, et infinitas iniquitates tuas, et XXXIX Abominantur etc."

64. *Super Isaiam*, 960.

65. Ibid.

66. On Aquinas's understanding of the purpose of divine and human *poena* see Sr. Elinor Gardner, OP, "Punishment as Medicine in the Thought of St. Thomas Aquinas," *The Thomist* 87, no. 1 (January 2023): 1–42.

67. *Super Isaiam*, 961.

scriptural texts that describe three different ways in which Christ can be understood to be this 'arm.' First, per Psalm 89:10, Christ is an arm (*brachio*) "for scourging demons."[68] Second, Isaiah 40:11 speaks of Christ the arm (*brachio*) as "supporting the weak."[69] Third, Wisdom 5:17 describes Christ as the arm (*dextera*) by which the Lord defends the faithful.[70] Moving on to Isaiah 53:2, Aquinas views the identification of the Servant as a "'tender sapling'" (*virgultum*) as signifying that "Christ is a rod" (*virga*).[71] Once more, he employs three scriptural citations which possess the word 'rod' (*virga*) in order to expound three meanings of Christ as a *virga*. Christ is a rod "for striking" (Nm 24:17), "for supporting" (Ps 23:4), and for "setting right" (Ps 45:6).[72] Aquinas then turns to the second clause in Isaiah 53:2 ("as a root out of a thirsty ground") to discuss what it means to say that "Christ is a root [*radix*]."[73] Again, the meanings of *radix* are discerned with the help of other scriptural texts that employ that term: Christ is a root "because he is hidden" (Sir 1:6), "because he supplies nourishment" (Jer 17:8), and "because he supports the entire tree" (Rom 11:18).[74]

Aquinas does not explicitly link these functions of Christ as the arm of the Lord (*brachium*), a rod (*virga*), and a root (*radix*) to his suffering and death. But a link is more than suggested by the context: as we have seen, Isaiah 53:1–2 (1) states what the remainder of the chapter is about (the revelation of the arm of the Lord), (2) gives a similitude of that content ("he shall rise up as a tender sapling [rod], and as a root out of thirsty ground"), and (3) finally proceeds to actually describe how that revelation and rising up will unfold, namely, through the humiliation and exaltation of the Servant. So, precisely by his humiliation and exaltation, Christ the *brachium* will scourge demons, support the weak, and defend the faithful. As *virga*, he will strike our enemies, support his sheep, and set right those who

---

68. Ibid., quoting Ps 89:10: "'With the arm of your strength you have scattered your enemies.'"

69. Ibid., quoting Is 40:11: "'he shall take up the lambs with his arm.'"

70. Ibid., quoting Wis 5:17: "'with his holy arm he will defend them.'"

71. Ibid., 962. Author's translation of "Item super illo 'virgultum,' quod Christus est virga."

72. Ibid.

73. Ibid., 963.

74. Ibid.

have gone astray. As *radix,* his divine majesty is hidden from view, yet he nevertheless supplies nourishment and support to the tree that grows up above him. It is thus not difficult to see how Aquinas's notes on these figures of Christ as *brachium, virga,* and *radix* point to the salvific functions that he carries out precisely in his humiliation and exaltation.

Having completed his notes on Isaiah 53:1–2, Aquinas now returns to where he left off and takes up an examination of Isaiah 53:5–6.[75] These verses contain three points concerning "the fruit" of Christ's humiliation and passion.[76] First, the "reason" (*rationem moventem*) or cause of Christ's suffering is identified as our sinfulness.[77] Whereas 53:4 indicates a mistaken perception of the cause of the Servant's suffering ("we have thought him as it were a leper, and as one struck by God and afflicted"), 53:5 clarifies the true nature of that cause: Christ was "'wounded' by thorns, nails, and lance 'for our iniquities' [*propter iniquitates nostras*]," so as to take them away (*tollendas*).[78] This means that Christ's suffering is not a consequence for his own sins, of which there are none. Rather, his suffering is the consequence of our sins. Second, the useful effect or fruit of Christ's suffering is identified as "the reconciliation of peace" between God and sinners.[79] By the "chastisement" (*disciplina*) that he endured in the passion Christ brings peace and "access to God."[80] Further, the bruises (*livore*) that Christ receives in his scourging bring about "the restoration of [our] broken health."[81] Aquinas here quotes 1 Peter 2:24, which has a clear reference to Isaiah 53:5: "by his bruises [*livore*] we are healed."[82] In a very basic sense, then, Aquinas identifies an element of exchange in Christ's saving work: his wounds bring about our healing, and his suffering causes our peace. At this point,

---

75. Is 53:5–6 states: "But he was wounded for our iniquities, he was bruised for our sins: the chastisement of our peace was upon him, and by his bruises we are healed. All we like sheep have gone astray, every one has turned aside into his own way: and the Lord has laid on him the iniquity of us all."

76. *Super Isaiam,* 964.

77. Ibid.

78. Ibid.

79. Ibid., 965.

80. Ibid.

81. Ibid.

82. Ibid., quoting 1 Pt 2:24.

though, Aquinas does not explain how this salvific exchange works. He does not indicate how the wounds and suffering of Christ bring about healing and peace for sinners.

The third point about the fruit of Christ's suffering is grounded in Isaiah 53:6, which for Aquinas points to the "imminent necessity" of Christ's passion "on our part."[83] That is, "all are sick, and thus all need a physician, and no one else can offer a sufficient remedy."[84] Here Aquinas sees a connection between Isaiah 53:6, "all we like sheep [*oves*] have gone astray," and 1 Peter 2:25, which states "for you were as sheep [*oves*] without a shepherd."[85] The universal infection of humanity with sin renders it such that all people are in need of "penance" (*paenitentia*).[86] So, the necessity of Christ's passion is grounded in the fact that sinners need a penance that will take away their sins. Here, Aquinas does not explain what exactly a penance is, nor does he describe how Christ's passion functions as a penance for sins. He does not even comment on the latter half of Isaiah 53:6, which states that as a result of our sinfulness "the Lord has laid on him the iniquity of us all." Though, as we have seen, earlier in his second lecture on Isaiah 9 Aquinas cites this latter half of Isaiah 53:6 and says that it refers to God laying upon Christ the task of offering satisfaction for human sins. So, for Aquinas, Isaiah 53:6 speaks of the need of sinners for penance and the fact that Christ provided the penance that they need through his work of satisfaction. Christ's passion was a penance that he undertook in order to heal humanity from sin and restore it to peaceful communion with God.

Aquinas views Isaiah 53:7 as the final verse in the chapter that pertains to Christ's humiliation.[87] Specifically, he reads this verse as speaking of various aspects of Christ's "meekness [*mansuetudinem*] in suffering."[88] The nature of Christ's meekness consists in the fact that he made a "voluntary offering of himself … to God the Father

---

83. Ibid., 966.

84. Ibid.

85. Ibid., quoting Is 53:6 and 1 Pt 2:25, respectively.

86. Ibid. Aquinas appeals to Rom 3:22–23 to support his point here.

87. Is 53:7 states: "He was offered because it was his own will, and he opened not his mouth: he shall be led as a sheep to the slaughter, and shall be dumb as a lamb before his shearer, and he shall not open his mouth."

88. *Super Isaiam*, 967.

as a victim for us."[89] Here, Aquinas cites Psalm 54:6 to emphasize that the root cause of Christ's suffering was not a violent external force working against him. Rather, Christ freely made of himself a sacrificial offering: "I will freely sacrifice to you."[90] Another aspect of Christ's meekness is displayed by the fact of "his patient suffering," for "'he opened not his mouth.'"[91] Aquinas views this passage as being fulfilled in the fact that Christ did not "contradict and contend" with the enemies who assaulted him, and he gave no reply during his trial with Herod.[92] This meekness of the Christ who refused to offer "resistance" to those who killed him is expressed in the "similitude" that speaks of the Servant being led "'as a sheep to the slaughter.'"[93] So too, the meek suffering of Christ was spoken of by the prophet Jeremiah, whom Aquinas here cites: "'I was as a lamb, that is carried to be a victim'" (Jer 11:19).[94] In sum, the meek love of Christ for sinners is manifested both in the free handing over of himself to the passion as well as in the innocence with which he endured that passion.

Before proceeding to the verses which pertain to the exaltation of the Suffering Servant, Aquinas first pauses to offer two further notes on Isaiah 53:3. This verse speaks of the Servant as "'the most abject of men'" and "'a man of pain [*dolorum*].'"[95] Aquinas identifies three scriptural texts for each of these phrases from Isaiah in order to draw out their Christological meanings. He says that Christ was "the most abject" of all men first due to "the bitterness of his pain" that he endured.[96] In order to emphasize the extent of this pain, Aquinas once again cites Lamentations 1:12.[97] Christ's extreme abjection also consists in the "shamefulness of his death" by public crucifixion (Wis 2:20) and in "the greatness of the charge imposed upon him"

89. Ibid.
90. Ibid., quoting Ps 54:6.
91. Ibid., quoting Is 53:7.
92. Ibid.
93. Ibid., quoting Is 53:7.
94. Ibid., quoting Jer 11:19. Author's translation of "Jer. XII 'Ego quasi agnus qui portatur ad victimam.'"
95. Ibid., 968 and 969, respectively, quoting Is 53:3. Here I consistently translate Aquinas's references to *dolor* as "pain," whereas St. Hilaire prefers "sorrow."
96. Ibid., 968.
97. Ibid., quoting Lm 1:12: "'O all you that pass by the way, attend, and see if there be any sorrow [*dolor*] like to my sorrow [*dolor*].'"

(Prv 30:2).[98] In addition to his extreme abjection, Christ "was full of pain" (*plenus doloribus*).[99] There were three reasons for his pain, the first of which is the "disease" (*morbi*) that covered his body "from the sole of the foot unto the top of the head.'"[100] The second reason is for the sake of the "effusion of grace" that proceeds from Christ,[101] and the third is "because of our obligation."[102] Aquinas does not flesh out the second and third reasons, and so their meaning remains vague. But his fundamental point is clear: in the experience of his passion, Christ suffered the most extreme abjection and pain that a person could suffer.

Having completed his notes on Isaiah 53:3 and his exposition of the humiliation that Christ endured in the passion, Aquinas turns to Isaiah 53:8. Here, the prophet "begins to set out the glory of his [Christ's] exaltation, which is the reward of his passion, as it says in Phil 2:9: 'for which cause, God also has exalted him.'"[103] Aquinas thus links Isaiah 53:8–12 with the Christological hymn in Philippians 2. Both speak of the vindication and exaltation of Christ by God as a result of his suffering and death.[104] Put simply, Christ is exalted following his passion because of his very endurance of that passion.

Aquinas draws out four principal points from Isaiah 53:8.[105] First, this verse speaks of the "reward" (*praemium*) that the exalted Christ receives from God.[106] This reward is Christ's own resurrection from the dead, and by this resurrection Christ escapes "'from' the 'distress' of his Passion, 'and from' the unjust 'judgment' by which he was judged by others."[107] Second, 53:8 signifies the source of the

---

98. Ibid.

99. Ibid., 969.

100. Ibid., quoting Is 9:6.

101. Ibid. Author's translation of "propter gratiarum effusionem."

102. Ibid.

103. Ibid., 970, quoting Phil 2:9.

104. This connection between Is 53 and Phil 2 has also been observed by modern exegetes. For instance, see Richard Bauckham, *Jesus and the God of Israel: God Crucified and Other Studies on the New Testament's Christology of Divine Identity* (Grand Rapids, Mich.: Eerdmans, 2009), 41–45 and 205–6.

105. Is 53:8 states: "He was taken away from distress, and from judgment: who shall declare his generation? Because he is cut off out of the land of the living: for the wickedness of my people have I struck him."

106. *Super Isaiam*, 971.

107. Ibid., quoting Is 53:8.

merit by which Christ merited his resurrection. This merit lies in the "dignity of the sufferer" (*patientis dignitatem*) and the "condition of the person" (*conditione personae*) who suffered.[108] The divine dignity of Christ is indicated by Isaiah's words "'who shall declare his generation?'"[109] These words point to the mystery of Christ's eternal, consubstantial generation from the Father. These same words can also point to Christ's mysterious "generation in time, which was from a mother without a father."[110] Isaiah's words indicate that no one can know of the manner of Christ's generation in eternity or even in time by the mere power of "natural reason," though the mystery of these generations can be known partially "by divine inspiration."[111] Third, the suffering of Christ in death at the hands of his enemies is once more stated through Isaiah 53:8's words "'because he is cut off out of the land of the living [*terra viventium*].'"[112] Aquinas identifies a parallel to these words of Isaiah in Jeremiah 11:19, which reads "Come … cut him off from the land of the living [*terra viventium*]."[113]

Lastly, in regards to Isaiah 53:8, Aquinas makes an interesting remark on the causal relation of God the Father to the event of Christ's suffering. He explains how Isaiah "sets out the acceptance of this suffering on the part of God the Father: 'for the wickedness of my people have I struck him,' that is, allowed him to be struck."[114] Here, Aquinas does not state that God the Father actively wills the suffering and death of Christ. Rather, we are simply told that God the Father "allows" or "permits" (*permisi*) Christ's passion and "accepts" (*acceptationem*) his suffering and death as a sacrifice "'for our sins [*pro peccatis nostris*]'" (1 Pt 3:18).[115] This means that the Father does not actively intervene in human history to afflict his Son with pain and death. Rather, according to Aquinas, the Father permits the Son to experience the pain and death that is inflicted upon him by his enemies. That is, the Father does not actively step in and rescue the

108. Ibid.
109. Ibid., quoting Is 53:8.
110. Ibid.
111. Ibid.
112. Ibid., quoting Is 53:8.
113. Ibid., quoting Jer 11:19.
114. Ibid., quoting Is 53:8.
115. Ibid., quoting 1 Pt 3:18.

Son from the hands of his enemies. At least one explanation for this absence of intervention by the Father is that the Son has freely chosen to endure the suffering that his enemies are inflicting upon him, and he has made this choice specifically for the sake of our sins.

Proceeding to Isaiah 53:9, Aquinas sees this verse as speaking of Christ's burial and his innocence.[116] Bound to the first clause of v. 9 in Latin, *Et dabit impios pro sepultura*, Aquinas interprets these words as saying that Christ was given to the Jews (who themselves where "in the hands of the Romans") to be entombed, in the sense that they set a guard over his tomb.[117] The "merit" from Christ's "life of innocence" in both deeds and words is indicated by Isaiah's statement that "'he has done no iniquity, neither was there deceit in his mouth.'"[118] Seeing a thematic and linguistic connection with a New Testament text, Aquinas links this latter half of Isaiah 53:9 with 1 Peter 2:22, in which the apostle says that Christ "'did no sin, neither was guile found in his mouth.'"[119] So, according to Aquinas, despite his perfect innocence in word and deed, Christ's corpse was handed over to be entombed by his impious enemies.

While continuing to discuss the merit of Christ, Aquinas turns to Isaiah 53:10, where he once more takes up the question of the relation between Christ's suffering and the will of God the Father. Aquinas's version of Isaiah 53:10 begins with the following, seemingly disturbing statement: "And the Lord willed [*voluit*] to bruise him in infirmity." On the surface, this passage makes it seem as if God delights in the suffering of his Servant and actively afflicts him with that suffering. But we have already seen how, while commenting upon Isaiah 53:8, Aquinas claimed that God merely allowed (*permisi*) Christ's suffering and death. Now, Aquinas must once again tackle a difficult text which seems to say that God 'desired,' 'willed,' or 'was pleased' (*voluit*) by Christ's suffering. Perhaps surprisingly, Aquinas's explicit engagement with this text of Isaiah 53:10 is quite

---

116. Is 53:9 states: "And he shall give the ungodly for his burial, and the rich for his death: because he has done no iniquity, neither was there deceit in his mouth."

117. *Super Isaiam*, 972. Author's translation of "'Et dabit impios Judaeos, in manus Romanorum, 'pro sepultura,' quia ipsum in sepulcro costodiri fecerunt."

118. Ibid., 972, quoting Is 53:9.

119. Ibid., quoting 1 Pt 2:22.

limited. He merely says, "And as to the obedience of his death: 'and the Lord,' the Father, 'desired [*voluit*],' and he was obedient [*obediens*] to the Father unto death, per Phil 2:8: 'becoming obedient unto death,' and 1 Cor 1:25: 'the weakness of God is stronger than men.'"[120] Unfortunately, Aquinas's meaning here is somewhat ambiguous. There are at least two ways to interpret what he is saying.

First, on the one hand, Aquinas may be saying merely that God the Father willed or desired (*voluit*) that the Son endure the passion, and that the Son obeyed this command of the Father. This interpretation seems to be the most consistent with the actual text of Isaiah 53:10. If this is what Aquinas is saying, then we must be cautious to not read any further into the statement. Aquinas does not say *why* the Father wills the Son to endure the passion, nor does he imply that the Father actively brings about the suffering of the Son. Rather, he simply is saying *that*, given the attacks which Christ's enemies are inflicting upon him, the Father wills that Christ as a man endure those attacks. That is, the Father is not going to actively intervene to save Christ nor does he want Christ to use his divine power to escape his suffering.

Second, on the other hand, it is entirely plausible here to interpret Aquinas as saying that what the Father fundamentally wills and desires (*voluit*) is the obedience (*obediens*) of Christ, an obedience that is prior to and beyond, yet also includes, Christ's endurance of suffering and death at the hands of his enemies. Aquinas's citation from Philippians 2 supports this interpretation, as there Paul depicts the exaltation of Christ as a reward for the obedience that Christ gave to the Father throughout his life, an obedience that was continually offered even leading up to and throughout his passion. Finally, in both interpretations offered above, one thing is clear: for Aquinas, the merit which Christ possesses from his passion lies in the fact that he endured his suffering out of obedience to the will of the Father. Not the suffering itself, but rather suffering voluntarily endured out of obedience, is the source of the merit that leads to the Suffering Servant's exaltation.

---

120. Ibid., quoting Is 53:10. This is the author's translation of *voluit*, which could also be rendered as 'willed,' whereas St. Hilaire typically prefers 'was pleased.'

Aquinas interprets the latter part of Isaiah 53:10 as once more speaking of the fruits of grace that are given to humanity as a result of Christ's free endurance of the passion. For Aquinas, the statement in 53:10—"'If he shall lay down [*posuerit*] his life'" points to the fact that, unless Christ freely chose to suffer and die, his passion would not have merited a reward of grace for humanity.[121] The voluntary, free nature of Christ's self-offering in death is thus a condition for and cause of the fruits that result from that death. Aquinas shows how Isaiah 53:10 is fulfilled, and that in fact Christ's death was voluntary, by citing John 10:17, in which Christ states "'I lay down [*pono*] my life.'"[122] Aquinas's claim that humanity's reception of certain graces is contingent upon Christ's free decision to lay down his life for us serves to emphasize the gratuitous, efficacious love of Christ for sinners.

Now, the "reward" (*praemium*) for Christ's voluntary death is that, per Isaiah 53:10, "'he shall see a long-lived seed.'"[123] According to Aquinas this means that "until the end of the world" Christ shall see "sons for him reborn out of the power of his death."[124] Given that Aquinas begins his treatment of v. 10 by stating that it concerns the "justification of men," the rebirth spoken of here would seem to be the justification of sinners in grace.[125] Aquinas cites John 12:24–25 in order to show how Christ himself understood that his death would bring about such a rebirth of souls: "'unless the grain of wheat falling into the ground die, itself remains alone. But if it dies it brings forth much fruit.'"[126] Aquinas concludes his exegesis of Isaiah 53:10 by saying that, in addition to "rebirth" (justification), Christ's death will ensure that "'the will [*voluntas*] of the Lord shall be directed in his hand.'"[127] This means that through the "work" (*opere*) of Christ in his passion, the "sanctification" (*sanctificatio*) of humanity

---

121. Ibid., 973, quoting Is 53:10.

122. Ibid., quoting Jn 10:17. Jn 10:18, which immediately follows the verse cited by Aquinas, supports his point even further: "No one takes it from me, but I lay it down of my own accord" (NRSV-CE).

123. *Super Isaiam*, 973, quoting Is 53:10.

124. Ibid.

125. Ibid.

126. Ibid., quoting Jn 12:24–25.

127. Ibid., quoting Is 53:10.

will be brought about.[128] Aquinas equates the "'will'" (*voluntas*) of God mentioned in Isaiah 53:10 with 'sanctification' on the basis of 1 Thessalonians 4:3, which states "'this is the will [*voluntas*] of God, your sanctification.'"[129] So, as a reward for his voluntary endurance of death, Christ merits from God an outpouring of grace upon sinners that brings about their justification (rebirth) and their sanctification.[130]

Isaiah 53:11 offers Aquinas an opportunity for further reflection upon Christ's work and the rewards of that work. Regarding the first part of this verse, Aquinas explains: "'because his soul has labored,' in preaching and discoursing, 'he shall see' the gentiles converted to him, 'and be filled [*saturabitur*]' as though having what he intended: 'I have meat to eat which you know not' (Jn 4:32)."[131] The citation from John here serves to show that the food that Christ eats and which renders him 'filled' is none other than the work of the Father that he accomplishes (Jn 4:34), a work that is fulfilled through the conversion of the gentiles, the justification of sinners and their sanctification in grace. So, here the teaching and preaching ministry of Christ is viewed as working in unison with his passion, for both are means by which the rebirth of sinners in grace is brought about. According to Aquinas, Christ "merits" grace for humanity and "justifies many" (Is 53:11) not only by his passion, but also "'by his knowledge'" (Is 53:11), that is, by "the exercise of preaching" and "his teaching."[132]

While most of Isaiah 53:11 has detailed the merits and justifying fruits of Christ's teaching, Aquinas interprets the final clause in this verse as speaking once more of the merit that Christ has from "the torment of death."[133] Commenting upon Isaiah's statement that the Servant "shall bear their iniquities," Aquinas understands this

---

128. Ibid.

129. Ibid., quoting Is 53:10 and 1 Thes 4:3.

130. This does not mean that, for Aquinas, prior to the occurrence of Christ's passion in human history no one possessed justifying grace or was filled with the Holy Spirit. In *ST* I-II, q. 107, a. 1, ad 2, he claims that there were some people during the period of the Old Testament who possessed "charity and the grace of the Holy Spirit" even as they awaited the fulfillment of further "spiritual and eternal promises" that would occur with the advent of Christ.

131. *Super Isaiam*, 973, quoting Is 53:11 and Jn 4:32.

132. Ibid., 974, quoting Is 53:11.

133. Ibid.

to mean that Christ will bear "the punishments for their iniquities" (*poenas pro iniquitatibus*).[134] We have already seen Aquinas use this terminology of Christ bearing the punishments (*poenas*) of sinners in his comments upon Isaiah 53:4. Here, he does not provide any further specification regarding the nature of these *poenas*. He simply identifies Christ's bearing of them as a further source of his merit. But he does not explain why and how Christ's carrying of our *poenas* is meritorious.

Aquinas now arrives at v. 12, the final portion of Isaiah 53. He identifies the general theme of this verse as Christ's "victory over his enemies,"[135] and in the service of this theme he draws out three subpoints. In order to better contextualize these three points, it is helpful to look at the entirety of Aquinas's version of Isaiah 53:12: "Therefore will I distribute to him very many, and he shall divide the spoils of the strong, because he has delivered his soul unto death, and was reputed with the wicked: and he has borne the sins of many, and has prayed for the transgressors."[136] Aquinas says that the first point of the above passage concerns "the subjection of the enemies" of Christ.[137] The "'very many'" whom God "'will distribute'" to Christ are "those held captive by demons," but whom in being given to Christ become believers in him.[138] Christ will "'divide'" these "'spoils of the strong'" to his disciples, precisely by "setting different disciples over different nations."[139] Thus Christ subdues the demons precisely by liberating their captives and setting them free with Christian faith. This setting free of the enslaved and entrusting them to his Church is the 'spoil' that Christ enjoys. Aquinas's second point is that Christ subdued his enemies and won his spoil "'because he has handed over'" his soul to death, and specifically a death "'with the wicked.'"[140] Aquinas here cites Luke 23:32 and Psalm 88:4 to show how Christ's death fulfills Isaiah 53:12: Christ was crucified

---

134. Ibid.

135. Ibid., 975.

136. Is 53:12, translation from the Latin: "Ideo dispertiam ei plurimos, et fortium dividet spolia, pro eo quod tradidit in mortem animam suam, et cum sceleratis reputatus est. Et ipse peccatum multorum tulit et pro transgressoribus rogavit."

137. *Super Isaiam*, 975.

138. Ibid., quoting Is 53:12.

139. Ibid., quoting Is 53:12.

140. Ibid., citing Is 53:12.

with "'two malefactors'" and was "'counted among them that go down to the pit.'"[141] That is, the cause of Christ's victory over his enemies was the fact that he was killed as if he were a grave sinner and criminal.

Aquinas's third and final point on Isaiah 53:12 concerns the nature of the salvation of those who are liberated from the devil and made subject to Christ. Aquinas explains, "He [Christ] does not subject them to himself like a tyrant to abuse them, but to save them."[142] Christ subdues sinners by liberating them from their sins. To submit to Christ is to be saved from sin. To say that Christ "'has borne the sins of many'" is thus simply to say that he has come to take away sins and thus bring humanity into subjection to himself.[143] Further, Christ has succeeded in his mission: the salvation which he has wrought is "efficacious" and "sufficient" for all sinners.[144] That Christ came to save us, and not to abuse us as a tyrant would, is manifested by the fact that he "'has prayed for the transgressors.'"[145] Aquinas ends his lecture on Isaiah 53 by quoting Luke 23:34.[146] On one level, this New Testament verse shows that Christ has fulfilled Isaiah's prophecy of the Suffering Servant who prays for sinners. On a deeper level, the text from Luke is further proof that Christ came not as a tyrant seeking to abuse sinners, but rather as a loving savior who seeks to free his sheep from the snares of sin: "'Father, forgive them, for they know not what they do.'"[147]

THE COMMENTARIES ON JEREMIAH AND LAMENTATIONS

We can now turn to Aquinas's brief engagement with the text of Isaiah 53 in the cursory commentaries on Jeremiah and Lamentations, respectively. Torrell explains that all cursory commentaries were meant to be "rapid by their very definition," and that "the commentaries

---

141. Ibid., quoting Lk 22:32 and Ps 88:4, respectively.
142. Ibid.
143. Ibid., quoting Is 53:12.
144. Ibid.
145. Ibid., quoting Is 53:12.
146. Ibid.
147. Ibid., quoting Lk 23:34.

on Jeremiah and Lamentations exactly correspond to that defini-tion."[148] As with the *Super Isaiam*, Aquinas likely wrote and taught on Jeremiah in Paris somewhere between 1251 to 1253.[149] If the *Super Threnos* is authentic, then it may also date to this time or to the ear-lier period in Cologne when Aquinas worked under Albert.[150] There are three references to Isaiah 53 in the *Commentary on Jeremiah* and one in the *Commentary on Lamentations*.[151] We will now look at each of these references and be attentive to how Aquinas uses the text of Isaiah 53 to shed light upon the mystery of Christ's passion.

Aquinas's initial two citations of Isaiah 53 in the *Commentary on Jeremiah* occur in his fourth lecture on Jeremiah 11. This lecture focuses upon Jeremiah 11:18–23. For Aquinas, the literal sense of this portion of Jeremiah 11 is about the violent persecution of the prophet by his enemies. In addition, "the persecution of Jeremiah prefigures the passion of Christ."[152] For "what is fulfilled in the pres-ent in Jeremiah, this he prophesied about the Lord in the future."[153] Both citations of Isaiah 53 occur in Aquinas's comments on Jeremiah 11:19, where the prophet compares his suffering to that of an inno-cent lamb who is ignorantly led to the slaughter.[154] Aquinas first cites Isaiah 53:7 ("'as a lamb before the shearer is silent, and opens not his mouth'") in response to Jeremiah's statement that he will be led to death "'like a lamb'" who "'did not know'" of the murderous plans that his enemies had for him.[155] Aquinas's points here are that even though both Jeremiah and Christ were violently persecuted as

148. Torrell, *Saint Thomas Aquinas*, 36.

149. Ibid., 35. See Weisheipl, *Friar Thomas D'Aquino*, 370, and Chenu, *Toward Understanding St. Thomas*, 245.

150. Torrell, *Saint Thomas Aquinas*, 35.

151. Aquinas himself makes a fourth reference in Latin to "Isaiah 53" in the *Commentary on Jeremiah*, but he is mistaken; he is actually quoting Is 55:6. See c. 29, l. 1.

152. Thomas Aquinas, *Commentary on the Prophet Jeremiah*, c. 11, l. 4. All further citations from this commentary will be abbreviated as *On Jeremiah* and will use the 1863 Parma Latin edition and the English translation by Ben Martin, edited by the Aquinas Institute. Both are available at aquinas.cc/la/en/~Jerem.C11.L4.7. References will identify the chapter and lecture number being cited.

153. *On Jeremiah*, c. 11, l. 4.

154. Jer 11:19 states: "And I was gentle, like a lamb brought as a sacrifice; and I did not know that they took counsel against me, saying: let us put wood in his bread, and let us destroy him from the land of the living, and his name shall be remembered no more."

155. *On Jeremiah*, c. 11, l. 4, quoting Is 53:7 and Jer 11:19, respectively.

innocent, seemingly ignorant lambs, in fact both had supernatural knowledge of the violent intentions of their enemies against them. Jeremiah knew "through the grace of revelation," and Christ "as man" knew through the hypostatic union, "by which he knew all things."[156] While Aquinas does not mention this, it is worth pointing out that Christ's knowledge of the malicious plans of his enemies and his foreknowledge that they would attempt to execute those plans is a further sign of the freedom with which he went to his passion. That is, he always knew of the suffering that was coming to him, and yet out of love for sinners he voluntarily chose not to use his divine power to escape that suffering.

Aquinas uses his second citation from Isaiah 53 in the context of a mystical, Christological interpretation of Jeremiah 11:19. Aquinas compares Isaiah 53:8's prophecy that the Suffering Servant will be "'cut off from the earth [*de terra*]'" to Jeremiah's description of his enemies' intentions.[157] When they say to one another "let us put wood in his bread, and let us destroy him from the land [*de terra*] of the living" (Jer 11:19), Aquinas views this "mystically" as referring to "the body of Christ on the wood of the cross."[158] That is, Christ's enemies destroy him and cut him off from the earth using the wood of the cross. The reference to the placement of the wood "'in his bread'" is likewise mystically interpreted in light of Isaiah 53:8 to mean that "through the wood of the cross let us stir up scandal at his doctrine, which is his bread."[159] In sum, what Isaiah 53:8 speaks of literally, Jeremiah 11:19 speaks of mystically: Christ's enemies cut him off from the land (*de terra*) of the living through the wood of the cross, and this destruction leads people to view him as a sinner whose teaching is scandalous.

Aquinas's third and final citation of Isaiah 53 comes in his second lecture on Jeremiah 40. He makes brief remarks on Jeremiah 40:7–12, in which the prophet describes how the Jewish people who fled during the Babylonian invasion of Jerusalem return and submit with confidence to the rule of Gedaliah, whom the Babylonians had

156. Ibid.
157. Ibid., quoting Is 53:8.
158. Ibid.
159. Ibid., quoting Jer 11:19.

put in governance after their departure. Aquinas points out how, in Jeremiah 40:10, Gedaliah assures the people of Judah that they have nothing to fear from him and that he will protect them against the Babylonians. He will ensure the "security" of Judah and will himself mediate with the Babylonians on their behalf.[160] Aquinas explains, "it is as though he [Gedaliah] were saying: I bear [*sustinebo*] the entire burden, that you may be in peace."[161] Immediately following this statement Aquinas first quotes 1 Corinthians 4:10 and then Isaiah 53:4, saying "'Surely, he has borne [*tulit*] our infirmities, and has himself carried [*portavit*] our griefs.'"[162] Aquinas thus connects Gedaliah's bearing (*sustinebo*) of the burden of dealing with the Babylonians for the good of the Judeans with Christ's bearing (*tulit, portavit*) of fallen humanity's infirmities for the good of sinners. Aquinas sheds further light on his meaning by quoting John 10:11 ("'a good shepherd lays down his life for his sheep'") immediately after his citation from Isaiah 53.[163] The point is that Christ bears a burden (lays down his life) for the good of his sheep; he dies so that we may live. By connecting Gedaliah with Christ, Aquinas depicts Christ's passion as the voluntary bearing of a painful burden that needed to be borne in order to acquire peace for sinners.

It now remains to examine Aquinas's lone citation of Isaiah 53 in his *Commentary on Lamentations*. This citation occurs in the lecture on Lamentations 4:1–21. Aquinas says that Lamentations 4:20 shows that even the kings of Jerusalem were not spared during the attacks of the chosen people's enemies. Specifically, he states that "'Christ the Lord is taken for our sins'" (Lam 4:20) refers principally to the Jewish king Josiah, whom the Egyptians killed, even though "he himself was just."[164] The "'Christ'" referred to by Lamentations could also refer to King Zedekiah.[165] But, Aquinas says that this verse of

---

160. *On Jeremiah*, c. 40, l. 2.

161. Ibid.

162. Ibid., quoting Is 53:4.

163. Ibid., quoting Jn 10:11.

164. Thomas Aquinas, *Commentary on the Lamentations of Jeremiah*, c. 4, l. 20, no. 86, quoting Lm 4:20. All references to this commentary will be abbreviated as *On Lamentations* and will cite the chapter, lecture, and paragraph number being referred to. All citations use the 1863 Parma Latin edition and the English translation by Mark Foudy and the Aquinas Institute, available online at aquinas.cc/la/en/~Lam.

165. *On Lamentations*, c. 4, l. 20, no. 86, quoting Lm 4:20.

Lamentations is understood "better" (*melius*) of Jesus Christ, and then he immediately quotes Isaiah 53:5: "'He was wounded for our iniquities.'"[166] So, while Josiah the just was killed as a consequence of his people's sins, so too was Jesus, as indicated by Isaiah. Yet, Jesus' death has the additional aspect of being for our protection from sin. As Aquinas explains, Jesus' death gave sinners "protection" by bringing them "'under [his] shadow.'"[167] Christ the king was physically killed as a result of his people's sins, and yet his bodily death results in the protection of his sinful people from the spiritual death of sin.

CONCLUSION AND SYNTHESIS

Aquinas's cursory *Super Isaiam* was his first scholarly engagement with the Suffering Servant text of Isaiah 53. While this commentary does not contain an exhaustive analysis of Isaiah 53, Aquinas nevertheless manages to draw out of that biblical text many significant theological points regarding the mystery of Christ's passion. In the first place, it is worth noting that Aquinas sets the stage for his reading of Isaiah 53 with his comments upon Isaiah 52:13–15. There he makes it clear that the Servant of whom Isaiah speaks is Christ, that Christ will suffer as a man, and that his suffering is an act of priestly sacrifice that will purify people from their sins and lead them into the presence of God. In his lecture on Isaiah 53 Aquinas once more interprets Isaiah's description of the Servant in Isaiah 53:1–12 as a straightforward and clear prophecy of the passion of Christ. Yet Aquinas also acknowledges that Christ's passion is a tremendous mystery that is difficult to believe and understand. This was especially the case for the contemporaries of Jesus who were expecting that the Messiah would come with great dignity, power, and prosperity. Instead, Isaiah foretold that Christ would come as a man who is rejected and filled with pain. So intense would be the suffering of Christ that for many it would serve to hide his divine dignity from their eyes. The nature of Christ's suffering included physical torture, hunger, thirst, death, and all of the sadness that accompanies these

166. Ibid., quoting Is 53:5.
167. Ibid., quoting Jer 4:20.

pains. These suffering are identified at least materially with the punishments (*poenas*) that sinners endure. Further, Christ's suffering consisted in the fact that he was misunderstood and considered as a criminal whose pains were a just punishment imposed upon him by God.

In reality, though, God the Father did not actively inflict the pains of the passion upon Christ. The Father did command Christ to live with a passible human nature and, consequently, to endure virtuously any suffering that came as a result of possessing such a nature. Christ freely obeyed this command. But this is distinct from saying that the Father actively willed that Christ would be arrested and put to death. Rather, the Father merely permitted the pain that Christ's enemies inflicted upon him in the passion. Christ voluntarily chose to endure his passion in order to save fallen humanity from its sins. Every human being is a sinner in need of salvation, but no sinner can perform a suitable penance for their sins. Hence, Christ offered himself in death as a penance for the sins of the world, and God the Father accepted this sacrifice. Christ's passion was thus a work of satisfaction for the sins of the world. For various reasons, Christ merited grace for himself and for sinners. The sources of this merit were the following: the divine dignity of Christ's personhood; his teaching and preaching ministry; the innocence of his words and deeds throughout his life and during his passion; the freedom with which he chose to endure his suffering, and the obedience to the Father he enacted in choosing to suffer; the great pain of his death, and the shame of his death among criminals. In all these ways, Christ merited his own resurrection from the dead. Further, he merited for sinners the grace of liberation from captivity to the devil, justification and spiritual rebirth, sanctification and peaceful access to the Lord.

Aquinas's citations of Isaiah 53 in his commentaries *On Jeremiah* and *On Lamentations* are few, and his engagement with the text in these circumstances is very brief. Even so, he provides us with some additional insights regarding the mystery of Christ's passion. Aquinas employs Isaiah to explain how even in his human nature Christ, in virtue of the omniscience that he possessed through the hypostatic union, knew full well of the malicious intentions of his enemies and of the slaughter that awaited him. Additionally, though he knew that his death would be a scandal to some and make them reject his teaching, Christ nevertheless freely chose to bear the burden of his passion for the good of sinners. By bearing the burden of his passion, Christ acquired peace, security, and protection for the sinners who dwell under his shadow.

4

The Commentary on the *Sentences*

In the previous chapter, I explored Aquinas's interpretations of the text of Isaiah 53 in his cursory lectures on Isaiah, Jeremiah, and Lamentations. Beginning with this chapter, the remainder of this book will focus on the references to Isaiah 53 that Aquinas makes in his major systematic works as well as in the detailed and theologically dense biblical commentaries that he produced as a *magister in sacra pagina*. In these works, Aquinas never departs from the substance of the foundational interpretation of Isaiah 53 that he offered in his *Super Isaiam*. Nonetheless, as is fitting, the theological depth of Aquinas's engagement with Isaiah 53 increases significantly in these later works in comparison to the level of analysis that he provided in his earlier, cursory biblical commentaries. Rather than contradicting his earlier interpretations, the interpretations of Isaiah 53 that we will see Aquinas offer in this chapter serve to clarify, build upon, and extend the readings that he offered in his cursory commentaries.

My focus in this chapter is on Aquinas's *Sentences* commentary (hereafter *SS*). The structure of this chapter contains the following divisions. First, I specify the number of references to Isaiah 53 in the *SS* and provide a brief historical overview of the origin, style, and purpose of that work. Second, I spend the majority of this chapter giving a detailed qualitative analysis of Aquinas's references to Isaiah 53 in the *SS*. I examine the cases of Isaiah 53 in the chronological order in which they appear in the *SS*. Finally, I conclude with a brief theological synthesis of the various Christological concepts that Aquinas draws out from the text of Isaiah 53 in the *SS*.

CONTEXT AND QUANTITATIVE ANALYSIS

Aquinas's commentary on on the *Sentences* of Peter Lombard contains seven explicit references to the text of Isaiah 53.[1] These references are found in books II, III, and IV of the *SS*, and each is used to testify to the nature and saving value of Christ's passion. Unlike the commentaries on Isaiah, Jeremiah, and Lamentations, the *SS* is not a cursory exposition of the immediate, literal meaning of a biblical text. Rather, it is a systematic, deeply speculative analysis of important theological questions and issues that are generated by the text of Lombard's *Sentences* as well as the writings of the Church Fathers and the Bible. Aquinas wrote the *SS* over a span of about four years (1252 to 1256) while at the University of Paris. His writing was based on a two-year (1252 to 1254) course of lectures that he gave on the *Sentences*.[2] He likely finished writing the final part, Book IV, after he had already been named a *Magister Sacra Pagina* in 1256.[3] As Weisheipl explains, the written commentary is not merely "a report of his day-to-day presentation[s] in the lecture hall. Rather, it is a carefully elaborated and edited version of questions discussed in the classroom, polished after the event."[4]

The nature of the *SS* and the manner in which it was composed are worth keeping in mind as we examine Aquinas's uses of the text of Isaiah 53 within. In this work, Aquinas's principal task is to provide a systematic answer to dense theological questions. He employs Isaiah 53 as a foundation for, and an aid to, his reasoning in response to these questions. So, in order to understand how Aquinas

---

1. The seven cases of Is 53 are found in (1) II, d. 36, q. 1, a. 4, ad 2; (2) III, d. 15, q. 1, a. 1, obj. 6; (3) III, d. 15, q. 2, a. 3, qc. 1, sc.; (4) III, d. 18, a. 5; (5) III, d. 19, a. 3, qc. 2, sc. 2, p. 2; (6) IV, d. 2, q. 1, a. 2, ad 4; (7) IV, d. 4, q. 2, a. 1, qc. 2, ad 1. Aquinas also refers to "Isaiah 53:21" in the prologue to the third book, and this reference has been preserved in the contemporary Latin text, but Aquinas was mistaken; the actual quotation is taken from Is 33:21.

2. Torrell, *Saint Thomas Aquinas*, 48.

3. Ibid., 386–87.

4. Weisheipl, *Friar Thomas D'Aquino*, 358–59.

is interpreting Isaiah 53 in a particular context, we will often have to step back and grasp the greater movement of the systematic analysis that he is undertaking in that context. Having established this context, we can now proceed to our qualitative analysis.

CASES OF ISAIAH 53 IN THE SS

First Case: II, d. 36, q. 1, a. 4, ad 2

In this article Aquinas takes up the question of "Whether every punishment [*poena*] is inflicted for sin?"[5] In order to understand Aquinas's use of Isaiah 53 in this context, we first need to highlight the major points that he articulates in the body of the article regarding the nature and cause of punishment. Aquinas first establishes that "every punishment [*poena*] is a kind of harm," and "one is only punished [*punitur*] by being deprived of something good for him."[6] He then explains that "a thing can be good for a man in two ways," namely, either "precisely as a man, or else in common nature, as an animal or as a living thing, and the like."[7] When treating of the cause of punishment, then, one must first specify the type of goods which the punishment deprives the person of.

First, the virtues are the unique good that a human possesses precisely as a human, as a rational animal. Regarding the virtues, Aquinas states, "no one has a punishment from the privation of these goods except by his own fault."[8] That is, a person's virtue can only be damaged by their own sinful decisions; sin alone deprives a person of virtue. The second category of goods that a person can possess are the "goods of the body, even external ones."[9] Humans share these goods in common with other animals and bodily creatures. While the loss of such goods is a type of punishment, Aquinas specifies that "not every punishment of this kind is introduced for his

---

5. Thomas Aquinas, *Commentary on the Sentences* (hereafter *SS*) III, d. 36, q. 1, a. 4. All citations of the *SS* are from the Latin editions, and the English translations by the Aquinas Institute, available online at aquinas.cc/la/en/~Sent.II. The Latin text of book II is the 1929 edition edited by P. Mandonnet.

6. *SS* II, d. 36, q. 1, a. 4, sc and co., respectively.

7. *SS* II, d. 36, q. 1, a. 4, co.

8. Ibid.

9. Ibid.

own sin, but it always does follow on some sin, at least the sin of the nature. For if human nature had not been infected by original sin, man would not suffer any disturbance or loss in these things."[10] This means that human beings suffer the loss of bodily and external goods due to the fallen, passible human nature that they possess as a result of original sin and, in addition, at times due to the actual sins of themselves or others.

With this context in mind, we can now adequately interpret Aquinas's citation of Isaiah 53:8 in his reply to the second objection. The second objection argues: "it says of Christ: 'he committed no sin' (1 Pt 2:22). Yet Christ bore many punishments [*poenas*]. Therefore not every punishment [*poena*] is inflicted for a fault."[11] In response to this objection, Aquinas makes two points. First, he says that Christ "in no way had any punishment that would be a punishment of man's precisely as man."[12] For, Christ possessed a "superabundance" of virtue and "suffered no defect in them."[13] Yet, second, Christ did have "a punishment as regards common nature."[14] Given that Christ suffered loss and damage to his bodily and external goods, but not to his virtues, Aquinas concludes: "Thus, it did not have to be the case that there was a fault in him but only that a fault preceded in human nature."[15] Immediately after this statement, he concludes his reply by quoting the following portion of Isaiah 53:8: "'I struck him for the transgression of my people.'"[16]

Aquinas is quoting Isaiah here because it supports his claim that Christ suffered due to others' sins and not his own. In addition, the argument that he has just provided in the reply to the second objection further clarifies what Isaiah 53:8 means when it says that Christ was struck "because" (*propter*) of the sins of the people. For Aquinas, the fundamental cause of the fact that Christ experiences damage to his bodily goods is the passible animal nature that he possesses in common with all people who are descended from Adam.

10. Ibid.
11. *SS* II, d. 36, q. 1, a. 4, obj. 2.
12. *SS* II, d. 36, q. 1, a. 4, ad 2.
13. Ibid.
14. Ibid.
15. Ibid.
16. Ibid., quoting Is 53:8.

Further, Christ suffers the loss of corporal goods as a result of the actual sins of the enemies who are inflicting punishment (*poena*) upon him. Aquinas interprets Isaiah 53:8 here as saying that Christ is struck because of the sins of those who have gone before him and of those who were against him during his own time.

Second Case: III, d. 15, q. 1, a. 1, obj. 6

Aquinas's question here is "whether Christ ought to have received a human nature with defects [*defectibus*] and infirmities [*infirmitatibus*]?"[17] In the sixth objection, the objector quotes Isaiah 53:2b and 53:3b ("'he had no form or comeliness that we should look at him,' and it follows 'we esteemed him not'") in order to argue that Christ should not have assumed infirmities.[18] The objector argues that Christ came in order to bring men knowledge of God, but his endurance of infirmities "led us away from knowledge of him," that is, from acceptance of Christ's teaching.[19] If, as the objector claims, Isaiah is saying that Christ's suffering was the reason why people did not believe in his teaching, then why did Christ allow himself to endure such suffering?

In his reply, Aquinas first establishes that Christ came to manifest the glory of his divine nature, not the glory of his human nature. Then, he states that Christ "made God's glory more transparent through the assumed infirmity, insofar as the weakness of God is more powerful than men."[20] So in this context, the text of Isaiah 53:2–3 is being employed because it raises a challenging theological question for Aquinas. He must look to another biblical text (1 Cor 1:25) to provide an answer to that question. While Isaiah indicates that Christ's passion was a stumbling block for some, Paul asserts that the foolishness of Christ reflected the wisdom of God, and the weakness of Christ demonstrated the strength of God. Aquinas's answer here is not necessarily meant to be exhaustive. The point is simply to demonstrate that scripture provides the resources that are needed to answer the questions posed by other parts of Scripture.

17. *SS* III, d. 15, q. 1, a. 1. The Latin text of Book III is the 1956 edition edited by M. F. Moos.
18. *SS* III, d. 15, q. 1, a. 1, obj. 6, quoting Is 53:2.
19. Ibid.
20. *SS* III, d. 15, q. 1, a. 1, ad 6.

For Aquinas, 1 Corinthians 1:25 sufficiently handles the issue raised by Isaiah 53:2–3.

Third Case: III, d. 15, q. 2, a. 3, qc. 1, sc.

In this article Aquinas asks "whether in Christ there was true pain [*dolor*] in the senses?"[21] Aquinas answers this question in the affirmative, and he does so initially with a *sed contra* that consists exclusively of a quotation from Isaiah 53:4: "'truly he himself has carried our pains [*dolores*].'"[22] Isaiah's prophecy provides the divinely revealed answer to the question being posed, and thus it serves as the foundation for the further theological reflection that Aquinas makes in response to the question.

In the remainder of *quaestiuncula* 1, Aquinas's theological reflection contains the following points. First, Christ had a true sense of touch and his body was truly wounded (*respondeo*). Even though Christ was God, he still suffered pain from the wounds to his flesh (ad 1). The fact that Christ voluntarily chose to suffer did not take away his experience of bodily pain (ad 2). Similarly, Christ's perfect contemplation of God did not eliminate his bodily pain (ad 3). For our purposes, the principal point here is that Aquinas has grounded these conclusions about Christ's experience of bodily pain in the text of Isaiah 53:4. More specifically, Aquinas cites Isaiah's assertion that the Servant of the Lord "'truly'" (*vere*) suffered. Isaiah shows that Christ's passion was not merely a docetic illusion; his pain was real, and thus it can serve as an object of Aquinas's systematic reflection.

Fourth Case: III, d. 18, a. 5

Here Aquinas asks "whether Christ merited for himself through his passion?"[23] In the body of the article, Aquinas states, "every voluntary act informed by charity is meritorious."[24] Then, in the conclusion to the body of the article, he quotes a portion of his version of Isaiah 53:7 ("'he was offered because he himself willed it'") in order

---

21. *SS* III, d. 15, q. 2, a. 3.
22. *SS* III, d. 15, q. 2, a. 3, qc. 1, sc., quoting Is 53:4.
23. *SS* III, d. 18, a. 5.
24. Ibid.

to support the claim that "Christ endured his passion voluntarily."[25] He then adds that this voluntary choice of Christ "was informed by charity," and so he concludes that "there is no doubt that he merited through his passion."[26] So the immediate function that Isaiah 53:7 performs here for Aquinas is simply that of establishing the foundation upon which he builds the rest of his answer. Theologically, Isaiah 53:7 testifies to the freedom with which Christ chose to suffer. Without his freedom, and without the charity that informed his free choice to undergo suffering, Christ's suffering would not have been meritorious. That is, Christ's passion was meritorious because he freely chose, from charity, to endure the suffering that was inflicted upon him by his enemies. Conversely, a person who is violently forced to undergo suffering against their will does not merit simply based on the fact that they are enduring pain.[27]

Fifth Case: III, d. 19, a. 3, qc. 2, sc.

The primary question that Aquinas addresses in this article is "'whether through Christ's passion we are freed from eternal punishment [*poena*]?"[28] The first *quaestiuncula* in this article clarifies that Christ freed us from sin, and since "sin is the cause of eternal death," this means that Christ freed us from hell as well.[29] The second *quaestiuncala* within a. 3 deals with a more difficult issue, namely, the relationship between Christ's passion and the human experience of suffering on this side of eternity. The objections which Aquinas fields here deny that Christ's passion has the power to take away the experience of "temporal punishment" on earth.[30]

In his initial response to these objections, Aquinas affirms that

---

25. Ibid., quoting Is 53:7.

26. Ibid.

27. This does not mean, however, that a person can only merit amidst suffering if they have freely chosen to suffer. For charity is the source of merit; hence, even if one is experiencing suffering against one's will, if one preserves and practices charity amidst that trial of suffering this would be a great source of merit. For example, the involuntarily imprisoned person who loves God and neighbor even amidst the pain of their imprisonment merits from the charitable way in which they have endured their suffering, even though they do not wish to suffer.

28. *SS* III, d. 19, a. 3.

29. *SS* III, d. 19, a. 3, qc. 1, sc. 1.

30. *SS* III, d. 19, a. 3, qc. 2, obj. 2.

Christ's passion does take away temporal punishment, and that it does so specifically through the mediation of the "keys of the Church."[31] Then, he employs the text of Isaiah 53:4 in the following argument: "Furthermore, God does not punish twice for the very same thing (Nah 1:9). But God placed on Christ the iniquities of all of us when he bore our pains [*dolores*] (Is 53:4). Therefore he freed us from temporal punishment through his passion."[32] The immediate sense of this passage can be somewhat jarring for a modern audience: Aquinas appears to be saying that Christ experienced all of the pains of temporal punishment that were due to sinners and, since God does not punish twice for the same offense, this means that sinners are freed from temporal punishment. That is, Christ has already endured the punishment (*poena*) that was owed to sinners, and so now there is no further need for sinners to suffer the pain that Christ suffered in their place. This reasoning from Aquinas, read in isolation, could be interpreted as somewhat legalistic, arbitrary, and even cruel—as if God vents his wrath on an innocent man and as a result is content to let the guilty go free. The text of Isaiah 53:4 would thus be used here to prop up a troubling account of the saving efficacy of Christ's suffering.

Fortunately, the remainder of Aquinas's response to *quaestiuncala* 2 clarifies his meaning and thus his use of Isaiah 53:4 in this context. There are several important points which need to be noted. First, "a punishment is called 'temporal' through which some temporal good is taken away."[33] Meaning, 'temporal punishment' simply refers to the loss of a temporal good. Second, following original sin, all humans will experience the loss of certain temporal goods as a result of the condition of their human nature. Aquinas explains that every postlapsarian person experiences the temporal punishments of "the necessity of dying, the ability to suffer, the disobedience of the flesh against the spirit, and the like," for "such things follow from the principles of the nature if the grace of innocence has been taken away."[34]

---

31. *SS* III, d. 19, a. 3, qc. 2, sc.
32. Ibid. I have translated *dolores* as "pains" in place of the Aquinas Institute's "sorrows."
33. *SS* III, d. 19, a. 3, ad qc. 2.
34. Ibid.

With these two foundational points established, Aquinas can then explain the relationship between Christ's endurance of the passion and our endurance of the pains that accompany the possession of a postlapsarian human nature. Even though Christ experienced the temporal punishment of suffering, as Isaiah 53:4 indicates, this does not mean that all human beings are immediately freed from the temporal punishments that are due to their postlapsarian nature. Nor does it mean that one day all people will be freed from the experience of these punishments. Rather, only those who are "partakers" of Christ's passion will experience liberation from such temporal punishments, and even they will do so only at the end of time when Christ raises their bodies from the dead.[35]

In addition to the temporal punishment that all humans incur in virtue of their postlapsarian nature, Aquinas says that "there are other punishments that are inflicted on certain men specifically."[36] One example of this involves "punishing a fault, insofar as fault makes one owe this penalty."[37] That is, sometimes temporal goods are lost as a consequence of a person's actual sins. Aquinas says that Christ saves us from having to endure these temporal punishments precisely by saving us from the sins that "cause" them.[38] Christ does this by making a person a "partaker" in his passion through baptism and "through a real conformity to him, namely, inasmuch as we suffer with the suffering Christ, which occurs through penance."[39] This active, penitential conformity to Christ can also occur after the commission of actual sins, as a means of reducing the debt of temporal punishment incurred by the sin committed. In this latter case, the penitent will not need to suffer as much as they otherwise would as long as they are united to Christ by charity and so share in the merit of his passion. The closer that a person is united to Christ in charity, the less temporal punishment is due to that person. In this way Christ "is said to remove these punishments insofar as he diminishes them."[40] One final form of temporal punishment which a Christian

35. Ibid.
36. Ibid.
37. Ibid.
38. Ibid.
39. Ibid.
40. Ibid.

can experience in this life involves the suffering of making satisfaction (*satisfaciat*) for others. Aquinas says that this type of suffering actually increases during this life for those who are united to Christ's passion in charity. Such people share in Christ's medicinal suffering on behalf of others. Even so, in eternal life, Christ will take away all such suffering from these people.[41]

We can now summarize the theological significance of this fifth case of Isaiah 53 in the *SS*. In the *sed contra* to *quaestiuncala* 2 (III, d. 19, a. 3), Aquinas employs Isaiah 53:4 in a way which suggests that we are freed from the experience of temporal punishment simply because Christ bore temporal punishments in our place. However, in the body of his reply to *quaestiuncala* 2, Aquinas clarifies and further fleshes out his meaning. Christ's liberating work on our behalf did not function in terms of a simple exchange: it is not that Christ suffered in our place, satisfied the demands of justice, and so now we do not need to suffer. Rather, for Aquinas, even though Christ suffered our pains, every postlapsarian person must still suffer the pains of nature in this life. Christ's endurance of pain on our behalf has opened up for fallen humanity the possibility of one day being definitively healed from these natural pains, but this healing will not occur until the eschaton. Further, all are called to participate in Christ's passion by suffering with him in this life in order to prevent sin, in order to repair the damages caused by one's own sins, and in order to satisfy for the sins of others. In fact, those who are more closely conformed to Christ in charity will suffer greater temporal punishment as a result of their efforts to make healing satisfaction for the sins of their neighbors. Aquinas employs Isaiah 53:4 here as a foundational biblical text in support of all of these soteriological points. Yes, the fact that Christ bore our pains is the sufficient and efficacious cause of our eventual liberation from all temporal punishment. But in order to receive this gift of liberation, everyone must first be united to Christ and bear his pain with him.

---

41. Ibid. See also ad qc. 2, ad 1.

Sixth Case: IV, d. 2, q. 1, a. 2, ad 4

Here Aquinas is discussing the degree to which the "sacrifices" (*sacrificia*) and "offerings" (*oblationes*) of the Old Testament can be said to prefigure the seven sacraments of the Church.[42] He states that these realities "signified, with a certain generality, our sacraments and their cause, namely, the Passion of Christ."[43] Then, he specifies that Jewish sacrifices signified the bodily death of Christ, and Jewish offerings signified "the disposition of the one suffering to his Passion, for he willingly offered himself to his Passion, as in Isaiah 53."[44] So, here Aquinas refers merely to Isaiah 53 as a whole, and not to any particular verse. He does so in order to indicate the fact that Christ freely chose to enter into his passion, and in doing so he made a voluntary sacrificial offering of himself to the Father. Christ's free sacrificial offering of himself is the antitype which the sacrifices and offerings of the Old Testament signify.

Seventh Case: IV, d. 4, q. 2, a. 1, qc. 2, ad 1

In this article, Aquinas considers "Baptism's effect as to the removal of evil."[45] In his response to *quaestiuncala* 1, Aquinas establishes that baptism takes away the fault incurred by both original sin and all actual sins. Then, in the response to *quaestiuncala* 2, he argues that baptism also takes away all of the temporal punishment that is owed to a person on account of their actual sins. Earlier, the first objection to this *quaestiuncala* made the following claim: baptism cannot take away all temporal punishments incurred by actual sin, for God must mete out punishment in response to sins when men fail to do so.[46]

Aquinas responds to this objection with a few points. First, he states that baptism incorporates a person into the mystical body of Christ. Second, Christ's endurance of punishment (*poena*) was an

---

42. *SS* IV, d. 2, q. 1, a. 2, ad 4. The Latin text of book IV is the 1956 edition edited by M. F. Moos.

43. Ibid.

44. Ibid.

45. *SS* IV, d. 4, q. 2, a. 1.

46. *SS* IV, d. 4, q. 2, a. 1, qc. 2, obj. 1.

act of satisfaction (*satisfactionem*) which is "reputed" (*reputatur*) to the person who is united to him in baptism.[47] For, third, all the members of the body suffer together with Christ in his suffering. Therefore, Aquinas concludes, "God in Christ punished [*punivit*] those sins, as is said: 'the Lord has laid on him the iniquity of us all' (Is 53:6)."[48] Aquinas's fundamental point here, which he grounds in Isaiah 53:6, is that God has not turned a blind eye to the evil of actual sins. Such sins have been met with an appropriate consequence which satisfies for the evil committed. That which satisfies for the actual sins of the baptized is the pain that Christ endured in his passion. Christ's passion provided the satisfaction that these sins required, and all those who are baptized into Christ share in this satisfaction. Hence, baptism remits the temporal punishment that was owed on account of their prebaptismal sins. In sum: those who have been baptized into Christ have no need to make satisfaction for their past actual sins, for in his passion, Christ has already made a perfect act of satisfaction for the sins of all people. Sin and the punishments due to sin are completely forgiven in baptism as a result of what Christ did for us on the cross.

CONCLUSION AND SYNTHESIS

In the *SS*, Aquinas employs Isaiah 53 on seven occasions in support of his systematic consideration of the mystery of Christ's passion. With the help of Isaiah 53, he affirms that Christ really experienced the punishments (*poena*) of suffering and death, and that he did so for two reasons. First, he possessed a passible, mortal animal nature in common with all of Adam's descendants. Second, he experienced the punishment of being physically assaulted by his enemies. Crucially, for Aquinas, Christ did not experience *poena* due to his own sins, but rather as a consequence of our sins—both original sin and actual sins. Aquinas acknowledges, in light of Isaiah 53, that the intense suffering and deformity which Christ experienced in his passion was an obstacle to some people's faith in his divinity. But

---

47. *SS* IV, d. 4, q. 2, a. 1, ad qc. 2, ad 1.
48. Ibid., quoting Is 53:6.

drawing upon Paul in 1 Corinthians 1, he says that the passion was still fittingly ordered toward Christ's revelatory mission, since the cross is a testimony to the wisdom and strength of God.

Christ's passion also merited for sinners the grace of salvation, and it did so precisely because he freely chose to suffer out of charity. As an act of perfect satisfaction for all of humanity's sins, Christ's passion results in the removal of all temporal punishments for sinners insofar as they participate in his passion. Christ's charity unto death accomplished what justice demanded in response to sin, and we participate in that satisfaction through faith, baptism, charity, and penance. Fallen humanity's punishment of possessing a passible, mortal nature will not be removed until the eschaton. But the punishments incurred as a result of actual sins are removed by baptism. Christ's grace empowers us to avoid further actual sin, and thus to avoid the temporal punishments that we would incur as a result of those sins. If we do sin, the need for temporal punishment is diminished in the repentant the more they are united to Christ in charity. But, conversely, the more conformed to Christ's charity we are, the more we will suffer precisely because we will labor to make satisfaction for the sins of others. Further, Aquinas interprets the offerings and sacrifices of the Old Testament as signs and foreshadowing of Christ's voluntary offering of his body and blood in sacrifice to God on our behalf.

5

The Commentary on the
Gospel of Matthew

My qualitative analysis of Aquinas's reception of Isaiah 53 now begins to turn toward the chronological and intellectual summit of Aquinas's theological career. We have already seen how Aquinas used the Suffering Servant text of Isaiah 53 in his cursory commentaries on Isaiah, Jeremiah, and Lamentations. We have also analyzed his use of Isaiah 53 in the early, systematic *Sentences* commentary. The next four works that I will examine, namely, the *Commentary on the Gospel of Matthew*, the *Commentary on the Gospel of John*, the collection of commentaries on the Pauline epistles, and the *Summa Theologiae*, may be considered the zenith of my project for a few reasons. First, these works are among the last that Aquinas produced, and so they bear witness to his mature thought. Second, they are his most theologically and exegetically rich works and they manifest his mature synthesis between biblical exegesis and theology. Third, each of these works contains at least fifteen cases of Isaiah 53. Up to this point, my consideration of Aquinas's works has been analogous to treading a long, level path, for I have examined several works which all featured relatively few cases of Isaiah 53. But beginning with the *Commentary on Matthew,* the number of references to Isaiah 53 that we will see in each chapter increases dramatically. It is as if our path has begun to ascend up a mountain with a high peak;

at the summit of that peak is the *Summa*. After enjoying the view from that summit, we will descend the mountain along the smooth and shorter road of Aquinas's commentary on the Psalms.

I will begin this chapter with a brief historical introduction to the *Super Matthaeum* and quantitative analysis of its references to Isaiah 53. Then I will explicate Aquinas's numerous references to Isaiah 53 throughout this biblical commentary. I will conclude with a theological synthesis of his interpretations of Isaiah 53 in the *Super Matthaeum*.

CONTEXT AND QUANTITATIVE ANALYSIS

Aquinas's *Super Matthaeum* is based on a course that he taught on the Gospel of Matthew. He most likely lectured on this Gospel during his second regency in Paris between the years of 1269 to 1270. The content of his lectures has come down to us as a *reportatio*.[1] In the *Super Matthaeum* Aquinas explicitly quotes the text of Isaiah 53 a total of twenty-four times.[2] He quotes Isaiah 53:7 most often, with a total of twelve explicit citations. The remaining quotations are as follows: v. 4 (four cases), v. 8 (three cases), v. 12 (two cases), vv. 2–3 (two cases), v. 5 (one case). In this chapter, I examine each of Aquinas's quotations of Isaiah 53 according to the order of the verses in that chapter of Isaiah. I begin with the two cases of Isaiah 53:2–3, and then proceed to the four cases of v. 4, and so forth.

---

1. Torrell, *Saint Thomas Aquinas*, 69–72 and 400–401. See also Weisheipl, *Friar Thomas D'Aquino*, 121–22, and Porro, *Thomas Aquinas*, 442. Note that until recently 5:11–6:8 and 6:14–19 of the *Commentary on Matthew* contained commentary that was from the thirteenth-century Dominican Peter de Scala, rather than from Aquinas. But the Leonine Commission has corrected this issue. The Latin text that I work with in this chapter (see the next note) contains these portions from the Leonine Commission. With that being said, Aquinas does not refer to Is 53 in his lectures on Mt 5 or Mt 6.

2. The *Lectura super Matthaeum* will henceforth be referred to as the *Super Matthaeum*. The Latin text cited is the 1951 Marietti edition and, for 5:11–6:8 and 6:14–19, the Leonine edition. The English translation, unless otherwise noted, is by Jeremy Holmes and Beth Mortensen and has been edited and revised by the Aquinas Institute. Both the Latin and English texts are available online at aquinas.cc/la/en/~Matt.

Cases of Isaiah 53 in the *Super Matthaeum*

Cases of Isaiah 53:2 and 53:3

Aquinas quotes Isaiah 53:2–3 once and makes an additional quotation of v. 3 only. The first quote occurs in the third lecture on Matthew 13. Aquinas quotes Isaiah 53 in the service of a Christological interpretation of the parable of the mustard seed. Drawing upon Hilary, Aquinas identifies Christ as the grain of mustard seed. Christ is filled with the Holy Spirit, and through his death he sows the Spirit into humanity (i.e., the field). As a result of the Spirit who lives within them, believers grow up and become perfected, like a mature tree that grew from a seed. This is despite the fact that they came from Christ, a seed that "was smallest of all on account of unbelievers' contempt."[3] In order to further testify to the fact that Christ was rejected and counted as one who is of little value, Aquinas quotes a combination of Isaiah 53:2 and 53:3: "'We have seen him, and there was no sightliness, that we should be desirous of him; despised, and the most abject of men, a man of sorrows, and acquainted with infirmity.'"[4] Aquinas uses Isaiah 53 here in order to indicate what it means to say that Christ the mustard seed was miniature and unimpressive in size: Christ was despised and scorned by countless unbelievers. And yet, through his rejection and death, he sowed the seed that would eventually develop into the mature tree that is the Church.

Aquinas quotes Isaiah 53:3 in the sixth lecture on Matthew 26. After describing Jesus' arrest in the garden of Gethsemane, Matthew 26:56 states: "'all this was done, that the Scriptures of the prophets might be fulfilled.'"[5] Commenting upon this verse, Aquinas boldly claims that Matthew does not specify which biblical texts are fulfilled through Christ's arrest since the passion of Christ "is found as it were in all" of the scriptures.[6] Nevertheless, in order to prove the evangelist's point, Aquinas himself quotes Psalm 22:17–18 and then loosely quotes Isaiah 53:3a, saying that the Servant of the Lord was

---

3. Aquinas, *Super Matthaeum*, c. 13, l. 3, 1164.
4. Ibid., citing parts of Is 53:2–3.
5. *Super Matthaeum*, c. 26, l. 6, 2266, quoting Mt 26:56.
6. Ibid.

"'considered the last of men, a man of pains.'"[7] Aquinas then explains that Christ's passion did not occur because the prophets predicted that it would, "but rather they predicted it for this reason, that it was to happen."[8] This simply means that Christ did not suffer and die in order to vindicate the prophecies contained in Isaiah 53 and numerous other Old Testament texts. Rather, these prophecies exist because God knew that he would become Incarnate, suffer and die for our salvation.

Cases of Isaiah 53:4

Aquinas quotes Isaiah 53:4 a total of four times. The first instance is found in the first lecture on Matthew 8. In Matthew 8:1–4 Jesus heals a man who is suffering from leprosy, and Aquinas uses this narrative to provide a reflection upon the spiritual symbolism of leprosy. He points out how the physical illness of leprosy produces external, visible effects upon the body of the ill person. Similarly, there are some spiritual illnesses of the will which cause sinners to perform external, public acts of evil.[9] These public acts point to the hidden, invisible sickness of the sinner's will. A spiritual leper may thus be defined as someone whose wicked will is publicly displayed for all to see. Aquinas quotes Isaiah 53:4 in order to give an example of such a spiritual leper, though his example is an ironic one: "'We have thought him as it were a leper.'"[10] The text of Isaiah 53 shows how the visible suffering of the Servant led people to believe that his invisible will was dominated by spiritual illness. The Suffering Servant appeared to be a spiritual leper, but in fact his external symptoms did not accurately manifest the interior health of his will. Christ is viewed as a spiritually ill sinner, when in fact he is the most righteous of all people.

The second case of Isaiah 53:4 occurs in the third lecture on Matthew 8. In 8:14–17, Jesus miraculously heals Peter's mother-in-law as well as numerous other ill and possessed people. Matthew

---

7. Ibid., quoting Is 53:3. Author's translation of "Et Is. LIII, 3: 'reputavimus eum novissimum virorium, virum dolorum.'"

8. Ibid.

9. *Super Matthaeum*, c. 8, l. 1, 682.

10. Ibid., citing Is 53:4.

interprets Jesus' healings as fulfilling Isaiah 53:4, which he quotes in the Gospel: "'he took our infirmities and bore our diseases.'"[11] Aquinas says that the evangelist quotes Isaiah here in order to provide additional scriptural testimony to the fact that Jesus healed people, for "it might seem extraordinary that he should cure so many."[12] Aquinas then explicates the meaning of the text of Isaiah 53:4 considered in itself, apart from the way it is used in Matthew 8:17. Isaiah's claim that the Suffering Servant "'took'" and "'bore'" our illnesses can mean that he "removed" or "took away" our sins from us.[13] In this case, Christ liberates us from both "'infirmities'" ("light sins") and "'diseases'" ("greater sins").[14] Another possible meaning of this prophecy is that it refers to the fact that Christ himself shared in the suffering and death that we all experience: In a seeming combination of these two meanings, Aquinas concludes this exegesis of Isaiah 53:4 by claiming that it speaks of how Christ "accepted passibility for taking away our infirmity and disease."[15] That is, Christ assumed a human nature that was subject to suffering and death for the purpose of taking away humanity's sins.

Having considered the meaning of Isaiah 53:4 in itself, Aquinas returns to its use in Matthew 8:17. He acknowledges that Matthew uses Isaiah 53:4 in connection with Jesus' physical healings, and this seems unfitting given that the Old Testament text itself is about how the Suffering Servant heals people from sin. Nevertheless, Matthew is justified in citing Isaiah 53:4 in response to Jesus' physical healings, for "often bodily diseases are caused by spiritual sins."[16] So, according to Aquinas, Isaiah 53:4 is cited by Matthew 8:17 for two reasons: first, to provide further biblical testimony to the fact that Jesus healed many people; second, to show that Jesus could heal people's bodies precisely because he could first heal their souls. By entering into solidarity with suffering, mortal humans, Jesus was able to take away both our sins and our physical ailments. Jesus is the physician who heals both the soul and the body.

---

11. *Super Matthaeum*, c. 8, l. 3, 715, citing Is 53:4 and Mt 8:17.

12. Ibid.

13. Ibid., citing Is 53:4.

14. Ibid., citing Is 53:4.

15. Ibid. This is another example of a pluriform literal sense.

16. Ibid.

The third quotation of Isaiah 53:4 is in the third lecture on Matthew 23. In 23:37, Jesus laments over the sins and unbelief of Jerusalem, saying "'How often would I have gathered together your children, as the hen gathers her chickens under her wings, and you would not?'"[17] Aquinas quotes Isaiah 53:4 in his explanation of why Christ may have chosen the metaphor of the hen and her chicks to describe his relationship to Jerusalem. He says, "It is said that there is no animal so compassionate to chicks as the hen. The hen defends them from the kite, and exposes her life for them, and gathers them under her wings. In the same way, Christ has pity on us: 'surely he has borne our infirmities and carried our sorrows.'"[18] Like the hen for her chicks, Christ the Suffering Servant exposes himself to pain and death in order to defend his spiritual children against spiritual evils and gather them into the safety of his mystical body. Christ bears the burden of his passion so that we may be spared the burden of sin and eternal death. Aquinas thus interprets the metaphor of the hen in a somewhat counterintuitive way. While the metaphor does signify the tender love of a mother for her children, this is not a merely comfortable love in which the hen snuggles her chicks safely under her wings. Rather, the love of the hen is a love which risks all and bears all pains for the protection and nourishment of her children.

The fourth and final case of Isaiah 53:4 in the *Super Matthaeum* occurs in the first lecture on Matthew 26. In 26:6, Jesus is said to have gone to Bethany and visited "'the house of Simon the leper.'"[19] Aquinas draws out a figurative, Christological sense from the name 'Bethany' as well as the fact that Simon was a leper. Aquinas claims that the name "'Bethania' means 'house of obedience.'"[20] This signifies the obedience of Christ, an obedience that he maintained up to and throughout his passion. Aquinas quotes from Philippians 2:8 in order to provide biblical testimony to Christ's unwavering obedience to the Father. In light of this allusion to Christ's obedience in the name 'Bethany,' Aquinas goes on to explain how "it was fitting

---

17. *Super Matthaeum*, c. 23, l. 3, 1899, citing Mt 23:37.
18. Ibid., citing Is 53:4.
19. *Super Matthaeum*, c. 26, l. 1, 2128, citing Mt 26:6.
20. Ibid.

that he be in a leper's house," for "'we have thought him as it were a leper.'"[21] The quotation of Isaiah 53:4 functions to associate leprosy with the obedience of Christ's passion. 'Bethany' signifies Christ's obedience unto death and 'leprosy' signifies the fact that the crucified Christ's peers viewed him as if he were a grave sinner and threat to society. Yet the truth is that the leprosy of Christ referred to by Isaiah 53:4 is actually the result of the unconditional obedience that he offered to the Father, an obedience referred to by Philippians 2:8. The obedience of Christ unto death is viewed as an abhorrent and dangerous leprosy by the world. Christ, the perfectly obedient one, is viewed as spiritually ill.

One case of Isaiah 53:5

The lone case of Isaiah 53:5 is found in the second lecture on Matthew 27. Aquinas uses Isaiah 53 in the service of a spiritual interpretation of the "'scarlet cloak'" that the soldiers placed upon Christ along with the crown of thorns.[22] Aquinas says that this scarlet cloak "can signify Christ's body, stained with his blood," and then he immediately quotes Isaiah 53:5: "'he was wounded for our iniquities, he was bruised for our sins.'"[23] The text from Isaiah here performs the simple function of providing an additional biblical witness to the reality of Christ's wounds and bruises, on account of which his body would have been covered with blood and red discoloration. Isaiah 53:5 testifies to the historical reality of which the scarlet cloak is a figure. Christ's body was covered in the red of wounds and the red of mockery, and he exposed himself to this suffering in order to save humanity from its sins.

Cases of Isaiah 53:7

The first of Aquinas's twelve quotations from Isaiah 53:7 is found in his second lecture on Matthew 1. Commenting upon the genealogy of Jesus, Aquinas presents a Christological interpretation of a name found in v. 4. The name "'Aminadab'" means "spontaneous,"

---

21. Ibid., citing Is 53:4.
22. *Super Matthaeum*, c. 27, l. 2, 2349, quoting Mt 27:28.
23. Ibid., quoting Is 53:5.

and it signifies Christ's free sacrificial offering of himself.[24] Aquinas provides biblical testimony to the reality of Christ's free offering by quoting Isaiah 53:7: "'he was offered because he himself willed it, and he opened not his mouth.'"[25] As we shall see, Aquinas will repeatedly quote Isaiah 53:7 throughout the *Super Matthaeum* in order to emphasize the freedom with which Christ endured his passion.

The second case of Isaiah 53:7 occurs in the fourth lecture on Matthew 2. Matthew 2:15 explains how Joseph, Mary, and the newborn Jesus went to live in Egypt and remained there until Herod died. The evangelist says that this sojourn in Egypt occurred in fulfillment of a prophecy contained in Hosea 11:1. In Aquinas's Latin version of Matthew, this prophecy reads as "'out of Egypt have I called my son.'"[26] Aquinas points out that the immediate context of Hosea 11:1 makes it clear that the 'son' referred to here is "'Israel.'"[27] That is, Israel is the beloved child of God. This observation requires Aquinas to explain Matthew's rationale in citing Hosea 11:1 in reference to Christ. Aquinas says that the New Testament cites some Old Testament texts because they "speak specially [*specialiter*] of Christ," such as Isaiah 53:7: "'he will be led as a sheep to the slaughter.'"[28] But the New Testament cites other Old Testament texts which merely "speak of certain things according as they introduced a figure of Christ," and such is the case with Hosea 11:1.[29] The "children of Israel … bore a likeness of the true only-begotten Son."[30] Whereas Hosea's prophecy speaks of Christ only in a figurative way, Isaiah's prophecy speaks of Christ in a straightforward and clear way. Hosea speaks directly of a reality (Israel) that bears a figurative likeness to Christ, but Isaiah 53 speaks directly of the reality of Christ himself.

The third occurrence of Isaiah 53:7 is in the second lecture on Matthew 10. In 10:16, Jesus tells his apostles that he is going to send

---

24. *Super Matthaeum*, c. 1, l. 2, 38.

25. Ibid. Author's translation of "'Aminadab,' qui interpretatur 'spontaneus' … et Isaiah LIII, 7: 'oblatus est, quia ipse voluit, et non aperuit os suum etc.'" The translation by the Aquinas Institute mistakenly renders the Latin of Is 53:7 into the English of Is 53:12.

26. *Super Matthaeum*, c. 2, l. 4, 216, citing Hos 11:1: "'Israel was a child, and I loved him: and I called my son out of Egypt.'"

27. Ibid., citing Hos 11:1.

28. Ibid., citing Is 53:7.

29. Ibid.

30. Ibid.

them on a mission and that they will be "'as sheep [*oves*] among wolves.'"[31] Aquinas points out that the apostles are thus compared to Christ himself, for in Isaiah 53:7 Christ is also called a sheep: "'he will be led as a sheep [*ovis*] to the slaughter.'"[32] Both Christ and his apostles are thus sent by God on a mission that involves them entering into danger. They enter into this dangerous context with "meekness," rather than with weapons, in order to display God's power.[33] "For," as Aquinas explains, "it was a great thing that by paupers, and the despised, and the unarmed so many were converted to the Lord."[34] Hence, Isaiah 53:7 and Matthew 10:16, read alongside one another, show how Christ and his apostles are both like peaceful sheep who do "no harm" to anyone.[35] Christ and his missionaries spread the Gospel peacefully, without violence, even at great cost to themselves. In this, the power of God is revealed.

The fourth instance of Isaiah 53:7 is in the first lecture on Matthew 12. In 12:18–21, the evangelist quotes Isaiah 42:1–4 in reference to Christ. Isaiah 42:2 says that the Servant of the Lord "will not … cry out.'"[36] Aquinas says that this text shows how Christ did not act out against those who opposed him, nor did he verbally complain or emotionally "murmur" about them.[37] Aquinas provides further biblical testimony to the merciful silence of Christ in the face of his opposition by quoting Isaiah 53:7, which states that the suffering Servant "'will be led as a sheep to the slaughter, and will be dumb as a lamb before his shearer, and he will not open his mouth.'"[38] Thus, Aquinas interprets Isaiah 53:7 alongside Isaiah 42:2 and concludes that both texts point to the peaceful nature of Christ's interaction with his opponents. Christ's emotions, words, and actions were completely free of violence toward those who rejected him and his message. Christ remained peacefully silent and passive in the face of those who persecuted him.

31. *Super Matthaeum*, c. 10, l. 2, 838, citing Mt 10:16.
32. Ibid., citing Is 53:7.
33. Ibid.
34. Ibid.
35. *Super Matthaeum*, c. 10, l. 2, 841.
36. *Super Matthaeum*, c. 12, l. 1, 1002, citing Is 42:2 and Mt 12:19.
37. Ibid.
38. Ibid., citing Is 53:7.

The fifth case of Isaiah 53:7 is in the second lecture on Matthew 20. In 20:17–19, Jesus warns his disciples of his imminent arrest and execution in Jerusalem. As Aquinas points out, Jesus gives this ominous prophecy while he and his disciples are traveling on their way to Jerusalem. This is significant, for it shows that Jesus enters into his passion freely. He is deliberately going to Jerusalem even though he knows that by doing so he is exposing himself to persecution and death. In order to emphasize the fact that Christ went to Jerusalem "by his own will," Aquinas quotes Isaiah 53:7: "'he was offered because he himself willed it.'"[39] Christ not only freely endured the violence that was inflicted upon him in the moments that it was inflicted; he also freely and knowingly chose beforehand to go to the place where he would be afflicted.

The sixth case of Isaiah 53:7 occurs in the second lecture on Matthew 21. In 21:39, amidst the larger context of Jesus' parable of the wicked tenants, we are told that the tenants take the son of the vineyard owner and kill him outside of the vineyard. Aquinas explains how this aspect of the parable points to the fact that Christ was crucified outside of the city gates of Jerusalem. Then he quotes Isaiah 53:7: "'He will be led as a sheep to the slaughter.'"[40] The function of the text of Isaiah here seems to be simply to reiterate the basic Christological interpretation of v. 39 in Jesus' parable, that is, that Jesus is the son who is killed by the tenants. Both Isaiah 53 and Matthew 21:39 are pointing to the fact that Jesus will be violently accosted and put to death.

The seventh case of Isaiah 53:7 is found in the third lecture on Matthew 25. In 25:31–46, Jesus describes how he will return to earth in the future to judge the nations. Just as a shepherd separates sheep from goats, so too Jesus will eternally separate the just from the unjust. He will "'set the sheep on his right hand, but the goats on his left.'"[41] Commenting upon this passage from Matthew 25:33, Aquinas inquires as to why Jesus compares the just to sheep. He identifies four reasons for this, and each reason pertains to a positive trait of sheep as described by scripture. Sheep provide abundant, good

---

39. *Super Matthaeum*, c. 20, l. 2, 1651, citing Is 53:7.
40. *Super Matthaeum*, c. 21, l. 2, 1745, citing Is 53:7.
41. *Super Matthaeum*, c. 25, l. 3, 2090, citing Mt 25:33.

fruits such as milk and wool. They are also innocent, obedient, and patient. Aquinas provides a biblical witness to the patience of sheep by quoting Isaiah 53:7: "'he will be led as a sheep to the slaughter, and will be dumb as a lamb before his shearer, and he will not open his mouth.'"[42] Isaiah 53:7 thus functions here as an interpretative aid for the significance of the sheep analogy employed by Jesus. The just sheep who will receive eternal life from Christ are those who, among other things, have shared in the patience of Christ. Just as Christ endured his suffering for the kingdom with patience, and merited resurrection and exaltation as a result, so too those sheep who exercise patience out of love for God will be eternally exalted with Christ.

The eighth instance of Isaiah 53:7 is in the second lecture on Matthew 26. In 26:24, Jesus tells his disciples at the Last Supper that one of them will betray him. He states: "'The Son of man indeed goes, as it is written of him, but woe to that man by whom the Son of man will be betrayed.'"[43] Aquinas says that the fact that Jesus prophesied his betrayal, and grounded his prophecy in scripture, indicates that his betrayal and death occurred "by his own will."[44] He then quotes Isaiah 53:7 in order to prove that Christ freely chose to endure betrayal and death: "'he was offered because he himself willed it.'"[45] Aquinas concludes his reflection upon the voluntary character of Christ's passion by saying "thus, nothing harms the Son of man, because he himself ordains what comes to pass."[46] Isaiah 53:7 as well as Matthew 26:24 bear witness to the absolute freedom and control of Christ over his destiny. Christ was betrayed and killed only because he allowed himself to be betrayed and killed and because he actively willed to refrain from using his divine power to escape the suffering and death inflicted upon him.

The ninth case of Isaiah 53:7 is in the third lecture on Matthew 26. In 26:26, the text states that during the institution of the Eucharist at the Last Supper Jesus "'broke'" the Eucharistic bread prior to giving it to his disciples to eat.[47] Aquinas says that this breaking of the bread

---

42. *Super Matthaeum*, c. 25, l. 3, 2089, citing Is 53:7.
43. *Super Matthaeum*, c. 26, l. 2, 2164–65, citing Mt 26:24.
44. *Super Matthaeum*, c. 26, l. 2, 2164.
45. Ibid., citing Is 53:7.
46. Ibid.
47. *Super Matthaeum*, c. 26, l. 3, 2177, citing Mt 26:26.

is symbolic of three things, namely, the incarnation, the passion, and the effects of both upon humanity. Christ broke the bread that became his Eucharistic body in order to symbolize the breaking of his body that would occur in the passion. As Aquinas explains, the broken bread "signifies the mystery of his future passion, for his members were pierced in the Passion."[48] He then quotes Isaiah 53:7: "'he was offered because he himself willed it,'" and then explains that Christ's body was broken in the passion "because he himself willed it."[49] That is, Christ freely willed to endure the suffering and death that was afflicted upon him in his passion. Thus Matthew 26:26 is the beginning of the realization of the event prophesied in Isaiah 53:7, namely, that the Servant of the Lord will voluntarily offer up his body to be broken for the honor of God and the forgiveness of our sins. Thus, when Christians participate in the sacramental breaking of the bread, they remember Christ's free handing over of his body to be broken for us, and they encounter that crucified and risen body in the sacrament.

The tenth and eleventh cases of Isaiah 53:7 are found in the first lecture on Matthew 27. In 27:11–14, Jesus is interrogated by Pilate and accused by his adversaries, and yet he remains silent and does not defend himself. Aquinas says that this silence of Christ "fulfilled" Isaiah 53:7, which he then quotes: "'[he will be] dumb as a lamb before his shearer, and he will not open his mouth.'"[50] Aquinas then claims that Pilate wished to free Christ, and so he continued to question him with the hope of finding sufficient cause to free him.[51] Then, Aquinas inquires as to why Christ did not respond to Pilate's questions.

In his explanation of possible answers to this inquiry, Aquinas quotes Isaiah 53:7 in the service of a rather jarring theological claim. The complexity of this use of Isaiah 53 makes it worthwhile to examine the entirety of the immediate context in which it occurs:

---

48. Ibid. Aquinas is here alluding to Ps 22:17–18.

49. Ibid., quoting Is 53:7.

50. *Super Matthaeum*, c. 27, l. 1, 2326, quoting Is 53:7. Author's translation of "per Is. LIII, 7: 'quasi agnus coram tondente se obmutescet, et non aperiet os suum.'"

51. *Super Matthaeum*, c. 27, l. 1, 2327.

As to why he did not respond, there can be a reason on Christ's part, because he was unwilling to be excused from his passion: for he could have been excused from it by speaking, and this is why he was unwilling to speak.[52] For 'he was offered because he willed it' [*quia voluit*] (Is 53:7). Also, to give us an example, that one should not slander when one is slandered. Also, because the Jews had seen so many signs that they could have converted, and so he considered them unworthy; 'where there is no hearing, pour not out words' (Sir 32:6). And one should notice that he speaks on several occasions, and is silent on several occasions, for if he always spoke he would have excused himself;[53] likewise if he was always silent, he would seem stubborn. However, he responds to Pilate sometimes, but never responds to the Jews, because Pilate was ignorant, and so he sometimes spoke the truth, but the Jews were obstinate.[54]

Aquinas appears to be saying that Christ rarely responded to Pilate because, among other things, he did not want to escape the prospect of being violently put to death. By speaking, Christ could have convinced Pilate to set him free. But, as Isaiah 53:7 indicates, Christ willed (*voluit*) to be handed over to death, and so he did not speak to Pilate. The problem here is that this seems to imply that Christ wants to be misunderstood and rejected by his enemies. He wants people to commit the sins of doubting him, hating him, and putting him to death. If he did not want this to occur, he would have responded to Pilate's questions, for this would have led Pilate to exonerate him. Such an interpretation is troubling because it indicates that God actively willed human ignorance and sin of the worst possible kind against God himself. Christ remained silent because he wanted his enemies to continue to doubt him, hate him, and put him to death. This would suggest a problematic conception of God, a conception that is both theologically inadequate and inconsistent with fundamental aspects of Aquinas's theological vision. If this is what Aquinas is claiming here, with the explicit help of Isaiah 53:7, then I think we need to reject this claim.

With that being said, there are several indicators that Aquinas is not particularly committed to this explanation of the reason for

---

52. *Super Matthaeum*, c. 27, l. 1, 2828. Author's translation of "quia noluti excusare passionem suam: poterat enim eam excusare loquendo; ideo noluit loqui."

53. Ibid. Author's translation of "quia si semper loqueretur, excusaret se."

54. Ibid.

Christ's silence. First, it is worth noting that Aquinas begins his explanation of Christ's silence with the qualification that "there can be [*potest esse*] a reason on Christ's part." That is, the suggestion that Christ was silent because he was unwilling to escape death *can be* an explanation of this event, but that does not necessarily mean it is an explanation that Aquinas is fully dedicated to. Further, what type of possibility does Aquinas mean here—is this explanation possible from a literary standpoint, a theological standpoint, or both? Perhaps such an explanation is possible from a literary standpoint, but it is not possible from a Catholic theological standpoint. Second, Aquinas's ensuing analysis of Pilate's behavior toward Christ highlights a different, more intelligible reason for Christ's silence. Pilate "'wondered exceedingly'" at Christ's silence, and Aquinas says one of the reasons for this is that Christ's silence indicated "that he was not terrified" in the face of criminal accusation and prospective death.[55] Christ did not respond to Pilate in order to show that he did not fear his enemies and their threats. From a theological standpoint, this is far more intelligible than saying that Christ was silent because he did not want Pilate to be persuaded to release him.

Third, and most significantly, Aquinas claims that Pilate tried to release Christ on multiple occasions, despite Christ's silence! When Pilate asks the people "'whom do you wish that I release to you?'" Aquinas says he did this because he wanted to release Jesus, and he was trying to lead the people to ask for Jesus' release.[56] Pilate did this because he preferred to release Jesus instead of Barabbas, since Barabbas was a violent criminal, but also because Pilate knew that Jesus had been brought to him out of envy.[57] If Jesus refused to answer Pilate because he did not want Pilate to try to release him, then Jesus' strategy failed miserably.

Aquinas provides a particularly important reason for which Pilate sought to release Jesus, namely, that his wife advised him to do so. Pilate's wife had "'suffered many things this day in a vision because of'" Jesus.[58] Aquinas offers two possible explanations for this

---

55. *Super Matthaeum*, c. 27, l. 1, 2329, quoting Mt 27:14.
56. *Super Matthaeum*, c. 27, l. 1, 2332, quoting Mt 27:17.
57. *Super Matthaeum*, c. 27, l. 1, 2332–33.
58. *Super Matthaeum*, c. 27, l. 1, 2334–36, quoting Mt 27:19.

dream: "we can [*possumus*] say that it was caused by God through good angels; or [*vel*] by the devil, who was bent on preventing the Passion."[59] If the dream is from God, then it was for the sake of preventing "the sin of murder" from being committed by those attempting to have Christ killed.[60] But, if the dream was from the devil, then this was "not because he wanted to prevent the sin" of murder, but instead because he wanted "to prevent the fruit of the Passion."[61] Intriguingly, Aquinas is saying that we do not know for sure who was the source of Pilate's wife's dream. Regardless, what is very clear is that those who are trying to get Christ killed are guilty of the sin of murder, and God does not actively will this sin. In fact, God may have even given Pilate's wife the dream in a final, supernatural attempt to persuade Pilate to ensure that the sin of murder was not enacted against Christ![62]

Therefore, when Aquinas employs Isaiah 53:7 in support of the possibility that Christ was silent before Pilate because he did not wish to be excused from impending death, this is a tenuous theological and exegetical move. Aquinas's own claim that Pilate repeatedly attempted to release Christ contradicts the very reason for which Christ is said to have been silent. It is also clear that those who sought to kill Christ were guilty of the sin of murder, and so Christ could not have in any way actively willed to help bring that sin about. Otherwise, Christ would seem to be guilty of both formal and material cooperation with evil. Further, the dream of Pilate's wife could very well have been a miraculous, divine intervention enacted in order to prevent the sin of murder from occurring. Such an intervention would directly contradict the action of Christ if he had indeed been silent before Pilate in an attempt to get himself killed. Hence, in conclusion, it seems that Aquinas's troubling use of Isaiah 53:7 in this context is put forth merely as an initial, literarily possible interpretation of the reason for Christ's silence. But then as his analysis continues, Aquinas himself severely undermines the theological legitimacy of the initial interpretation that he proposed.

59. *Super Matthaeum*, c. 27, l. 1, 2336.

60. Ibid.

61. Ibid.

62. Aquinas further details Pilate's attempts to release Jesus in *Super Matthaeum*, c. 27, l. 1, 2338–42.

The twelfth and last case of Isaiah 53:7 is found in the second lecture on Matthew 27. Aquinas employs Isaiah 53 in the service of another spiritual, figurative interpretation of Christ's clothes. Matthew 27:31 notes that once the soldiers had finished mocking Christ they took away the scarlet cloak and put his own clothes back on him. Aquinas makes a very brief note on this passage, saying that Christ "is mocked in another's clothing but led away [*ducitur*] in his own; which signifies that to be mocked was not his own, but to be killed."[63] Aquinas does not provide any further explicit explanation of what he means here. He simply quotes Philippians 2:8, and then says "For his [Christ's] strength was made apparent there."[64] After this statement Aquinas quotes Psalm 118:16 and then Isaiah 53:7: "'he will be led [*ducetur*] as a sheep to the slaughter.'"[65] Unfortunately, the theological point that Aquinas is attempting to make here is vague, and so as a result the precise reason for which he is quoting Isaiah 53 is also unclear.

At the very least, Aquinas appears to be observing a linguistic connection between Matthew 27:31 and Isaiah 53:7, both of which speak of Christ being 'led away' to be killed. Aquinas does not explicitly cite the portion of the Latin text of Matthew 27:31 that contains this phrase, but he alludes to it at the beginning of paragraph 2355, when he says that Christ was 'led away' (*ducitur*) to be crucified in his own clothing. The text of Matthew says that the soldiers "led him away [*duxerunt*] to crucify him." Thus Isaiah 53:7 and Matthew 27:31 both testify to the same event, albeit from different historical standpoints. Christ was led away to the slaughter like a helpless sheep.

Cases of Isaiah 53:8

The first of Aquinas's three references to Isaiah 53:8 occurs in the first lecture on Matthew 1. Aquinas is commenting upon Matthew 1:1, where the evangelist begins to set out "'the book of the generation of Jesus Christ.'"[66] Aquinas points out that this attempt to

---

63. *Super Matthaeum*, c. 27, l. 2, 2355.
64. Ibid.
65. Ibid., quoting Is 53:7.
66. *Super Matthaeum*, c. 1, l. 1, 15, citing Mt 1:1.

describe Christ's genealogy appears to be "contrary" to Isaiah 53:8, which asks of the suffering Servant: "'who will declare his generation?'"[67] Following Jerome, Aquinas solves this problem by distinguishing between Christ's eternal generation from the Father and his temporal, human generation from Mary. The former "cannot be recounted," for not even the angels "can comprehend the manner in which he is begotten" of the Father.[68] It is this eternal, divine generation that Isaiah 53:8 speaks of, while Matthew 1:1 is concerned with Christ's human genealogy.[69] Hence, while Isaiah alludes to Christ's divine nature, Matthew's genealogy highlights Christ's human nature.

The second case of Isaiah 53:8 is found in the fourth lecture on Matthew 22. In 22:42, Jesus asks the Pharisees "'what do you think of the Christ? Whose son is he?'"[70] Commenting on this verse, Aquinas says "this question was most difficult," and then he identifies the source of the difficulty by quoting Isaiah 53:8: "most difficult, because it says, 'who will declare his generation?'"[71] Aquinas is using the text of Isaiah here in order to show how scripture testifies to the fact that many would be unable to fully identify who the Christ was descended from. Isaiah's prophecy previews the inadequacy of the Pharisees' response to Jesus in Matthew 22:42, where they say that the Christ is the son of David. Their answer is true in regards to Jesus' humanity, but on its own, this answer is incomplete. For, as Aquinas points out, Jesus is also the divine, eternally begotten Son of the Father. In fact, it was specifically in order "to show that he was God" that Jesus asked the question "'what do you think of the Christ?'"[72] The Pharisees could only answer this question in regards to Jesus' humanity, and so Aquinas concludes that "they responded insufficiently," for "they knew him insufficiently."[73] Hence, Aquinas uses the text of Isaiah 53:8 here in order to point to the eternal, divine generation of Christ, a generation which many like

---

67. Ibid.

68. Ibid.

69. Ibid.

70. *Super Matthaeum*, c. 22, l. 4, 1822, citing Mt 22:42.

71. Ibid., citing Is 53:8.

72. Ibid., citing Mt 22:42.

73. *Super Matthaeum*, c. 22, l. 4, 1823.

the Pharisees do not believe. This divine generation is what Christ speaks of in Matthew 22:41–45 through his Christological exegesis of Psalm 110:1. Christ is both the temporal son of David in his humanity and the eternal son of God in his divinity.

The third case of Isaiah 53:8 occurs in the fifth lecture on Matthew 26. Following the Last Supper, Jesus and his disciples go out to the Mount of Olives. There, Jesus tells his disciples that they are going to abandon him, and then he quotes Zechariah 13:7, which states: "'I will strike [*percutiam*] the shepherd, and the sheep of the flock shall be dispersed.'"[74] Aquinas explains that Christ is the shepherd, and he is "struck" (*percusses*) in the sense that "God handed him over, for 'he who spared not even his own Son.'"[75] Aquinas then quotes Isaiah 53:8 in order to explain why Christ was handed over to his passion: "this was on account of our sins, 'for the wickedness of my people have I struck [*percussi*] him.'"[76] Both Zechariah and Isaiah 53:8 say that God struck (*percussi*) Christ with the passion, and Isaiah makes it clear that this happened as a result of our sins and for the sake of saving us from sin. Further, Aquinas emphasizes that Christ freely chose to endure being struck. He says that when Jesus quotes Zechariah as saying "'I will strike the shepherd'" he is speaking "in his own person."[77] That is, Christ is the 'I' who will do the striking and he is the shepherd who will be struck. Similarly, when Isaiah 53:8 says that God strikes the Servant due to the wickedness of the people, the divine agency of God here can be attributed to both the Son and the Father. Now, as we have already seen a number of times, this does not mean that God actively willed the murder of his Son. Rather, it simply means that God did not save Christ from the suffering that was inflicted upon him, and that Christ himself as God freely chose to possess a passible human nature and to endure the suffering that life in the world brought him. In conclusion, Aquinas is using Isaiah and Zechariah here in order to show that Christ freely entered into his passion and that his passion occurred as a remedy for our sins.

74. *Super Matthaeum*, c. 26, l. 5, 2209, quoting Mt 26:26 and Zech 13:7.
75. Ibid., quoting Rom 8:32.
76. Ibid., quoting Is 53:8.
77. Ibid., quoting Zech 13:7.

Cases of Isaiah 53:12

The first of Aquinas's two quotations from Isaiah 53:12 is found in the second lecture on Matthew 1. In 1:3, while detailing the human genealogy of Jesus, Matthew mentions that among the descendants of Abraham there was a man named "'Phares'" who "'begot Esron.'"[78] Aquinas interprets the name Esron as a figure of Christ. 'Esron' can mean "hall" (*atrium*), and this name is Christological because it signifies the "breadth of [Christ's] charity."[79] Christ's charity is wide, like an atrium, because he loved both his friends and his enemies. In order to prove this point, Aquinas quotes several biblical texts, among which is Isaiah 53:12: "'he has prayed for the transgressors.'"[80] Thus Aquinas employs Isaiah 53 here in order to provide biblical witness to the reality of Christ's unconditional love for humanity. Christ does not only seek the salvation of the righteous, but also prays for those who are far from God; all are objects of Christ's loving concern and beneficiaries of his intercession.

The second case of Isaiah 53:12 is also Aquinas's final quotation from Isaiah 53 in the *Super Matthaeum*. This case occurs within the context of Aquinas's comments on Matthew 27:38. The evangelist relates how two thieves were crucified with Christ, and Aquinas explains how this fact indicates that Christ was considered to be "an evildoer."[81] In support of this he quotes Isaiah 53:12, which states "'and he was reputed with the wicked.'"[82] Matthew's narrative of Christ's crucifixion alongside two thieves thus fulfills the prophecy contained in Isaiah 53, a prophecy which states that Christ would be counted among the wicked and treated accordingly. Despite his perfect innocence, Christ is condemned as if he were a violent criminal. In this we see the radical depths of Christ's solidarity with humanity. Christ knows what it is like to be completely innocent, and yet to suffer persecution as a sinner, an enemy of the faith and of the state.

---

78. *Super Matthaeum*, c. 1, l. 2, 36, citing Mt 1:3.
79. Ibid.
80. Ibid., citing Is 53:12.
81. *Super Matthaeum*, c. 27, l. 2, 2367.
82. Ibid., quoting Is 53:12.

The Christ of Isaiah 53:12 is in solidarity with all those who are errantly accused, condemned, and punished.

CONCLUSION AND SYNTHESIS

Aquinas is confident that the text of Isaiah 53 is about Jesus Christ. Isaiah testifies to the fact that the Christ would suffer, be rejected by his peers, and die. Isaiah speaks of Christ's suffering in a literal and straightforward way, rather than through the use of symbolic figures. Christ's historical passion in the first century in Israel fulfilled the prophecy of Isaiah as well as various other Old Testament prophecies and so manifested God's foreknowledge of Christ's suffering. The prophecy contained in Isaiah 53 also points to the incomprehensibility of Christ's eternal generation from the Father. The Suffering Servant is also the eternal, divine Son of God. In terms of his humanity, Isaiah 53 shows that Christ was not a man of appealing looks or reputation. His appearance was repulsive, he was weighed down with infirmities, and he was despised by his peers. He was condemned as a spiritual leper, a man whose invisible will was dominated by evil. Yet the truth is that Christ never wavered in his obedience to the Father. Even amidst his complete lack of physical and social glory Christ still offered himself in perfect obedience to God, and this perfect obedience amidst utter rejection functioned as the principle that would give spiritual life to the Church.

Aquinas interprets Isaiah's statement that Christ bore our diseases as referring primarily to the fact that God the Son entered into our mortal human state. The Son assumed a passible human nature for the ultimate goal of taking away our sins. Further, as witnessed in Matthew 8:17, Christ also takes away our infirmities in the sense that he physically heals the sick. By entering into our suffering, Christ is able to liberate us from both spiritual and physical evil. As a hen exposes herself to danger to care for her young, so Christ entered into solidarity with us in suffering precisely in order to take away the causes of our pains. Christ's suffering was real. He was truly wounded and bruised, bloodied and beaten. He was covered with a red cloak of blood and crucified among thieves. Yet, amidst all the pain which he endured in his body and the pain of being errantly condemned by his peers, Christ nevertheless continued to love both his friends and his enemies. Like an innocent sheep he approached death peacefully and patiently, and he refused to do any harm to those who sought his life. Emotionally, verbally, and in concrete action, Christ refrained from lashing out against his enemies. Further, he refused to use violence of any kind to defend himself and his message. He completely rejected the sword, and this testifies to the power of God at work in his life and death. For the crucified one and his apostles were able to convert many despite their refusal to defend themselves or use coercion in support of their message. Rather than cursing his enemies, Christ prayed for those who unjustly condemned him, and he interceded on behalf of all sinners.

Aquinas repeatedly interprets the text of Isaiah 53:7 as a witness to the voluntary character of Christ's passion. Christ knew what would happen to him in Jerusalem even before he freely made his final journey to the city of David. He knew that he would be betrayed by one of his own apostles and that he would be arrested and put to death outside of the city. Yet he freely handed himself over to this fate, for he chose to assume a passible human nature and to abstain from using his divine power to save himself. In that sense, Christ is both the shepherd who is struck and the one who does the striking. Christ's voluntary choice to undergo his passion was sacramentally enshrined at the Last Supper when he gave his disciples his broken body in the Eucharist, the same body that he would hand over to be broken upon the cross. While his human enemies were the immediate material cause of Christ's suffering and death, the fact is that they could carry out their evil designs only because Christ freely chose to endure the brutalities that they inflicted upon him. In doing so, Christ experienced radical solidarity with all those who are errantly persecuted and who experience suffering for the sake of righteousness.

In conclusion, the *Super Matthaeum* features by far the most cases of Isaiah 53 that we have seen in a single work of Aquinas's up to this point. Of those cases, Isaiah 53:7 accounts for half of Aquinas's references to the Suffering Servant text. As in earlier works, Aquinas consistently interprets Isaiah 53 as a literal Christological prophecy which testifies to Christ's eternal generation from the Father, his real solidarity with passible humans, and his assumption of human pains for the sake of our salvation. In addition, Aquinas stresses the fact that Christ experienced human condemnation as if he were a grave sinner, and yet he loved and prayed for his enemies and freely chose to hand over his body to be broken for the salvation of sinners.

6

The Commentary on the Gospel of John

This chapter is about Aquinas's use of the text of Isaiah 53 in his second and final Gospel commentary, the *Lectura Super Ioannem*. As in the previous chapter, here I begin by briefly identifying the literary nature of the *Super Ioannem* as well as its time and place of composition. I will then provide a quantitative analysis, followed by an examination of the quality of each of Aquinas's references to Isaiah 53 in the *Super Ioannem*. I will then conclude the chapter with a theological synthesis of Aquinas's interpretations of Isaiah 53 in the *Super Ioannem*.

Aquinas's *Super Ioannem,* like his *Super Matthaeum,* dates to the mature years of his theological career. Both Gospel commentaries are the written reports of lectures that Aquinas gave as a *magister in sacra pagina* during his second stint at the University of Paris toward the end of his life. While the lectures that make up the *Super Matthaeum* likely date to 1269 to 1270, the course that resulted in the *Super Ioannem* was given shortly after, probably sometime between 1270 to 1272. The contents of the lectures given in this latter course were written down by the Dominican friar Reginald of Piperno.

Further, Thomas himself may have edited chapters 1–6.[1] While Aquinas references Isaiah 53 a total of twenty-four times in his exegesis of Matthew, he cites this Suffering Servant text only fifteen times in his lectures on John.

The fact that the *Super Ioannem* features ten fewer quotations from Isaiah 53 than the *Super Matthaeum* may be at least partially due to the distinct ends which Aquinas discerns in these different Gospels. In the prologue of the *Super Ioannem,* Aquinas claims that the primary purpose of the synoptic Gospels is to detail Jesus' humanity. Conversely, the primary end of John's Gospel is to expound the divinity of Christ. While John also contains teachings about Christ's humanity, his treatments of the human words and deeds of the Lord are always ultimately ordered toward the end of explicating Christ's divinity.[2] This emphasis upon Christ's divinity makes Aquinas's *Super Ioannem* "a particularly rich source for his theological speculation, notably on the Trinity, the Incarnation, and grace."[3] In order to explain these divine, heavenly matters Aquinas provides lengthy and intricate theological expositions of the words of the fourth Gospel. Hence, as Weisheipl states, the *Super Ioannem* "is sublime in its theological profundity," and "it is a mature work for theologians as well as for students of Scripture."[4] For our purposes the point is simply that, given how Isaiah 53 is primarily about the human suffering of Christ, it is not unfitting that Aquinas employed Isaiah 53 more in the *Super Matthaeum* than he did in the *Super Ioannem.* Isaiah 53 is certainly more relevant to expositions of Christ's human life than it is to expositions of the Trinity, the hypostatic union, and grace.

Nonetheless, despite the difference in quantity, the quality of Aquinas's references to Isaiah 53 throughout his two Gospel commentaries is quite similar. In both works, Aquinas consistently employs Isaiah's text in order to help him explain or support the veracity

1. Torrell, *Saint Thomas Aquinas,* 229–32 and 401. See Weisheipl, *Friar Thomas D'Aquino,* 246–47.

2. See Boyle, *The Order and Division of Divine Truth,* 43–44.

3. Timothy F. Bellamah, "The Interpretation of a Contemplative. Thomas' Commentary *Super Iohannem,*" in *Reading Sacred Scripture with Thomas Aquinas* (ed. Roszak and Vijgen), 231.

4. Weisheipl, *Friar Thomas D'Aquino,* 246.

of the Gospel narratives. Isaiah 53 functions like a key which helps Aquinas to unlock the meaning of particular passages in the Gospels as well as a foundation upon which he builds specific exegetical arguments. Throughout both Gospel commentaries, Aquinas typically turns to Isaiah 53 in order to make an exegetical or theological point regarding the nature, purpose, and fruits of Christ's passion.

CASES OF ISAIAH 53 IN THE *LECTURA SUPER IOANNEM*

Just as in the *Super Matthaeum*, Isaiah 53:7 accounts for the majority of Aquinas's references to Isaiah 53 in the *Super Ioannem*. Aquinas quotes this verse a total of eight times. His remaining quotations from Isaiah 53 are of the following verses: v. 1 (two cases), v. 4 (one case), v. 8 (two cases), and v. 12 (two cases). In what follows I examine each of these cases according to their verse order in Isaiah.

Cases of Isaiah 53:1

The first of Aquinas's two references to Isaiah 53:1 is contained in the seventh lecture on John 8. In John 8, Jesus rebukes those who do not believe in his teaching and who are seeking to kill him. He calls such unbelievers children of the devil, and in v. 46 he asks them, "'If I say the truth to you, why do you not believe me?'"[5] Commenting upon this verse, Aquinas claims that Isaiah also "complains" about those who do not "adhere to the truth" about Christ.[6] He then quotes Isaiah 53:1, which states "'Lord, who has believed our report?'"[7] Aquinas thus interprets Isaiah 53:1 as an additional witness to the fact that there are people who do not believe in the truth about Jesus. There are those who will reject the truth of Christ, whether they heard it directly from Jesus' mouth, from the preaching of the Church, or from the prophecies of the Old Testament. Isaiah knew that the revealed truth of Christ would not be accepted by all.

---

5. Thomas Aquinas, *Super Ioannem*, c. 8, l. 7, 1254, quoting Jn 8:46. All references to the *Super Ioannem* are based on the 1972 Marietti edition of the Latin text. Unless otherwise noted, I use the English translation by Fabian Larcher, edited and revised by the Aquinas Institute. The Latin and English texts are available at aquinas.cc/la/en/~Ioan.

6. *Super Ioannem*, c. 8, l. 7, 1254.

7. Ibid., quoting Is 53:1. Author's translation of "'Domine, quis credidit auditui nostro?'"

Aquinas's second reference to Isaiah 53:1 is in his seventh lecture on John 12. In this lecture Aquinas is commenting upon John 12:37–41, which states the following:

And whereas he had done so many miracles before them, they believed not in him: that the saying of Isaias the prophet might be fulfilled, which he said: 'Lord, who has believed our report? and to whom has the arm of the Lord been revealed?' (Is 53:1). Therefore they could not believe, because Isaias said again: 'he has blinded their eyes, and hardened their heart, that they should not see with their eyes, nor understand with their heart, and be converted, and I should heal them' (Is 6:10). These things said Isaias, when he saw his glory, and spoke of him.[8]

In these verses, the evangelist quotes two distinct passages from Isaiah. While only the first passage is from Isaiah 53, Aquinas's analysis of the reference to Isaiah 6:10 sheds light upon his understanding of Isaiah 53. Hence, I will examine Aquinas's comments upon both of these biblical references in John 12.

Aquinas claims that John 12:37–41 is primarily about the "unbelief" of those who rejected Christ during his earthly ministry.[9] He says that the evangelist quotes the prophecies from Isaiah in order to show that this unbelief "came about not without reason or by chance."[10] Specifically, the prophecy from Isaiah 53 foretells the fact of this unbelief, while the prophecy from Isaiah 6 explains "the reason for their unbelief."[11] Aquinas carefully clarifies that Isaiah's prophecy in chapter 53 is not itself the "cause" or reason why many people chose not to believe in Christ.[12] People did not reject Jesus "because" Isaiah said they would.[13] Rather, Isaiah knew that people would reject Jesus, and so he gave a prophecy that "signifie[d] a future event."[14] This means that the people who rejected Christ did so freely. The prophecy did not predetermine their choices and thus eliminate their responsibility for them. On the contrary, as Aquinas explains, "God, knowing the future beforehand, foretold

8. Jn 12:37–41, as given at the beginning of *Super Ioannem* c. 12, l. 7. The translation of Is 53:1 is my own.

9. *Super Ioannem*, c. 12, l. 7, 1688.

10. Ibid.

11. *Super Ioannem*, c. 12, l. 7, 1690.

12. *Super Ioannem*, c. 12, l. 7, 1691.

13. Ibid.

14. Ibid.

their unbelief in the prophecy, but he did not bring it about; for God does not force one to sin just because he already knows one's future sins."[15] So the existence of the prophecy in Isaiah 53:1 is not a cause that took away people's freedom and made them unwittingly reject Christ. Rather, God gave Isaiah knowledge of the future, and the text of Isaiah 53 testifies to this knowledge. Isaiah knew that people would freely choose to reject Christ.

Aquinas proceeds to further specify the object of unbelief and the content of the 'report' that Isaiah 53:1 mentions. He first points out that "belief comes in two ways."[16] People can come to believe in Christ by hearing others proclaim him or by receiving a divine revelation directly from God.[17] When Isaiah says, "'Lord, who has believed our report?,'" Aquinas claims that this refers to the first way of coming to believe in Christ.[18] That is, Isaiah is saying that many will not believe what he teaches in chapter 53 about the "birth and passion" of Christ.[19] The birth and passion of Christ are the subjects of "this entire chapter of Isaiah," and yet many will reject this teaching.[20] This line from Isaiah 53 can also be interpreted as referring to the preaching of the Church. On this interpretation, Isaiah is speaking in the person of the Church. He is prophesying the future reality that many will hear the Church's teaching and yet respond to it with unbelief.[21] So the "report" of which Isaiah 53:1 speaks is the human transmission of the divine revelation about the birth and passion of Christ. This report is given by Isaiah himself in chapter 53 and it is proclaimed in every age by the Church. What Isaiah 53:1 is saying is that there are people who will hear this Christological report and yet refuse to believe in it.

Upon finishing his analysis of the first half of Isaiah 53:1, Aquinas turns to the latter portion of the verse, which says: "'and to whom has the arm of the Lord been revealed?'"[22] He claims that this sec-

---

15. *Super Ioannem*, c. 12, l. 7, 1692.

16. *Super Ioannem*, c. 12, l. 7, 1693.

17. Ibid.

18. *Super Ioannem*, c. 12, l. 7, 1694, quoting Is 53:1.

19. Ibid.

20. Ibid.

21. Ibid. Again, Aquinas's interpretation here grants a pluriform literal sense.

22. *Super Ioannem*, c. 12, l. 7, 1695, quoting Is 53:1.

tion of v. 1 is about "the special way belief comes, by revelation."[23] Here, Isaiah is referring to the fact that he has received a divine revelation about Christ directly from God. The "'arm of the Lord'" that has been revealed to Isaiah is the Son himself.[24] Isaiah has not heard about the birth and passion of this arm from another human teacher, but rather he has received these truths directly from God. The same can be said about the apostles, who are among the "few" to whom such a revelation was given.[25] Like the apostles, Isaiah knew the Son because he received a revelation from God about him.

Aquinas explains why he thinks the "'arm'" (*brachium*) of Isaiah 53:1 is a reference to God the Son.[26] The Son is appropriately called the arm of the Father since the Son is the one "through whom the Father does all things, just as we accomplish things through our arm."[27] Aquinas quotes John 1:3 in order to provide biblical support for this claim that the Father does all things through the Son. This biblical text states that the Son is the one through whom the Father created all things. Aquinas then quotes two biblical passages which refer to the 'arm' of God in functional ways. Job 40:9 says "'have you an arm [*brachium*] like God, and can you thunder with a voice like his?'"[28] Luke 1:51 states that God "'has shown strength with his arm [*brachio*].'"[29] So Isaiah 53 and these other biblical texts refer to the Son as the *brachium* of the Father because it is through the Son that the Father creates all things and displays his power in human history.

Yet Aquinas notes that both Sabellius and Arius claimed that the biblical references to the Son as the arm of the Father supported their Christological heresies. Sabellius said that the Son must be the same person as the Father, since an arm and the person to whom it belongs constitute one person. Arius said that the Son must be "inferior" to the Father, for "an arm is not equal to the person."[30] In response, Aquinas says that Sabellius and Arius took this biblical

---

23. Ibid.
24. Ibid., quoting Is 53:1.
25. *Super Ioannem*, c. 12, l. 7, 1696.
26. *Super Ioannem*, c. 12, l. 7, 1695, quoting Is 53:1.
27. Ibid.
28. Ibid., quoting Job 40:9.
29. Ibid., quoting Lk 1:51.
30. *Super Ioannem*, c. 12, l. 7, 1696.

metaphor of the arm too literally. Citing Dionysius, he says that "symbolic theology is not argumentative."[31] In symbolic expressions "the similarities are not really adequate, for what we find in creatures does not perfectly represent what is in God."[32]

Thus it may be true that in humans the arm is not its own distinct person and, insofar as it is merely one of many corporal parts of a person, it is not equivalent to the person *per se*. But scripture is not saying that the Son is literally the arm of the Father. Rather, scripture is using the notion of arm in a symbolic way, as a metaphor that is meant to highlight a specific aspect of the way in which the Father and Son exercise their divine economy. Isaiah 53:1 and other biblical texts refer to the Son as the *brachium* of the Lord simply in order to draw attention to the fact that "the Father does all things through him [the Son]."[33] This specific point about the Son is clear within the broader context of Isaiah 53. That chapter is all about the active work of the Son on behalf of sinners; it is about how the Father saves humanity from sin through the passion and exaltation of the Son. The Son is the arm by which the Father lifts humanity up out of the pit of sin and death. Hence, it is appropriate that Isaiah 53 refers to the Son as the *brachium* of the Father.

After commenting upon the reference to Isaiah 6 in John 12:40, Aquinas concludes his lecture by examining John 12:41, which states "'these things Isaias said when he saw his glory and spoke of him.'"[34] For Aquinas, this statement from the evangelist indicates that Isaiah 53 and Isaiah 6 ("these things Isaiah said") are the written record of a revelation that Isaiah received about Christ ("he saw his glory and spoke of him").[35] Isaiah saw the glory of God and of Christ in the vision that he writes about in 6:1: "'I saw the Lord seated on a high and lofty throne.'"[36] Specifically, in this vision Isaiah saw the glory of "the entire Trinity" and "he saw at the same time that the Jews would be blinded" and refuse to believe in Christ, the arm of the Lord.[37]

---

31. Ibid.
32. Ibid.
33. Ibid.
34. *Super Ioannem*, c. 12, l. 7, 1703, quoting Jn 12:41.
35. Jn 12:41.
36. *Super Ioannem*, c. 12, l. 7, 1703, quoting Is 6:1.
37. *Super Ioannem*, c. 12, l. 7, 1704 and 1703, respectively.

Aquinas clarifies that Isaiah did not see "the essence of the Trinity" as a saint would in the Beatific Vision, but instead he received "an imaginary vision, with understanding," and he employed "signs" to describe the glory that was revealed to him.[38] Isaiah's vision of the Trinity and reception of a divine revelation, albeit received and written about through figurative images, is significant because it shows that he had direct, divinely revealed knowledge from God about Christ.

Consequently, as Timothy Bellamah states, Aquinas had "confidence in Isaiah's capacity for speaking literally of Jesus Christ."[39] For Aquinas, the literal sense of the prophecy in Isaiah 53 is about Christ. The fact that Isaiah saw Christ's glory refutes "the error of Theodore of Mopsuestia, who said that all the prophecies of the Old Testament bore on some current event, but that the apostles and evangelists appropriated them to the life of Christ."[40] Theodore's error, explains Aquinas, "is excluded by the statement 'and spoke of him,' just as Christ said of Moses that 'he wrote of me.'"[41] Aquinas is saying that the words of John 12 indicate that Isaiah intended to write about Christ in his prophecy of the Suffering Servant. Isaiah was not speaking about the suffering and rejection of some merely human figure from his own time period. In his vision of the heavenly throne room recorded in Isaiah 6, Isaiah received a revelation about the incarnation and passion of Christ. Therefore, when Christians read Isaiah 53's words in reference to Christ they are not applying these words to a referent of which Isaiah was ignorant. Isaiah also realized that he was writing about Christ, for he himself had seen Christ's glory. Consequently, for Isaiah himself as well as for God, Christ is the first and primary *res* to which the *verba* of Isaiah 53 refer.

One Case of Isaiah 53:4

Aquinas's only quotation of Isaiah 53:4 comes in his fourteenth lecture on John 1. Commenting upon 1:29, Aquinas proposes two possible ways of interpreting the statement that Jesus "'takes away the

---

38. *Super Ioannem*, c. 12, l. 7, 1704. In the *ST*, Aquinas describes three different ways in which humans can receive visions of God. See *ST* I, q. 12.

39. Timothy F. Bellamah, "The Interpretation of a Contemplative: Thomas' Commentary *Super Iohannem*," 250.

40. *Super Ioannem*, c. 12, l. 7, 1705.

41. Ibid., quoting Jn 12:41 and 5:46.

sins of the world.'"[42] First, Jesus can take away our sins in the sense that he "removes" them. Second, it can be said that Jesus takes away our sins in the sense that he "takes upon himself" the sins of humanity.[43] In order to further explicate and biblically ground this second explanation, Aquinas quotes from 1 Peter 2:24 and then Isaiah 53:4, which states "'he bore our pains and carried our infirmities.'"[44] Aquinas provides no further explanation here regarding what precisely it means to say that Christ takes our sins, pains, and infirmities upon himself. So it is difficult to say with certainty how exactly he is interpreting Isaiah 53:4 in this context. Yet it does appear that the first interpretation of John 1:29 that he proposes seems to complement and shed light upon the second. In this light, we can say that Jesus removes our sins precisely by assuming a human nature that bears the marks of sin, that is, a human nature that is passible and subject to death. Jesus chose to take upon himself and carry the yoke of human pain and infirmity, and he used this infirmity as a means through which he could take away the various sins and infirmities that press down upon us.

Cases of Isaiah 53:7

The first of Aquinas's eight quotations of Isaiah 53:7 comes in the fourteenth lecture on John 1. Once again, Aquinas's reference to Isaiah 53 comes in the context of his comments upon John 1:29, though this time he is dealing with the fact that John the Baptist calls Jesus the "'Lamb of God.'"[45] Aquinas identifies three characteristics of lambs that can be appropriately applied to Jesus. Lambs are pure, gentle, and they bear the fruit of clothing and food for human beings. In order to illustrate the "gentleness" of Christ the lamb, Aquinas quotes Isaiah 53:7: "'like a lamb before the shearer, he will not open his mouth.'"[46] Christ approaches his death in peace and treats his enemies with gentleness. Then, slaughtered like a lamb, he becomes clothing and food

---

42. *Super Ioannem*, c. 1, l. 14, 259, quoting Jn 1:29.

43. Ibid.

44. Ibid., quoting Is 53:4. Author's translation of "'Is. LIII, 4: dolores nostros ipse tulit, et languores nostros ipse portavit.'"

45. *Super Ioannem*, c. 1, l. 14, 257, quoting Jn 1:29.

46. *Super Ioannem*, c. 1, l. 14, 258, quoting Is 53:7.

for sinners. We "'put on the Lord Jesus Christ'" and we consume the flesh that he gives us "'for the life of the world.'"[47] Isaiah 53:7, interpreted alongside Romans 13 and John 6, shows that Christ is the gentle lamb who becomes our spiritual clothing and whose flesh becomes our spiritual food.

The second case of Isaiah 53:7 occurs in the third lecture on John 2 in the context of Aquinas's comments on John 2:19. In this verse Jesus says: "'destroy this temple and in three days I will raise it up.'"[48] In these words, Christ foretold his death at the hands of his enemies, for he "died and was killed by others."[49] At the same time, though, Aquinas emphasizes that Christ died freely; Jesus was killed by others, "yet with him willing it."[50] In the service of this point he quotes Isaiah 53:7: "'he was offered because he himself willed it.'"[51] So the text of Isaiah 53 ensures that one does not fall into the error of thinking that Christ was merely a completely helpless human victim in his passion. The truth is that Christ knew he would be killed, and yet he permitted this sin to be inflicted upon him. When Christ says "'destroy this temple'" he was not actively commanding the people to kill him, but was rather stating a "prediction" and a "permission."[52] That is, he was prophesying that he would be violently put to death by his peers, but his death would only occur because he allowed it to occur. Aquinas says that it is as if Jesus were here saying "do with my body what you will, I submit it to you."[53] So, once again, Aquinas here draws upon Isaiah 53:7 in order to support the claim that Christ voluntarily chose to undergo his passion. Aquinas makes the additional specification here that Christ's decision to undergo the passion does not mean that he actively pursued suffering and death, but rather that he permitted himself to endure the violence that was inflicted upon him.

Aquinas's third quotation of Isaiah 53:7 is found in his first lecture on John 12. He employs Isaiah 53 while commenting on John 12:1, which states "Jesus therefore, six days before the Pasch, came

47. Ibid., quoting Rom 13:14 and Jn 6:52, respectively.
48. *Super Ioannem*, c. 2, l. 3, 402, quoting Jn 2:19.
49. Ibid.
50. Ibid.
51. Ibid., quoting Is 53:7.
52. Ibid., quoting Jn 2:19.
53. Ibid.

to Bethany.'"[54] Bethany is in Judea and lies very close to Jerusalem. Hence, Aquinas explains, "when the paschal season was at hand, during which the symbolic lamb was immolated, he, as the True Lamb, came to the place where he would suffer and of his own free will be immolated for the salvation of the world."[55] Aquinas then quotes Isaiah 53:7 in order to provide a biblical testimony to the fact that Christ freely chose to be immolated: "'he was offered because he himself willed it.'"[56] Unlike the actual lambs that were sacrificed in Jerusalem for the feast of Passover, Christ is the lamb who voluntarily chose to be immolated. Isaiah 53 shows that Christ was not ignorantly led to death like every other paschal lamb. Rather, he is the paschal lamb who knows his destiny and endures it freely.

The fourth case of Isaiah 53:7 is in the fifth lecture on John 12. In 12:27, Jesus laments, "'Now is my soul troubled. And what shall I say? Father, save me from this hour? But for this cause I came unto this hour.'"[57] Aquinas says that Christ's words here express the fact that he experienced fear and sadness in the "sentient part" of his soul at the prospect of death, but these natural passions did not trouble the "rational part" of his soul.[58] That is, the passions of Christ's sensitive will were not in themselves contrary to the order of reason and they did not lead Christ to act contrary to reason.[59] Christ chose to experience troubling passions in order to demonstrate the truth of his humanity and to provide an example to us of how to remain steadfast even amidst the terrifying presence of death.[60] Despite his natural experience of the fear of death, Christ resolves to endure his passion. Aquinas explains that Christ, in the final sentence of v. 27, is essentially saying "it is not right that I be freed from this time of suffering, because I came to suffer; and not as compelled by the necessity of fate or forced by the violence of men, but by willingly offering myself."[61] Aquinas then immediately quotes Isaiah 53:7, "'he was

---

54. *Super Ioannem*, c. 12, l. 1, 1590, quoting Jn 12:1.
55. Ibid.
56. Ibid., quoting Is 53:7.
57. *Super Ioannem*, c. 12, l. 5, quoting Jn 12:27.
58. *Super Ioannem*, c. 12, l. 5, 1651 and 1653.
59. Ibid.
60. *Super Ioannem*, c. 12, l. 5, 1652.
61. *Super Ioannem*, c. 12, l. 5, 1659.

offered because he himself willed it,'" and then he concludes with a quotation from John 10:18: "'no one takes my life away from me, but I lay it down of myself.'"[62] Here Aquinas employs Isaiah 53:7 in order to emphasize the freedom of Christ even amidst the pain of fear and sadness. Christ experienced the natural dread of death, and yet he nevertheless freely chose to persevere in his mission and to endure the pain that would be inflicted upon him by his enemies. Neither fate nor human violence forced Christ to suffer. Rather, as Isaiah 53, John 10, and John 12 show, Christ experienced the pain of his passion only because he freely chose to do so.

The sixth lecture on John 12 contains Aquinas's fifth quotation from Isaiah 53:7. In John 12:34 Jesus' interlocutors say "'we have heard out of the law that Christ abides forever. How can you say: the Son of man must be lifted up?'"[63] Aquinas says that there are two possible reasons why the people knew that when Jesus "spoke of being lifted up, he was referring to [his] death on the cross."[64] The first reason is simply that people realized that Jesus often spoke to them using "figurative language," and so they became accustomed to understanding "much of what was said in that way."[65]

The second reason is that in their "wickedness" some of Jesus' audience "had already thought of doing that very thing," namely, crucifying Jesus.[66] So when they heard Jesus speak about being lifted up, they recognized this figure of speech because they already intended the action to which it refers. Aquinas thinks that this wickedness of Jesus' interlocutors made them choose their words very carefully. They did not claim that according to the law Christ "does not suffer," but rather simply that Christ should live forever.[67] Aquinas says that the reason they do not say that the Christ should not suffer and die is because they know that such a claim is refuted by the Old Testament, which on numerous occasions bears witness to the suffering, death, and resurrection of Christ. In support of this,

62. Ibid., quoting Is 53:7 and Jn 10:18, respectively.
63. *Super Ioannem*, c. 12, l. 6, quoting Jn 12:34.
64. *Super Ioannem*, c. 12, l. 6, 1678.
65. Ibid.
66. Ibid.
67. *Super Ioannem*, c. 12, l. 6, 1679.

Aquinas quotes Psalm 3:7 and then Isaiah 53:7: "'like a lamb that is led to the slaughter.'"[68] The text of Isaiah 53:7 testifies against those who would claim that the Christ will not suffer and die. Here, scripture shows that Christ will be slaughtered like a lamb. It is true that he will rise from the dead and afterward live on forever, but first he must undergo the agony of death.

Aquinas's sixth use of Isaiah 53:7 is in his fifth lecture on John 13. During the Last Supper, after the devil inspires Judas to betray Jesus, Jesus says to Judas "'that which you do, do quickly.'"[69] Aquinas says that with these words Jesus did not give Judas "a command or a counsel" to betray him, for "sin cannot be commanded or counseled."[70] The Lord did not actively will and try to bring about his betrayal by Judas. Rather, his words to Judas simply signify "a permission."[71] The devil is the one who commands Judas to betray Jesus, not God. Judas acted out of malice and intellectual darkness.[72] "Yet," Aquinas explains, Judas would not have been able to betray Christ "unless Christ himself gave permission."[73] Aquinas justifies this statement by quoting John 10:18 and Isaiah 53:7: "'he was offered because he himself willed it.'"[74]

Care is needed here in order to identify Aquinas's essential point and avoid an errant reading of his exegesis of Christ's words. Aquinas does not appear to be saying that Judas was able to betray Christ only because Christ gave him explicit, verbal permission to do so. It is not as if Judas was asking for Christ's permission, and that Christ gave it, but that if he had not, Judas would have abstained from betraying him. Rather, Judas already intended to betray Christ, and Christ's words to him simply manifested that Christ was not going to actively prevent Judas from carrying out his malicious plans. Aquinas's essential point, therefore, is that Christ knowingly and freely allowed himself to be betrayed and handed over to death. This is what Isaiah 53:7 and John 10:18 indicate. Judas's betrayal did not take Christ by

68. Ibid., quoting Is 53:7.
69. *Super Ioannem*, c. 13, l. 5, 1815, quoting Jn 13:27.
70. Ibid.
71. Ibid.
72. *Super Ioannem*, c. 13, l. 5, 1824.
73. *Super Ioannem*, c. 13, l. 5, 1815.
74. Ibid., quoting Is 53:7.

surprise, and the event of the betrayal occurred only because Christ freely allowed it to occur. He chose to abstain from using his power to prevent Judas's betrayal, for he freely willed to experience the suffering that came to him as a passible human being. Isaiah 53 testifies to this absolute freedom of Christ in the face of betrayal and death.

The seventh case of Isaiah 53:7 is in the first lecture on John 18. In this lecture, Aquinas analyzes 18:1–9, which describes how Judas arrives in Gethsemane with a band of soldiers to arrest Jesus. When Jesus identifies himself the soldiers go "'backward'" and fall "'to the ground.'"[75] Among other things, the backward fall of the soldiers demonstrates Jesus' miraculous power, for even though "his enemies came against him" he repelled them with merely his words.[76] Jesus' miraculous display of power was meant to give Judas and the soldiers "a reason to be converted," but they did not respond with faith.[77] After displaying his power over the soldiers, Jesus then identifies himself a second time as the one whom they are seeking to arrest. Aquinas says that Jesus does this in order to show that he "voluntarily offered himself to be taken by them" and that "he was captured because he willed it."[78] Here Aquinas quotes Isaiah 53:7: "'he was offered because he himself willed it.'"[79] Once more, we need to say that this does not mean that Jesus actively willed the soldiers to arrest him; such a reading would mean that Jesus willed them to sin. On the contrary, it simply means that Jesus "gave them the power to capture him," whereas he "saved his disciples by his own power."[80] Jesus was in complete control of the situation in Gethsemane, and Aquinas uses the text of Isaiah 53:7 to help him demonstrate this point. Jesus used his miraculous power to ensure the safe escape of his apostles, but he freely chose to allow the soldiers to arrest him despite his miraculous ability to overcome them.[81] He was violently taken by Judas's band only because he freely chose to abstain from using the power that he had to save himself.

---

75. *Super Ioannem*, c. 18, l. 1, 2282, quoting Jn 18:6.
76. *Super Ioannem*, c. 18, l. 1, 2283.
77. Ibid.
78. Ibid.
79. Ibid.
80. Ibid.
81. *Super Ioannem*, c. 18, l. 1, 2284.

Aquinas's eighth and final reference to Isaiah 53:7 in the *Super Ioannem* is found in his second lecture on John 19. In John 19:9, Pontius Pilate asks Jesus "'where are you from?,'" but Jesus does not answer the question; he remains silent.[82] Aquinas provides two explanations for Jesus' silence. First, Jesus refuses to answer Pilate's question because "he was unwilling to overwhelm by words and to make excuses, since he had come to suffer."[83] Rather than give Pilate a detailed account of his origin or enter into a dialogical argument regarding his innocence, Christ simply preferred to focus upon continuing to bear his suffering righteously. Second, Aquinas says that "at the same time he is an example of patience," and he "fulfilled what is found in Isaiah: 'like a sheep that before its shearers is dumb, so he opened not his mouth.'"[84] Like a silent sheep, Christ's silence before Pilate is not the silence of guilt but rather the silence of an innocent and "gentle person" who is "being sacrificed for the sins of the others."[85] Isaiah 53:7 and John 19:9 depict the same reality: Christ is an innocent lamb who exercises patience and gentleness as he is violently led to the slaughter. His gentleness and patience serve as an example to sinners of how to bear suffering virtuously.

Cases of Isaiah 53:8

The first of Aquinas's two quotations from Isaiah 53:8 is found in the third lecture on John 7. In 7:27, Jesus' interlocutors argue that Jesus cannot be the Christ, for they know where he is from, and "'when the Christ comes, no man knows where he comes from.'"[86] Aquinas inquires why the crowds make this statement about the Christ given that the location of the Messiah's birth is clearly prophesied in Micah 5:2. He answers that Jesus' interlocutors must have been drawing upon the text of Isaiah 53:8, which states "'who shall declare his generation?'"[87] In the context about which John 7 speaks, Jesus' interlocutors are misinterpreting Isaiah 53:8 as if it applies

---

82. *Super Ioannem,* c. 19, l. 2, 2390, quoting Jn 19:9.

83. *Super Ioannem,* c. 19, l. 2, 2391.

84. Ibid., quoting Is 53:7.

85. Ibid.

86. *Super Ioannem,* c. 7, l. 3, 1056, quoting Jn 7:27.

87. Ibid., quoting Is 53:8. Author's translation of "'generationem eius quis enarrabit?'" In this chapter I consistently translate this Latin phrase in the above manner.

to Jesus' human origin. On the basis of Isaiah 53:8, their logic is: "the Christ should have a hidden origin; but the origin of this man is known; therefore, he is not the Christ."[88] Aquinas explains that Isaiah 53:8 is actually about Jesus' eternal, divine origin from the Father. Hence, the fact that they know where Jesus is from on a human level does not mean that Jesus cannot be the Christ.[89] Their argument is founded upon an errant interpretation of Isaiah 53:8.

The second case of Isaiah 53:8 is in the second lecture on John 8 and it occurs in the context of Aquinas's commentary on 8:14. In this verse, Jesus says that the Pharisees who reject his testimony do so because they "'do not know where I come from or where I go.'"[90] Aquinas interprets this saying from Jesus as a reference to his divinity. His opponents do not believe in Christ's teaching because of "their ignorance" of his divinity and his "eternal procession from the Father."[91] Aquinas quotes Isaiah 53:8 in support of this interpretation: "'who shall declare his generation?'"[92] Isaiah testifies to the fact that many will not believe in the eternal generation of the Son from the Father and in the consequent divinity of the former. This eternal Son of the Father is the one who will bear humanity's pains and be handed over to death in order to save sinners. The cross is the death of God.

Cases of Isaiah 53:12

The first of two *Super Ioannem* references to Isaiah 53:12 is in the third lecture on John 8 and occurs in the service of Aquinas's interpretation of 8:21–22. In these verses Jesus tells his interlocutors that "'Where I go, you cannot come,'" and in response they say to one another "will he kill himself, because he said, 'where I go, you cannot come?'"[93] Regarding the concern that Jesus would kill himself, Aquinas proposes the idea (attributed to Origen) that the people asked this because they had heard Jesus himself say that he would

---

88. *Super Ioannem*, c. 7, l. 3, 1055.
89. *Super Ioannem*, c. 7, l. 3, 1056.
90. *Super Ioannem*, c. 8, l. 2, 1150, quoting Jn 8:14.
91. Ibid.
92. Ibid., quoting Is 53:8.
93. *Super Ioannem*, c. 8, l. 3, 1173, quoting Jn 8:21–22.

die and because "they had learned from their traditions that the Christ would die willingly."[94] Aquinas claims that this Jewish tradition about the death of the Messiah is "especially" contained in Isaiah 53:12, which he then quotes: "'I will give him many things, and he will divide the spoils of the strong, because he delivered himself to death.'"[95] So Aquinas thinks it is plausible that at least some of Jesus' Jewish interlocutors believed, on the basis of Isaiah 53:12, that the Messiah would be killed. But they do not properly understand the manner in which he will die; they think Jesus is saying that he is going to kill himself. Instead, Aquinas explains, the truth is that Christ delivers himself to death in the sense that "his soul [is] going to depart, leaving his body, when he wishes."[96] Christ not only freely assumes a passible human nature and willingly endures the violence that is inflicted upon him. In addition, he himself determines the exact moment when he allows this violence to finally overcome his bodily life and cause his soul to depart in death. As Aquinas puts it, in an understated way, "we are unable to do this."[97] This power of Christ over even the exact moment of his death testifies to the voluntary character of his passion, and it is to this trait that Isaiah 53:12 bears witness. Ultimately, we were not able to kill Christ by our own power; his body was destroyed only because he allowed it to be at a time of his choosing. In this way Aquinas affirms the omnipotence and freedom of the Son even amidst the latter's seeming helplessness.

The second reference to Isaiah 53:12 is also the final case of Isaiah 53 in the *Super Ioannem*. This case is in the third lecture on John 19 and it occurs in Aquinas's exegesis of 19:18, which states that Jesus was crucified with "'two others, one on each side, and Jesus between them.'"[98] Aquinas thinks that Jesus was crucified with "criminals" in order to add to his "dishonor."[99] Specifically, he was crucified in the middle of the two criminals so that it would be "implied that the cause of his death was similar to that of the criminals," that is, that he

94. Ibid.
95. Ibid., quoting Is 53:12.
96. Ibid.
97. Ibid.
98. *Super Ioannem*, c. 19, l. 3, 2417, quoting Jn 19:18.
99. Ibid.

was being crucified on account of proportionately grave crimes. In order to further support this point, Aquinas quotes Isaiah 53:12: "'he was numbered with the transgressors.'"[100] This text from Isaiah 53:12 points to multiple aspects of Christ's passion: first, Christ was crucified, which is a punishment meant for criminals; second, he was crucified in the midst of other crucified criminals and thus was associated with their crimes. In these two ways, Christ was counted and treated as if he was a wicked evildoer. In these two ways, he publicly suffered excruciating dishonor. In conclusion, Isaiah 53 and John 19 depict the ironic and tragic fact that the divine, eternally begotten one, the gentle and patient lamb, was publicly condemned and punished as if he was a violent threat to human flourishing. God was nailed to a tree with criminals.

CONCLUSION AND SYNTHESIS

In the *Super Ioannem* Aquinas once again argues that the literal sense of Isaiah 53 is about Christ himself. Isaiah had direct, divinely revealed knowledge of the incarnation and passion of Christ, and he knowingly wrote about these divine mysteries in his prophecy of the Suffering Servant. Yet, within this same prophecy, Isaiah makes it clear that many will not accept these truths about which he has written and about which the Church preaches. Isaiah knew that there would be sinners who would freely choose not to believe in the truth about the suffering and death of the eternal Son of God.

Isaiah calls Christ the 'arm' of the Lord because Christ is the one through whom God creates all things and manifests his power to creation. God works through Christ's passion to rescue humanity from sin just like a man employs his arm to rescue a drowning person from the abyss. Yet Christ is not a merely human instrument through which God works; he is also the eternal, only begotten Son of the Father. The Son's divine generation and nature is a mystery; many in Jesus' time reject his teaching because they are ignorant of or refuse to believe that he is the divine Son of the Father. As true God and true man, Christ goes to his death with gentleness,

---

100. Ibid., quoting Is 53:12.

patience, and peace; he acts like an innocent lamb led to the slaughter. Christ's death, like that of a lamb, produces food and clothing for others. His crucified and risen flesh gives us spiritual nourishment and clothes us with the power of the Holy Spirit. The gentleness, patience, and peace with which Christ endured the passion is an example to humanity of how to bear suffering virtuously.

Just as in previous works, in the *Super Ioannem* Aquinas repeatedly turns to Isaiah 53:7 in order to emphasize and explain the nature of Christ's voluntary acceptance of the passion. Christ manifested his free acceptance of death on numerous occasions: when he prophesied the destruction of the temple of his body; when he went to Jerusalem even though he knew he would be killed there; when he expressed his acceptance of death even as his sensitive will experienced revulsion at the prospect of the passion; when he permitted Judas to betray him; and when he allowed the soldiers to seize him in Gethsemane. In all these ways, Christ foresaw and freely permitted his passion; he did not command or encourage Judas to betray him and soldiers to seize him. To have done so would have been to command sin, and God cannot do this. Christ had the power to save himself, and yet he allowed himself to be handed over to suffering and destruction even though he did not actively will that he be handed over. Aquinas draws upon Isaiah 53:7 in order to support all of these exegetical and theological claims about the passion of Christ. Further, Aquinas appeals to the text of Isaiah 53:12 in order to explain that Christ's control over the events of his passion was so complete that he was even able to decide the exact moment in which he would pass over from this world to the next. In this sense too, he freely handed himself over to death.

In accord with previous works, in the *Super Ioannem* Aquinas reads Isaiah 53:12 as a testimony to Christ's radical solidarity with those who are unjustly persecuted. Christ was crucified, a punishment fit for grave criminals. Further, he was crucified in between criminals, as if he shared in their sin and guilt. Hence, though completely innocent, Christ experienced the dishonor of being judged and sentenced as an evildoer. He experienced the shame, humiliation, pain, and injustice of being errantly condemned by both civil and religious authorities. Thus, Christ is the model for those who must endure unjust suffering and even death at the hands of worldly powers.

In conclusion, despite its focus upon the divinity of Christ, Aquinas's *Super Ioannem* nevertheless offers significant reflections upon the nature and fruit of Christ's passion. In this work, Aquinas often interprets and uses Isaiah 53 in familiar ways which are consistent with the interpretations that he offered in previous works. But at times, Aquinas's reading of Isaiah 53 in the *Super Ioannem* has an exegetical and theological depth to it that surpasses his interpretations in previous works. This is especially evident in his engagement with Isaiah 53:7. He consistently looks to this verse to illuminate the meaning of those difficult Gospel texts which testify to Jesus' conscious and voluntary acceptance of the passion. In those instances, Aquinas employs Isaiah 53:7 in support of sophisticated, carefully distinguished theological points regarding the nature of Christ's free, deliberate endurance of death.

7

The Commentaries on
the Pauline Epistles

This chapter details Aquinas's use of Isaiah 53 in his commentaries on the New Testament Pauline epistles. The first part will discusses the historical origin and literary style of these commentaries before providing a brief quantitative analysis. Then I will examine each case of Isaiah 53 in each Pauline commentary in the order in which the cases appear in that particular commentary. Finally, I will synthesize the theological content of Aquinas's Pauline engagement with Isaiah 53.

CONTEXT AND QUANTITATIVE ANALYSIS

Like the *Super Matthaeum* and *Super Ioannem*, Aquinas's commentaries on the epistles of Paul are undoubtedly the product of the scriptural courses that he taught as a *magister in sacra pagina*. Each of the Pauline commentaries most likely began to circulate from Naples around 1272 or 1273, and they did so as a single, unified work.[1] Torrell claims "it is ... certain that Thomas thought of this commentary as a whole. The proof of this is given in the Prologue that he placed at the head of this whole" and which he "refers to ...

1. Torrell, *Saint Thomas Aquinas*, 293.

at the start of each epistle."[2] However, the specific time and place in which Aquinas originally composed each particular commentary is uncertain. Torrell quotes (and approves of) the recent conclusion of Wielockx, who says regarding all of the Pauline commentaries: "For now, nothing allows us to fix the date of the course (and of its *reportatio*), that of its revision or that of its publication."[3]

That being said, Torrell himself proposes a few solutions. He "suggest[s]" as a "hypothetical" that "Thomas taught the Pauline corpus while in Orvieto, excepting, of course, the courses on the Epistle to the Romans, the first part of 1 Corinthians, and the epistle to the Hebrews, which were taught only later, in Naples."[4] Further, he proposes that the commentaries on 1 Corinthians 11 up to and including Hebrews that have come down to us are a *reportatio* made by Reginald of Piperno.[5] Conversely, the first thirteen chapters of the *Super Romanos* that we have today appears to have been revised by the hand of Thomas himself.[6] The uncertainty and complexity regarding when and where Aquinas originally composed each particular commentary makes it difficult to determine where to examine them in a chronological presentation such as my own. I have decided to treat them here in chapter 7 based on the prevailing view that Aquinas considered the various commentaries to be a unified whole, and that they began to circulate as such from Naples around 1272 or 1273. I thus examine them here as the first expression of Aquinas's thoughts on the text of Isaiah 53 during his time in Naples.

Aquinas makes twenty-one explicit references to Isaiah 53 across eight specific commentaries on the Pauline corpus. Those commentaries are Romans, 1 Corinthians (beginning with 1 Cor 11), 2 Corinthians, Galatians, Ephesians, 2 Thessalonians, 2 Timothy, and Hebrews.

2. Ibid., 296.

3. Ibid., 402.

4. Ibid., 292.

5. Ibid., 402.

6. Ibid., 293. See Torrell's summary on 401–2 on the composition dates and places of the Pauline commentaries.

CASES OF ISAIAH 53 IN THE
PAULINE COMMENTARIES

Cases of Isaiah 53 in the *Commentary on Romans*

The first of Aquinas's two cases of Isaiah 53 in the *Super Romanos* occurs in lecture 5 on Romans 9. In 9:32, Paul says that some of the Israelites have "'stumbled at the stumbling stone'" because they sought righteousness through the works of the law rather than through faith in Christ.[7] Aquinas identifies this stumbling stone as Christ, and he explains why Paul uses this metaphor: "just as a stone against which a man stumbles is not guarded against because it is small, so the Jews, seeing Christ clothed with our weakness, did not guard against stumbling over him."[8] Aquinas then immediately quotes Isaiah 53:3, stating "'his look was as it were hidden and despised. Whereupon we esteemed him not.'"[9] Aquinas turns to Isaiah's text in order to provide a biblical explanation for why some of the Israelites stumbled over Christ. The human defects which Christ experienced, especially during his passion, veiled his divinity and thus led some to reject him. As a result of his weakness and misery, some of the Israelites did not take Christ seriously, and so they did not sufficiently guard themselves against the spiritually destructive effects of rejecting him. It is easy for people to disregard the weak and despised Christ, and yet the very act of disregarding Christ leads them to stumble against him. The passion of Christ is thus a stumbling block.

The second and final case of Isaiah 53 in the *Super Romanos* occurs in lecture 3 on Romans 12. In 12:19, Paul exhorts Christians to abstain from seeking revenge against those who hurt them, saying "'revenge not yourselves.'"[10] Aquinas says that in this verse

---

7. Thomas Aquinas, *Super ad Romanos*, c. 9, l. 5, 811, quoting Rom 9:32. All ensuing references to Aquinas's commentaries on the Pauline Epistles are taken from the Latin and English texts published by the Aquinas Institute and available at aquinas.cc/la/en/~Rom. For each commentary I will specify the edition of the Latin text and the names of the English translators. References to the *Super ad Romanos* are from the 1953 Marietti edition of the Latin text and the English translation by Fabian Larcher, edited by the Aquinas Institute.

8. *Super ad Romanos*, c. 9, l. 5, 811.

9. Ibid., quoting Is 53:3.

10. *Super ad Romanos*, c. 12, l. 3, 1011, quoting Rom 12:19.

Paul is simply reiterating Jesus' command to turn the other cheek (Mt 5:39) and he is instructing Christians to imitate the example of Jesus himself. In order to illustrate how Christ treated his enemies, Aquinas quotes Isaiah 50:6 and then Isaiah 53:7, which states "'like a sheep that before its shearers is dumb, so he opened not his mouth.'"[11] Aquinas explains that Christ's teaching and example do not necessarily mean that Christians must literally say to their enemies "here is the other cheek," for during the passion Christ himself said "'if I have spoken ill, give testimony of the evil; but if well, why do you strike me?'"[12] More fundamental than turning the other cheek, Christians are always called to practice "patience" and "benevolence" toward their enemies for the sake of the latter's "correction and concord."[13] Hence, Isaiah's description of Christ as a silent and helpless lamb who was led to death should be interpreted as a description of Christ's patience and benevolence toward his enemies. Rather than seeking revenge through violent words and deeds, Christ exercised silence and nonviolence toward his enemies for the sake of their conversion and salvation.

Cases of Isaiah 53 in the Commentaries on
1 and 2 Corinthians

Aquinas makes six explicit references to the text of Isaiah 53 in his *Commentary on 1 Corinthians* (hereafter *Super I ad Corinthios*). These references are contained in his treatment of 1 Corinthians 11, 14, and 15.[14] The first reference occurs in Aquinas's fifth lecture on 1 Corinthians 11. Here he is commenting upon Paul's recounting of the Lord's institution of the Eucharist at the Last Supper (1 Cor 11:23–24). The fact that Christ "'took bread,'" Aquinas says, is meant to signify "that he voluntarily accepted the passion, of which this sacrament is the memorial."[15] Immediately following this statement, Aquinas quotes Isaiah 53:7: "'he was offered because he himself

---

11. Ibid., quoting Is 53:7.

12. Ibid., quoting Jn 18:23.

13. Ibid.

14. The *Commentary on 1 Corinthians* will henceforth be referred to in its Latin form, *Super I ad Corinthios*. The Latin text of the *Super I ad Corinthios* is the 1953 Marietti edition; the English translation is by Fabian Larcher, edited by the Aquinas Institute.

15. *Super I ad Corinthios*, c. 11, l. 5, 656, quoting 1 Cor 11:23.

willed it.'"[16] Aquinas thus wants to interpret the institution of the Eucharist, at least in part, as a sign that Christ knew full well that he was going to be handed over to his enemies and that he freely chose to endure that handing over. Aquinas uses the text of Isaiah 53:7 here in order to further support this notion that Christ voluntarily chose to endure his passion.

The second reference to Isaiah 53 in the *Super I ad Corinthos* is a passing citation at the conclusion of Aquinas's fourth lecture on 1 Corinthians 14. Commenting on Paul's statement that prophecies are a "'sign ... not to unbelievers, but to believers,'" Aquinas quotes Isaiah 53:1 ("'Lord, who has believed our hearing?'") simply in order to provide an example of people "who do not believe."[17] The text from Isaiah refers to those who do not believe in the report regarding the Suffering Servant. While Aquinas himself does not say this, his connection of 1 Corinthians 14 with Isaiah 53 suggests that Isaiah's prophecy of the Suffering Servant functions as a sign for believers, though not for unbelievers. That is, those who believe in Christ will see Isaiah 53 as a prophetic sign of Christ, while those who reject Christ will see no such sign.

Aquinas's next three citations of Isaiah 53 all occur in his first lecture on 1 Corinthians 15. Aquinas employs Isaiah's text in his exegesis of 1 Corinthians 15:3–4, where Paul discusses the essential content of the apostolic tradition that he has handed over to the Corinthian community.[18] Aquinas cites Isaiah 53:8 ("'he was stricken for the transgressions of my people'") in order to support Paul's statement that Christ died "'for our sins.'"[19] This insistence that Christ died for our sins refutes "two suspicions which can arise about the death of Christ."[20] The first errant suspicion is that Christ "died for his own actual sins, or [from] original sin."[21] The second suspicion "is that the death of Christ was by chance or by the violence of the Jews."[22]

---

16. Ibid., quoting Is 53:7.

17. Super *I ad Corinthios*, c. 14, l. 4, 858, quoting 1 Cor 14:22 and Is 53:1, respectively.

18. 1 Cor 15:3–4 states: "For what I received I passed on to you as of first importance: that Christ died for our sins according to the Scriptures, that he was buried, that he was raised on the third day according to the Scriptures" (NRSV-CE).

19. *Super I ad Corinthios*, c. 15, l. 1, 895, quoting 1 Cor 15:3.

20. Ibid.

21. Ibid.

22. Ibid.

Paul further refutes this second suspicion by saying that Christ died "'according to the Scriptures.'"[23] Aquinas supports this idea that Christ's death was foretold in scripture by citing Isaiah 53:7, which explains how the Suffering Servant was "'like a lamb'" who "'was led away to the slaughter.'"[24] The final case of Isaiah 53 in this lecture occurs in support of Paul's statement that Christ "was buried" (1 Cor 15:4). Isaiah 53:9 provides a biblical support of the truth of Paul's teaching, as it says that the Suffering Servant's enemies "'made his grave with the wicked.'"[25] This point is important to emphasize, Aquinas claims, because it is the basis for Paul's ensuing claim that Christ rose from the dead.[26] So, in this lecture Aquinas employs Isaiah 53:7–9 in order to show that Paul is firmly grounded in the witness of the scriptures when he says that the death and burial of Christ were foreseen and providentially willed by God on account of our sins, and not on account of any human chance or sinfulness on Christ's part.

The sixth and final occurrence of Isaiah 53 in the *Super I ad Corinthios* occurs in the seventh lecture on 1 Corinthians 15. Here Aquinas reflects upon why Paul refers to Christ as the "'last [*novissimus*] Adam.'"[27] He says that Christ is referred to in this way in order to show that he ushered in the last or final state which human beings can experience. Whereas the "'first [*primus*] Adam'" brought about a state of guilt into the world, Christ the last Adam brought a state "of true glory and life," and "after that state no other one followed in that life."[28] That is, humanity's temporal journey on earth is marked by only two states of being: the state of guilt in Adam or the state of glory and life in Christ. No further states of being will be possible on this side of eternity, and Christ's state is the final, consummate, 'last' state that a human being can reach prior to eternity. Aquinas then loosely quotes a combination of Isaiah 53:2b–3a in this context because Isaiah's text also refers to Christ as the 'last,' saying

---

23. Ibid., quoting 1 Cor 15:3.
24. Ibid., quoting Is 53:7.
25. *Super I ad Corinthios*, c. 15, l. 1, 896, quoting Is 53:9.
26. Ibid.
27. *Super I ad Corinthios*, c. 15, l. 7, 992, quoting 1 Cor 15:45.
28. Ibid., quoting 1 Cor 15:45.

"'we desired him, despised and last [*novissimum*] of men.'"[29] The Suffering Servant's peers perceived him to be 'last' in the sense of being the least and worst among humans, but Paul shows that in fact Christ is 'last' in the sense of being the ultimate, perfect, final realization of the human potential for glory and life in God.

There is one case of Isaiah 53 in Aquinas's *Commentary on 2 Corinthians*. This case occurs in the fifth lecture on 2 Corinthians 5, where Aquinas grapples with the following statement from Paul: "Him who knew no sin, he has made sin for us: that we might be made the justice of God in him" (2 Cor 5:21). Aquinas identifies three ways to interpret the claim that God "'made Christ sin for us.'"[30] The first way of interpreting this verse is to say that Christ 'became sin' in the sense that he offered himself as a sacrifice in reparation for our sins. Second, Christ can be called 'sin' insofar as he endured the "punishment of sin," which simply means that he assumed the "mortal and suffering flesh" that all sinners possess on account of their fallen human nature.[31] Third, one can say that Christ was made 'sin' in the sense that "one thing is said to be this or that, not because it is, but because man considers it such."[32] That is, Christ is "regarded as a sinner" by those who persecuted him and witnessed his suffering.[33] Aquinas cites Isaiah 53:12 in support of this third interpretation, for Isaiah tells us that the Suffering Servant "'was numbered with the transgressors.'"[34] Thus when Paul says that Christ was 'made sin' for us, this does not mean that Christ actually committed sin, or was guilty, or that God actively willed the suffering that was inflicted upon him in his passion. Rather, as Isaiah 53 indicates, Paul's saying simply means that Christ was judged to be a sinner by his peers. Further, despite his utter innocence, Christ endured pains

---

29. Ibid., loosely quoting Is 53:2–3.

30. Thomas Aquinas, *Super II ad Corinthios*, c. 5, l. 5, 201, quoting 2 Cor 5:21. The Latin text cited here is the 1953 Marietti edition; the English translation is by Fabian Larcher, edited by the Aquinas Institute.

31. *Super II ad Corinthios*, c. 5, l. 5, 201.

32. Ibid. Aquinas's threefold interpretation of 1 Cor 5:21 is an example of his acceptance of the possibility of a pluriform literal sense. See Johnson, "Another Look at the Plurality of the Literal Sense," 140.

33. *Super II ad Corinthios*, c. 5, l. 5, 201.

34. Ibid., quoting Is 53:12.

which sinners endure, and he offered himself as a sacrifice in order to save humanity from sin.

One Case of Isaiah 53 in the *Commentary on Galatians*

Aquinas's lone reference to Isaiah 53 in his *Commentary on Galatians* comes in the context of his exegesis of Galatians 6. Commenting on Galatians 6:2 ("Bear [*portate*] one another's burdens, and so you shall fulfill the law of Christ"), Aquinas identifies "charity" as the "law" to which the apostle refers.[35] He then explains how Christ himself "fulfilled" this law and "left us an example [of] how to follow it; for he bore [*tulit*] our sins out of charity."[36] Aquinas then cites Isaiah 53:4 in order to provide further biblical testimony to the fact that Christ "bore" our sins through his passion: "'surely he has borne [*tulit*] our infirmities.'"[37]

Aquinas's point is that charity should induce us to endure suffering, to bear burdens, for the good of our neighbors. The charitable person takes up the yoke from his neighbor in order to alleviate their burden. Christ did this for us when he assumed our passable nature and voluntarily endured the passion in order to release us from the burden of sin and all of its consequences. Aquinas concludes by saying that if we want to fulfill the law of charity "then we ought to carry one another's burdens."[38]

Cases of Isaiah 53 in the *Commentary on Ephesians*

Aquinas's *Commentary on the Epistle to the Ephesians* features four references to Isaiah 53. The first case is in the first lecture on Ephesians 3. Aquinas quotes Isaiah 53:1 ("'Who has believed our report? And to whom is the arm of the Lord revealed?'") in order to support what Paul says in Ephesians 3:5, namely, that Christ was not revealed to the people of the Old Testament period in the same way as he "is now revealed to his holy apostles and prophets in the Spirit."[39]

---

35. Thomas Aquinas, *Super ad Galatas*, c. 6, l. 1, 348. The Latin text cited here is the 1953 Marietti edition; the English translation is by Fabian Larcher, edited by the Aquinas Institute.

36. *Super ad Galatas*, c. 6, l. 1, 348.

37. Ibid., quoting Is 53:4.

38. Ibid.

39. Thomas Aquinas, *Super ad Ephesios*, c. 3, l. 1, 141, quoting Is 53:1. The Latin text cited

That is, the actual incarnation and passion of Christ in history was a more "clear and complete" revelation of the mystery of Christ than even the very explicit prophecy contained in Isaiah 53.[40] One way to think about what Aquinas is saying is to recall the distinction between *verba* and *res*. In the Old Testament, people could hear and read the *verba* of Isaiah 53, but it was not until the coming of Christ that they could hear and see and touch the living *res* to which the *verba* referred. In this sense, the revelation of the incarnate Lord in first-century Israel was certainly superior to the revelation that was given through Isaiah.

There are two cases of Isaiah 53 in Aquinas's treatment of Ephesians 5:2, where Paul says that Christ "loved us and has delivered himself for us, an oblation and a sacrifice to God for an odor of sweetness." Citing Gregory the Great, Aquinas first establishes the principle that love is proven through concrete action. Then, he reasons that Christ truly loved us, for he "'delivered himself for us.'"[41] That is, Christ made the deliberate choice to endure his passion for us, and this demonstrates his love for us. Aquinas here cites Isaiah 53:12 in order to further illustrate this active love of Christ for us: "'He has delivered his soul unto death and was reputed with the wicked.'"[42] Isaiah and Paul are thus both showing that Christ did not merely say he loved us, but he lived out that love in a most radical way.

Proceeding to the latter clause of Ephesians 5:2, Aquinas explains how the active love of Christ "was both advantageous and necessary for us" as "an 'oblation and a sacrifice.'"[43] Aquinas first interprets these labels for Christ's passion by turning to Leviticus 3–4, which he interprets as stipulating that sinners were "obliged" (*debebat*) to offer certain sacrifices and oblations in reparation for their particular sins.[44] Further, referring to Leviticus 3:9 and 3:16, Aquinas claims that "when someone gave thanks to God, or wished to obtain some

---

here is the 1953 Marietti edition; the English translation is by Matthew Lamb, edited by the Aquinas Institute.

40. *Super ad Ephesios*, c. 3, l. 1, 141.
41. *Super ad Ephesios*, c. 5, l. 1, 270, quoting Eph 5:2.
42. Ibid., quoting Is 53:12.
43. Ibid., quoting Eph 5:2.
44. Ibid.

favor" they had to offer a sweet smelling sacrifice.[45] Aquinas says that Christ "accomplished" each of these types of prescribed sacrifices "through the actions he performed during his life."[46] In support of this point, he then quotes Isaiah 53:7, which states that Christ "'was offered because he himself willed it, et cetera.'"[47] So, Aquinas quotes Isaiah 53:7 here in order to show that Christ's voluntary deliverance of himself over to the passion and the manner in which he conducted himself throughout his suffering was a sweet smelling sacrifice offered to the Father in atonement for sins, in thanksgiving, and in petition on behalf of sinners. Aquinas concludes this treatment of Ephesians 5:2 by pointing out that sinners "ought to offer spiritual sacrifices to God: 'a sacrifice to God is an afflicted spirit.'"[48] Thus, through contrition, we participate in the pleasing sacrifice of Christ of which Paul and Isaiah speak. ·

The fourth and final occurrence of Isaiah 53 in the *Super ad Ephesios* is found in the eighth lecture on Ephesians 5. Here, Aquinas engages Paul's famous exhortation to husbands to love their wives "as Christ also loved the Church" (Eph 5:25). Aquinas explains: "the sign of Christ's love for the Church is that 'he delivered himself up for her.'"[49] He then quotes Isaiah 53:12: "'He has delivered his soul unto death.'"[50] The text of Isaiah functions here to further illustrate the point from Ephesians about Christ freely delivering himself over to death. Aquinas's overall point is that husbands who truly love their wives will lay down their lives for them, just as Christ's true love for the Church led him to lay down his life for his mystical bride.

Cases of Isaiah 53 in the Commentaries on
2 Thessalonians and 2 Timothy

Aquinas makes one reference to Isaiah 53 in both his *Commentary on 2 Thessalonians* and his *Commentary on 2 Timothy*. In 2 Thessalonians 3:2, Paul states that "'not all men have faith.'"[51] Aquinas reads

<hr>

45. Ibid.
46. Ibid.
47. Ibid., quoting Is 53:7.
48. Ibid., quoting Ps 51:19.
49. *Super ad Ephesios*, c. 5, l. 8, 323, quoting Eph 5:25.
50. Ibid., quoting Is 53:12.
51. Thomas Aquinas, *Super II ad Thessalonicenses*, c. 3, l. 1, 65, quoting 2 Thes 3:2. The

this as referring to "false apostles" and "persecutors" of the Church who appear to have faith but in reality do not.[52] He then quotes Isaiah 53:1 as a biblical text which speaks of those who lack faith in Christ: "'Lord, who has believed what we have heard?'"[53] Thus, once again Aquinas reads Isaiah 53:1 as a reference to those unbelievers who have refused to believe in the good news about Christ.

In 2 Timothy 2:9, Paul says that he has labored on behalf of Christ "even unto chains, as an evildoer." Here, according to Aquinas, Paul is describing himself to Timothy "as an example of martyrdom."[54] Paul's martyrdom includes enduring the "pain" (*poena*) of "shame before unbelievers," and this is what Paul means by calling himself an "'evildoer.'"[55] For, Aquinas explains, in the days of Paul "Christians were regarded as the worst of criminals."[56] Aquinas then concludes with the following comment upon Isaiah 53:12: "For Christ was also condemned as an evildoer: 'he was reputed with the wicked.'"[57] Paul has been rejected by unbelievers and persecuted as a criminal for his faith in Christ. In this way, Paul shares in the suffering of Christ who, as Isaiah 53 shows, was also falsely judged and condemned as a criminal. Christians thus need to take heart in the fact that when they are errantly treated as evildoers due to their faith in Christ they are in fact sharing in the suffering of Christ. For they are suffering the same type of unjust rejection that Christ suffered, and thus they participate in the merit of Christ's cross.

Cases of Isaiah 53 in the *Commentary on Hebrews*

The last Pauline commentary that I will examine in this chapter is Aquinas's *Commentary on the Epistle to the Hebrews*, which features five references to Isaiah 53. The first occurs in the first lecture on

---

Latin version of Aquinas's text is the 1953 Marietti edition; the English translation is by Fabian Larcher, edited by the Aquinas Institute.

52. *Super II ad Thessalonicenses*, c. 3, l. 1, 65.

53. Ibid., quoting Is 53:1.

54. Thomas Aquinas, *Super II ad Timotheum*, c. 2, l. 2, 50. The Latin text cited here is the 1953 Marietti edition; the English translation is by Fabian Larcher, edited by the Aquinas Institute.

55. *Super II ad Timotheum*, c. 2, l. 2, 51, quoting 2 Tm 2:9.

56. Ibid.

57. Ibid., quoting Is 53:12.

Hebrews 7. The context needed to understand Aquinas's analysis of these verses begins with Hebrews 6:20, which states that Christ is a "high priest forever according to the order of Melchizedech." In order to explain what it means to say that Christ is of the "order of Melchizedech," Hebrews 7 highlights certain aspects of the description of this priestly figure in Genesis 14. For Aquinas, Christ is of the order of Melchizedech because the "qualities" of the latter made him a "similitude" (*similitudinem*) of Christ.[58] One such Christological quality is mentioned in Hebrews 7:3, which states that Melchizedech was "without mother, without genealogy, having neither beginning of days nor end of life." Hebrews says this, Aquinas reasons, "because in Scripture no mention is made of his [Melchizedech's] father or mother or genealogy."[59] One of the reasons for this silence on the part of scripture "is because the generation of Christ is ineffable: 'who shall declare his generation?'"[60] Aquinas quotes Isaiah 53:8 here in reference to Christ's "eternal generation" from the Father, a generation that "is spiritual, as splendor from the sun."[61] In this spiritual way, the Son was born of the Father before all time.[62] So, for Aquinas, both Isaiah 53 and Hebrews 7 point to the incomprehensible, eternal generation of the Son from the Father.

The second reference to Isaiah 53 in the *Super ad Hebraeos* occurs in the fourth lecture on Hebrews 7. The text of 7:27–28 contrasts the numerous sacrifices of the Levitical priesthood with the one sacrifice of Christ. Whereas Levitical priests had to offer sacrifices in reparation for their own sins as well as those of the people, Aquinas says that this was not the case with Christ. For Christ "did not offer for his own sins but for ours: 'he was wounded for our iniquities.'"[63] Aquinas's purpose here is to contrast the imperfection of the Levitical priests with the perfect priesthood of Christ.[64] Christ

58. Thomas Aquinas, *Super ad Hebraeos*, c. 7, l. 1, 326. The Latin text cited here is the 1953 Marietti edition; English translation by Fabian Larcher, edited by the Aquinas Institute.

59. Super *ad Hebraeos*, c. 7, l. 1, 333; see Gn 14:18–20 and Ps 110:4.

60. Ibid., quoting Is 53:8.

61. Ibid.

62. Ibid.

63. Super *ad Hebraeos*, c. 7, l. 4, 376, quoting Is 53:5.

64. For a thorough study of Aquinas's *Super ad Hebraeos,* and in particular for its

was sinless, and therefore he had no need to offer sacrifices on his own behalf, much less to repeatedly offer new sacrifices in response to his daily sins. Rather, as Isaiah 53:5 shows, Christ is the unique priest who offers sacrifice solely in response to the sins of others. Thus, in this context Aquinas quotes Isaiah 53:5 in order to explain why Christ died, namely, for the good of sinners, and not for himself. In this sense, Isaiah 53:5 bears witness to the completely disinterested love of Christ on the cross.

Aquinas next quotes Isaiah 53 in his fifth lecture on Hebrews 9, while commenting on Hebrews 9:27–28. These verses state, "as it is appointed unto men once to die, and after this the judgment, so also Christ was offered once to exhaust the sins of many." Aquinas acknowledges that Christ, insofar as he died only once, is like all other people. But, there is also a way in which Christ's experience of death differs from the rest of humanity's way of dying. For Christ "did not contract original sin," Aquinas explains, and so "consequently, he was not obliged by that statute: 'for in what day soever you shall eat of it, you shall die the death' (Gn 2:17)."[65] Rather, "he underwent death by his own will."[66] Aquinas then points to the statement of Hebrews 9:28 that "Christ was offered [*oblatus*] once" and connects this with Isaiah 53:7: "'he was offered [*oblatus*] because he himself willed it.'"[67] Isaiah 53:7 shows that Christ endured death because he freely chose to do so. Unlike all other human beings, Christ did not have to die, but in freedom, he chose to die for us. We are created and born with a passible nature that is subject to death, apart from our decisions. Conversely, Christ freely chose to be conceived and born as a man who would be subject to suffering and death, and his eventual succumbing to death by crucifixion only occurred because he allowed it to happen. In this way, the absolutely gratuitous love of Christ for us is revealed.

The fourth use of Isaiah 53 occurs in Aquinas's first lecture on

---

treatment of the priesthood of Christ, see Antoine Guggenheim, *Jésus-Christ, Grand Prêtre de l'Ancienne et de la Nouvelle Alliance: Étude du commentaire de saint Thomas d'Aquin sur l'Épître aux Hébreux* (Langres: Parole et Silence, 2004).

65. *Super ad Hebraeos*, c. 9, l. 5, 477, quoting Gn 2:17.

66. Ibid.

67. Ibid., quoting Is 53:7.

Hebrews 12. Aquinas comments on Paul's exhortation that Christians should look to the way Jesus endured his passion as an example and always strive to "think diligently upon him that endured such opposition from sinners against himself" (Heb 12:2). Aquinas says that Paul exhorts such reflection because "the remedy for every tribulation is found in the cross," and "an example of every virtue is found in the cross."[68] He then quotes Isaiah 53:7 as a text that witnesses to the virtue of "patience in adversity" that Christ enacted in his passion: "'he shall be led as a sheep to the slaughter, and shall be dumb as a lamb before his shearer, and he shall not open his mouth.'"[69] Isaiah describes Christ enduring his passion quietly, innocently, and nonviolently. Christ does not even verbally lash out against his enemies as they assault him. Rather, he is a model of the Christian call to persevere in justice even amidst the worst circumstances.

The fifth and final reference to Isaiah 53 in the *Super ad Hebraeos* occurs in the fourth lecture on Hebrews 12. Commenting upon the statement in Hebrews 12:24 that the blood which Christ shed in his passion "speaks better than that [blood] of Abel,'" Aquinas first establishes the basic point that in the Old Testament Abel's death and the deaths of every just person at the hands of sinners "prefigured" the "shedding of Christ's blood."[70] But prefigurement does not mean strict equivalency, for, as Aquinas explains, "Christ's blood speaks better than Abel's blood, because Abel's blood cries for vengeance, but Christ's blood cries for pardon."[71] In order to support this statement, Aquinas proceeds to quote, among other biblical texts, Isaiah 53:12: "'he prayed for the transgressors.'"[72] Isaiah's text shows that the shedding of Christ's blood was not followed by an act of divine vengeance against the enemies of Christ, but rather by an act of divine mercy.

68. *Super ad Hebraeos*, c. 12, l. 1, 667.
69. Ibid., quoting Is 53:7.
70. *Super ad Hebraeos*, c. 12, l. 4, 712, quoting Heb 12:24.
71. Ibid.
72. Ibid., quoting Is 53:12.

CONCLUSION AND SYNTHESIS

In the commentaries on the epistles of Paul, Aquinas uses Isaiah 53 as an aid in his theological exegesis of Paul's teaching on Christ's passion. Both Hebrews and Isaiah witness to the fact that Christ, the Suffering Servant, is eternally born of the Father in a divine generation which lies beyond the comprehension and experience of humanity. Yet the passion of Christ hid his divinity from the eyes of some of his contemporaries. Christ's misery was thus a stumbling block which caused his enemies to fall into unbelief and sin.

Nonetheless, Isaiah shows that the eternally begotten Son of the Father freely offered himself up upon the cross, just as Paul indicates when recounting the fact that Christ instituted the sacramental memorial of his passion on the night before he died. Nevertheless, there are many who have doubted and rejected belief in the voluntary, saving death and exaltation of God incarnate. This was especially the case during the Old Testament, when the prophetic revelation of the incarnation and passion of Christ in Isaiah was imperfect in comparison to its historical realization in the person of Jesus. Even so, Isaiah makes it clear that Christ did not die from chance: scripture foretold his passion and burial, which were willed by God for the sake of saving us from sin and which were the necessary preconditions for his resurrection. For both Paul and Isaiah, Christ is the 'last' Adam, not in the sense of being the least, most despicable of men, as his enemies thought, but rather in the sense of ushering in and personally realizing the final, glorified state which has been made accessible to all sinners.

Isaiah 53 testifies to the reality of Christ's love, for it shows that he actively chose to deliver himself up for sinners and bear their burden of suffering and infirmity. Similarly, Christians who wish to participate in Christ's charity and passion must bear one another's burdens and deliver themselves up for one another. In addition, all Christians who must endure the shame of being falsely judged as an evildoer by their peers share in the martyrdom of Christ, for he too had to bear the shame and punishment of false judgment. In this way, it can be said that Christ was 'made sin' for us, insofar as he was falsely regarded as a sinner by those who condemned him. The reality is that Christ was completely free from sin, and so unlike the Levitical priests who offered sacrifices for their own sins, Christ's sacrifice was offered exclusively to take away our sins. The Levitical, liturgical sacrifices for sin, thanksgiving, and petition are all fulfilled by Christ's free sacrifice of his body and blood. Christ's passion is also the model of all the moral virtues, for he never failed to exercise perfect justice toward all even amidst his suffering. He exercised benevolence and patience toward his enemies and prayed for them so as to bring about their conversion and correction. In this, the profound mercy of God is revealed.

8

The *Summa Theologiae*

In previous chapters, the vast majority of my analysis has focused upon the way in which Aquinas interpreted and used the text of Isaiah 53 in his biblical commentaries. In addition to the lecture upon Isaiah 53 and the five cases of Isaiah 53 in the *Super Isaiam*, I have explored seventy-one references (out of a total of 110) to Isaiah 53 that constitute the object of this study. Sixty-four of those seventy-one cases occurred in biblical commentaries, and thirty-nine of those seventy-one cases occurred in merely two biblical commentaries, namely, the *Super Matthaeum* and the *Super Ioannem*. Only seven of the seventy-one cases were in a work of systematic theology, namely, the *Sentences* commentary. But now that we have arrived at the *Summa Theologiae*, the proportion of references to Isaiah 53 in Aquinas's systematic works increases significantly. For, as this chapter will detail, Aquinas refers to Isaiah 53 a total of twenty-seven times throughout the *Summa*.[1] That is the most cases of Isaiah 53 in any individual work of Aquinas's.

The structure of this chapter unfolds as follows. The first part will historically situate the *Summa* and provide a quantitative analysis of Aquinas's references to Isaiah 53 throughout that work. I will

---

1. In the Index Thomisticus, only twenty-five of these references come up when one searches for "Isaias LIII" and its variants. This is because in *ST* III, q. 47, a. 3, co., Aquinas quotes three different verses from Is 53 (see cases 21–23 in table 8-1.) but he only mentions "Isaiae LIII" prior to the first verse that he quotes. Hence, a word search for "Isaias LIII" will not show these latter two references.

152

identify the number of times that Aquinas explicitly quotes Isaiah 53, the specific places in which those references occur, and particular verse numbers that are being quoted. The second part is a qualitative analysis that explicates the various ways in which Aquinas interprets and uses the Suffering Servant text throughout the *ST*. For reasons discussed below, this analysis is organized in accord with the chronological order of the various sections of the *ST* in which the cases of Isaiah 53 are found. Just as was the case in my examination of the *SS*, so too here in the *ST* it is often necessary to examine the primary points that Aquinas makes in a particular article before we can examine his reference to Isaiah 53, as references to this biblical text in the *ST* are always in the service of specific, systematic theological points that are being argued in the article. Finally, the third part will consist of a synthetic exposition of the various Christological and soteriological truths that Aquinas draws out from the text of Isaiah 53 throughout the course of the *ST*.

CONTEXT AND QUANTITATIVE ANALYSIS

Aquinas began to compose the *ST* around 1265 or 1266 for the sake of his Dominican students at the newly established *Studium* in Rome. His task was to theologically prepare Dominicans for the ministries of preaching and hearing confessions, and he determined that a new theological text was needed for this enterprise.[2] He sought to create a manual of theology that would, as Torrell explains, "treat of the whole of theology, both dogmatic and moral, in a comprehensive and organically structured way."[3] Aquinas completed the *Prima Pars* in 1268 in Rome and then proceeded to compose the *Prima Secundae* (1271) and the *Secunda Secundae* (1271 to 1272) in Paris. He likely began writing the *Tertia Pars* in Paris in 1271 or 1272. He continued working on it in Naples until December of 1273, at which point he permanently ceased writing.[4] All of the *Summa*'s references to Isaiah 53 are found in the *Secunda Secundae*

---

2. Torrell, *Saint Thomas Aquinas*, 169–70.

3. Torrell, *Aquinas's "Summa": Background, Structure, and Reception*, trans. Benedict M. Guevin (Washington, D.C.: The Catholic University of America Press, 2005), 10.

4. Torrell, *Saint Thomas Aquinas*, 389.

and the *Tertia Pars,* with the overwhelming majority coming in the latter.

Aquinas composed the *Secunda Pars* (1271 to 1272) and the *Tertia Pars* (1271 to 1272 or 1273) shortly after the *Super Matthaeum* (1269 to 1270) and around the same time as the *Super Ioannem* (around 1270 to 1272). His composition of the *Tertia Pars* also may have coincided with the period in Naples during which he composed some, if not all, of the Pauline commentaries. All of these works from his time in Paris and Naples feature a combined total of eighty-seven references to Isaiah 53, or seventy-nine percent of the 110 total references to this scriptural text that Aquinas makes throughout his biblical commentaries and major systematic works apart from the *Super Isaiam.* Hence, the text of Isaiah 53 is most prominent in the biblical commentaries and *Summa* that Aquinas composed in 1269–73.

Of the twenty-seven cases of Isaiah 53 in the *Summa,* the only portion of Isaiah 53 that Aquinas does not quote is v. 11. The remaining eleven verses of Isaiah 53 are each quoted the following number of times: 53:1 (one case, or x1), 53:2–3 (x1), 53:3 (x2), 53:4 (x7), 53:5 (x1), 53:6 (x2), 53:7 (x6), 53:8 (x2), 53:9 (x1), 53:10 (x1), and 53:12 (x2). Aquinas also makes a reference to Isaiah 53 without quoting or discussing a specific verse. This is actually the first of the twenty-seven cases. As in previous works, here v. 7 plays a large role. However, surprisingly, it is v. 4 that is most often cited in the *ST.* Of the remaining cases, only vv. 3, 6, 8, and 12 are quoted multiple times.

Aquinas uses Isaiah 53 in the *Tertia Pars* far more than he does in any other portion of the *ST.* He quotes Isaiah 53 only two times in the *Secunda Secundae.* His remaining twenty-five references to Isaiah 53 are all found in the *Tertia Pars*; twenty-four of those quotations come between questions 14 and 52. The remaining, final quotation is in question 68, which concerns the salvific effects of baptism. Hence, as is fitting, Aquinas turns to Isaiah 53 above all when he is addressing questions concerning the incarnate being and work of Christ. In the table below, I identify the location of the articles in the *ST* where cases of Isaiah 53 are found, the question posed by the article, and the specific verse(s) of Isaiah 53 that are quoted in those articles:

TABLE 8-1. CASES OF ISAIAH 53
IN THE *SUMMA THEOLOGIAE*

ST case # and location	The question posed by the article (notably, I have slightly reworded some of these questions for the sake of brevity)	Isaiah text cited:
#1: II–II, q. 2, a. 7, ad 2	Does salvation always require explicit faith in Christ?	53; no verse
#2: II–II, q. 10, a. 1, co.	Is unbelief a sin?	53:1
#3: III, q. 14, a. 1, obj. 4	Should the Son of God have assumed bodily defects?	53:2–3
#4: III, q. 14, a. 1, co.	Ibid.	53:4
#5: III, q. 14, a. 1, ad 3	Ibid.	53:5
#6: III, q. 14, a. 2, obj. 1	Did he assume the obligation of subjection to these defects?	53:7
#7: III, q. 15, a. 1, ad 4	Was there sin in Christ?	53:6
#8: III, q. 15, a. 5, sc.	Was there sensible pain in Christ?	53:4
#9: III, q. 15, a. 6, obj. 4	Was there sorrow in Christ?	53:7
#10: III, q. 18, a. 6, obj. 2	Was there any contrariety of wills in Christ?	53:7
#11: III, q. 22, a. 2, ad 1	As a priest, what victim did Christ offer?	53:7
#12: III, q. 22, a. 6, ad 3	Should Christ be called "a priest according to the order of Melchizedech?"	53:8
#13: III, q. 31, a. 3, obj. 1	Is Christ's genealogy suitably traced by the evangelists?	53:8
#14: III, q. 35, a. 6, obj. 2	Did Christ's mother suffer in childbirth?	53:4
#15: III, q. 36, a. 1, sc.	Should Christ's birth have been made known to all?	53:3
#16: III, q. 43, a. 1, obj. 2	Should Christ have worked miracles?	53:3
#17: III, q. 46, a. 1, obj. 2	Was it necessary for Christ to suffer for men's deliverance?	53:7
#18: III, q. 46, a. 6, ad 4	Was the pain which Christ endured the greatest?	53:4
#19: III, q. 46, a. 11, sc.	Was it fitting for Christ to be crucified with robbers?	53:12
#20: III, q. 47, a. 3, obj. 2	Did the Father deliver Christ up to suffer?	53:12
#21: III, q. 47, a. 3, co.	Ibid.	53:6
#22: Ibid.	Ibid.	53:10
#23: Ibid.	Ibid.	53:7
#24: III, q. 49, a. 3, sc.	Did Christ's passion free us from our debt of punishment?	53:4
#25: III, q. 51, a. 1, ad 2	Was it fitting for Christ to be buried?	53:9
#26: III, q. 52, a. 1, co.	Was it fitting for Christ to descend into hell?	53:4
#27: III, q. 68, a. 5, ad 1	Do the baptized need to do works of satisfaction?	53:4

The above table shows that in the entire *ST*, Aquinas quotes Isaiah 53 in sixteen different questions and twenty-two different articles. Fourteen of those questions and twenty of those articles are contained in the *Tertia Pars*. Aquinas uses Isaiah 53 in the *Tertia Pars* primarily in order to reflect upon the causes, essence, and saving value of Christ's passion. Nineteen of the twenty-five cases in the *Tertia Pars* are in articles that are explicitly concerned with the nature, origin, end, or soteriological consequences of Christ's suffering and death. Only the articles in which cases 7, 10, 13, and 14–16 are contained are not specifically about Christ's suffering or its salvific effects.

CASES OF ISAIAH 53 IN THE
SUMMA THEOLOGIAE

I will now conduct a qualitative analysis of the twenty-seven cases of Isaiah 53 in the *ST*. Unlike in the last two chapters, here I will not examine Aquinas's references to Isaiah 53 in the chronological order of verses within that biblical text. The reason for this is that in the *ST* as a whole, and particularly within specific questions, understanding a particular article often requires one to be familiar with the basic content of the articles that have come before it. So, for example, it would be unfitting to examine the reference to Isaiah 53:4 in *ST* III, q. 68, prior to the reference to 53:7 in q. 46, a. 1, even though v. 4 precedes v. 7 in the actual text of Isaiah 53. Consequently, in this chapter, I will simply organize my qualitative analysis in accord with the chronological order of questions in which those cases occur in the *ST*. I will label each subsection within this qualitative analysis after the topic(s) which Aquinas addresses in the questions under consideration.

Cases 1–2: II-II, qq. 2 and 10 (On Faith and Unbelief)

Aquinas's first and second references to Isaiah 53 in the *ST* are found in two questions from the *Secunda Secundae* on the act of faith and the nature of unbelief, respectively. The first case is found in II-II, q. 2, a. 7, ad 2. In this article, Aquinas considers whether or not "it is necessary for the salvation of all" that they "believe explicitly" in Christ.[5] The second objection argues that explicit faith in Christ cannot be necessary for salvation, for even John the Baptist did not "appear to have known the mystery of Christ explicitly" given the question that he asks the Lord in Matthew 11:3.[6] Aquinas responds by arguing that the Baptist's own words, as recorded in John 1:34 and 39, testify to the fact that he was explicitly aware of the Son's incarnation and "future Passion."[7] Further, the Baptist would have known about Christ's passion from the fact that "other prophets had foretold it, as may be seen especially in Isaiah 53."[8] Aquinas does not mention a specific verse from Isaiah 53. Rather, he simply refers to the chapter as a whole and uses it as the principal example of an Old Testament prophecy concerning Christ's passion. The words of Isaiah's prophecy can generate explicit faith in Christ's passion, and that is exactly what they did for John the Baptist.[9] So while Aquinas does not use the phrase "literal sense" here, his analysis in this context suggests once more that the passion of Christ is the first and principal reality to which the words of Isaiah 53 refer.

The second case of Isaiah 53 in the *Secunda Secundae* occurs in q. 10, a. 1, where Aquinas considers the question of whether or not unbelief is sinful. His answer hinges upon a distinction between two kinds of unbelief. The first kind, which consists of "pure negation," is not sinful.[10] This type of unbelief is present in those "who have heard nothing about the faith."[11] The second, sinful type of unbelief consists in "opposition to the faith," such as when "a man refuses to hear the faith, or despises it."[12] At this point, Aquinas quotes Isaiah 53:1 in order to provide a biblical illustration of the nature of sinful

5. Aquinas, *ST* II-II, q. 2, a. 7. All quotations from the *ST* are taken from the Leonine edition of the Latin text and, unless otherwise noted, the English translation by Laurence Shapcote. These Latin and English texts are available at aquinas.cc/la/en/~ST.II-II.

6. Aquinas, *ST* II-II, q. 2, a. 7, obj. 2. In Mt 11:3 John the Baptist asks: "Are you the one who is to come, or are we to wait for another?" (NRSV-CE).

7. *ST* II-II, q. 2, a. 7, ad 2.

8. Ibid.

9. On Aquinas's distinction between implicit and explicit faith, and on the degree to which the latter is necessary, see *ST* II-II, q. 2, aa. 5–7.

10. *ST* II-II, q. 10, a. 1, co.

11. Ibid.

12. Ibid.

unbelief: "'who has believed our report?'"[13] Isaiah's text shows that the sin of unbelief consists in denying the divine message, or, the divine report. This is the case even when the divine report is difficult and challenging to believe, such as Isaiah's report about the suffering of the Christ.

As is evident from the above analysis, Aquinas uses Isaiah 53 in the *Secunda Secundae* in relatively simple and inconsequential ways. The remainder of his references to Isaiah 53 are found in the *Tertia Pars*. There, Aquinas frequently employs Isaiah 53 in the service of theologically rich Christological and soteriological arguments.

Cases 3–10: III, qq. 14, 15, and 18
(On Christ's Human Defects and Pain)

Aquinas's first eight references to Isaiah 53 in the *Tertia Pars* are found in his questions on the bodily defects (q. 14) and defects of soul (q. 15) that Christ experienced in his human nature as well as on the unity of of Christ's will (q. 18). The first four cases are in q. 14, the next three are in q. 15, and the final case is in q. 18.

The first three cases of Isaiah 53 in the *Tertia Pars* are found in III, q. 14, a. 1. The first of these cases is in the fourth objection to the question of whether God the Son should have assumed bodily defects in his human nature. This objection argues that one of the ends of the incarnation, namely, to bring people to the knowledge of God, was frustrated by the fact that Christ assumed bodily defects. For "by these infirmities men were kept back from knowing him."[14] This claim is followed by a lengthy quotation from Isaiah 53:2–3, which reads, in part, "'there was no sightliness in him that we should be desirous of him,'" and he appeared "'hidden and despised, whereupon we esteemed him not.'"[15] In his response to this objection, Aquinas grants that Christ's bodily infirmities

---

13. Ibid., quoting Is 53:1.

14. *ST* III, q. 14, a. 1, obj. 4.

15. Ibid., quoting Is 53:2–3. The full quotation states: "'[There was no sightliness] that we should be desirous of him. Despised and the most abject of men, a man of sorrows and acquainted with infirmity, and his look was, as it were, hidden and despised, whereupon we esteemed him not.'"

"concealed his Godhead," but he claims that they also "made known his manhood."[16]

Thus bodily defects do not ultimately frustrate the revelatory end of the incarnation, for it is precisely through Christ's humanity that we come to know and believe in his divinity. His humanity is "the way" to "the Godhead."[17] In support of this claim, Aquinas quotes Romans 5:1–2, where Paul identifies Christ as the one through whom we gain access to God. In the body of the article, Aquinas identifies another proof of this principle in the appearance of the risen Christ to Thomas the apostle. Thomas was "recalled to the faith" through "the sight of his [Christ's] wounds."[18] Hence, with the help of the text of Isaiah 53:2–3, Aquinas provides a phenomenological order in regards to the way that we come to know Christ: through our encounter with Christ's bodily infirmities, we come to know his humanity, and through our encounter with his humanity, we come to know his divinity.

The second case of Isaiah 53 in the *Tertia Pars* (and the fourth in the *ST* as a whole) occurs in the body of q. 14, a. 1. In the *sed contra,* Aquinas claims that God the Son did indeed assume a human nature which was vulnerable to bodily defects. Christ did so in order "to suffer and be tempted" just as other humans are.[19] By sharing in their pain and temptation, yet without sin, Christ is able to help all those who suffer and who are tempted to bear their trials as he did. In the body of the article, Aquinas further specifies how it is that Christ's bodily defects enable him to help sinners. He says that Christ came "to satisfy for the sin of the human race," and that "one satisfies for another's sin by taking on himself the punishment [*poenam*] due to the sin of the other."[20] He then specifies that the "punishment [*poena*] for sin" that all sinners must pay are "bodily

16. *ST* III, q. 14, a. 1, ad 4.

17. Ibid.

18. *ST* III, q. 14, a. 1, co.

19. *ST* III, q. 14, a. 1, sc.

20. *ST* III, q. 14, a. 1, co. On the relationship between punishment and satisfaction in Aquinas's account of the cross, see Waldow, "Aquinas on the Nature of Christ's Punishments"; Van Nieuwenhove, "St. Thomas Aquinas on Salvation"; Brandon Peterson, "Paving the Way? Penalty and Atonement in Thomas Aquinas's Soteriology," *International Journal of Systematic Theology* 15, no. 3 (2013): 265–83.

defects, namely, death, hunger, thirst, and the like."[21] All of these defects were "brought into the world by Adam."[22] That is, as a result of sin Adam lost the grace of original justice for himself and all of his descendants. This grace included the gift of being immune to physical suffering and death. Deprived of this grace, Adam and his descendants became subject to the *poena* of natural bodily defects.[23]

As a fellow descendant of Adam who lacked the grace of original justice, Christ also experienced the *poena* of natural bodily infirmity. Aquinas explains this concept with the help of a quotation from Isaiah 53:4: "it was useful for the end of the incarnation that he [Christ] should assume these penalties [*poenalitates*] in our flesh and in our stead, according to Isaiah 53:4: 'surely he has borne our infirmities.'"[24] The text of Isaiah 53:4 here witnesses to the fact that Christ endured the same basic types of bodily defects that all sinners must endure. Christ experienced the natural passibility of his human nature in solidarity with all of postlapsarian humanity. This is what Aquinas means in this context when he speaks of the "punishment" that Christ endured on our behalf. The immediate source of Christ's bodily pain was simply the passible nature that he freely assumed; he was not actively inflicted with pain by the Father. The Father was not actively afflicting additional suffering upon Christ as a punishment for his own sins or for the sins of others. Aquinas's next use of Isaiah 53 further clarifies this point.

The fifth case in the *ST* occurs in the third objection of III, q. 14, a. 1. This objection claims that "penalty [*poena*] is the consequence of fault," and that Christ never had any faults.[25] Hence, Christ should not have experienced any bodily defects, for such defects are penalties (*poenales*). In his response to this objection, Aquinas affirms that *poena* is always a consequence of sin, though it can be a consequence of actual sins or original sin. Then, he specifies that such

---

21. *ST* III, q. 14, a. 1, co.

22. Ibid. For a Thomistic account of original sin and its consequences see J.A. Di Noia, "Not 'Born Bad': The Catholic Truth about Original Sin in a Thomistic Perspective," *The Thomist* 81, no. 3 (July 2017): 345–59.

23. See Bertrand de Margerie, "Mort sacrificielle du Christ et peine de mort chez Thomas d'Aquin, commentateur de Saint Paul," *Revue Thomiste* 83 (1983): 396–97.

24. *ST* III, q. 14, a. 1, co., quoting Is 53:4.

25. *ST* III, q. 14, a. 1, obj. 3.

poena can be endured by the sinner himself or by someone else who offers satisfaction on behalf of the sinner. In terms of the human nature that Christ assumed, the vulnerability of this nature to bodily defects is ultimately due to the sin of Adam, the father of the human race. Further, Christ chose to assume such a passible human nature and thus be subject to bodily *poena* in response to both Adam's sins and all of the actual sins committed throughout human history. In order to emphasize this point, Aquinas quotes Isaiah 53:5: "'He was wounded for our iniquities; he was bruised for our sins.'"[26] Christ was not a sinner; he did not owe a debt of punishment and satisfaction in response to his own sins. The text of Isaiah 53:5 makes the origin of Christ's suffering clear: he experienced pain in order to enact satisfaction for *our* sins. Christ himself never did anything that was displeasing to God, and God never had any reason to vent his wrath upon Christ's body. Rather, Christ freely chose to endure bodily *poenas* for our sakes, as a fitting means of satisfying for our sins.

The sixth instance of Isaiah 53 is in III, q. 14, a. 2.[27] Having established that Christ assumed a human nature that was vulnerable to bodily defects, Aquinas now asks whether or not Christ assumed an obligation to endure these defects. The first objection answers this question in the negative, and it does so with the help of Isaiah 53:7, which states "'he was offered because he himself willed it.'"[28] The objection argues that this text refers to Christ's voluntary willing of the passion, and that "will is opposed to necessity."[29] Since Christ freely chose to suffer bodily pain, as Isaiah 53:7 seems to indicate, then he could not have been bound by any necessity or obligation to suffer those pains. Aquinas provides a thorough response to this objection in the body of the article.

He begins by establishing that the Son of God freely chose, with his divine will, to assume a human nature that would be naturally "subject to the necessity of death and other like defects" in virtue of its substantial matter.[30] Consequently, this passible human nature was

---

26. *ST* III, q. 14, a. 1, ad 3, quoting Is 53:5.

27. Unless otherwise noted, all further references in this chapter to question and article numbers which feature cases of Is 53 come from the *Tertia Pars*.

28. *ST* III, q. 14, a. 2, obj. 1, quoting Is 53:7.

29. Ibid.

30. *ST* III, q. 14, a. 2, co.

also "subject to necessity in regard to the nail that pierced and the scourge that struck."[31] Further, the human, sensitive will of Christ would have been subject to the natural, necessary experience of "repugnance" at the prospect of "death and bodily hurt."[32] But, again, Christ necessarily experiences these bodily defects and interior revulsion at them as a consequence of his prior, free, eternal, and divine decision to assume a human nature subject to these defects. Additionally, even as a human Christ willed, "following the deliberation of reason," to experience these defects.[33] That is, his rational will was completely conformed to the eternal decision of his divine will, even as his sensitive will experienced natural repugnance at the prospect of pain and death. Aquinas summarizes this argument and returns to the text of Isaiah 53:7 in his response to the first objection. He states, "Christ is said to be 'offered because he himself willed it,' namely, with his divine will and deliberate human will."[34] In conclusion, the text of Isaiah 53:7 does not mean that Christ's human body and sensitive will were completely free from the necessity of undergoing defects. Rather, this biblical text simply indicates that Christ freely chose, as both God and man, to subject himself to this natural necessity.

Aquinas's seventh reference to Isaiah 53 is in III, q. 15, a. 1. In the body of this article Aquinas argues that Christ was not guilty of actual or original sin.[35] But, as the fourth objection points out, this conclusion seems to contradict the testimony of 2 Corinthians 5:21, which states that "'he that knew no sin,' namely, Christ, 'for us was made sin.'"[36] In his response to this objection, Aquinas turns

---

31. Ibid.

32. Ibid.

33. Ibid.

34. *ST* III, q. 14, a. 2, ad 1. This could be considered Aquinas's twenty-eighth explicit reference to the words of a verse from Is 53 in the *ST*. But here Aquinas does not explicitly mention that these words come from 'Isaiah,' and so they will not turn up on a search for 'Isaiah' using the Index Thomisticus. Further, Aquinas is quoting these scriptural words because they were quoted in the objection that he is responding to. And so, it raises the question of whether or not one should count a quotation once or twice if it occurs in an objection and then is repeated verbatim in the response to the objection. I have chosen to count such occurrences as simply one quotation.

35. *ST* III, q. 15, a. 1, co.

36. *ST* III, q. 15, a. 1, obj. 4.

to Isaiah 53 and several other biblical texts in order to explain the proper meaning of 2 Corinthians 5:21.[37] He states:

God "made Christ sin," not, indeed, in such sort that he had sin, but that he made him a sacrifice for sin, just as it is written in Hosea 4:8: "They shall eat the sins of my people," that is, the priests, who by the law ate the sacrifices offered for sin. And in that way it is written in Isaiah 53 that "the Lord has laid on him the iniquity of us all," namely, because he gave him up to be a victim for the sins of all men. Or, "he made him sin," meaning that he had "the likeness of sinful flesh," as it is said in Romans 8. And this is because of the passible and mortal body he assumed.[38]

In this passage, Aquinas quotes Isaiah 53:6. He does not think that this verse is saying that Christ sinned. Nor does Isaiah's text mean that God placed upon Christ the cumulative interior effects of every human sin, such as the endurance of a disordered will, guilt, and shame. Isaiah 53:6 also does not mean that in his own being Christ experienced all of the bodily pain that every human sin in history has ever caused. Rather, that which God has laid on Christ's shoulders is the task of offering himself as a sacrifice in atonement for the sins of all of humanity. Christ has received from the Father the heavy responsibility of making an offering which suitably atones for every sin that has been and ever will ever be committed by human beings.

The eighth case of Isaiah 53 is in III, q. 15, a. 5, which inquires whether Christ experienced "sensible pain."[39] In the body of the article, Aquinas clarifies the meaning of the question. For, while it is one thing to say that Christ's body was harmed, it is another thing to say that he felt the pain that comes from that harm, or, that he had "the sense of hurt."[40] In the *sed contra,* he establishes the biblical foundation for his answer by simply quoting Isaiah 53:4: "'Surely he has borne our infirmities and carried our pains.'"[41] Building off of this quotation, in the body of the article Aquinas claims that Christ

---

37. Aquinas also uses Is 53 in order to explain the meaning of 2 Cor 5:21 in his *Commentary on 2 Corinthians.* See the discussion in chapter 7 on *Super II ad Corinthios,* c. 5, l. 5, 201.

38. *ST* III, q. 15, a. 1, ad 4, quoting Hos 4:8, Is 53:6, and Rom 8:3.

39. *ST* III, q. 15, a. 5.

40. *ST* III, q. 15, a. 5, co.

41. *ST* III, q. 15, a. 5, sc., quoting Is 53:4. I have translated *dolores* into "pains," rather than the given "sorrows."

really did experience sensible pain. He really endured "the sense of hurt" and felt "true pain."[42] The reason for this is that Christ actually possessed a real soul with all of its "natural powers," including the power to feel pain.[43] The Son of God did not assume merely a body in the manner of a pilot who controls a drone that is disconnected from his own being. Rather, Christ assumed a human body and soul that were intimately united. He possessed a complete human nature. Hence, when damage and harm was inflicted upon Christ's body, he felt the experience of pain in his soul. In short, he really did experience the sensory pain of which Isaiah 53:4 speaks.

The ninth occurrence of Isaiah 53 is the third and final reference to this text in III, q. 15. In a. 6, Aquinas asks if Christ experienced "sorrow" (*tristitia*).[44] In order to understand how he uses Isaiah 53 in this article, we first need to examine the basic answer to the question that Aquinas explicates in the body of the article. He explains that sorrow, like sensible pain, exists in the "sensitive appetite" of the human soul.[45] But sorrow and sensible pain are distinct in terms of their causes. The soul feels sensible pain in response to harm that is "perceived by the sense of touch, such as when anyone is wounded."[46] The soul feels sorrow in response to "anything hurtful or evil interiorly apprehended by the reason or imagination, as when anyone grieves over the loss of grace or money."[47] To put it simply, the soul experiences sensible pain in response to bodily harm, and it experiences sorrow in response to the intellectual recognition of any type of harm and evil. So, all sensible pain is accompanied by sorrow, but not all sorrow results from sensible pain. Given this definition, Aquinas reasons that Christ certainly experienced sorrow. For "Christ's soul could apprehend things as hurtful either to himself, as his passion and death, or to others, as the sin of his disciples, or of the Jews that killed him."[48] Christ felt the interior pain of sorrow precisely because he intellectually recognized the evil and

---

42. *ST* III, q. 15, a. 5, co.
43. Ibid.
44. *ST* III, q. 15, a. 6.
45. *ST* III, q. 15, a. 6, co.
46. Ibid.
47. Ibid.
48. Ibid.

harmful things that were done to him or to others and by others. Christ grieved in the face of these evils, just as he grieved outside of the tomb of his friend Lazarus.

We can now appreciate the use of Isaiah 53 in the fourth objection to this article. This objection is grounded in a quotation from St. Augustine which states that sorrow is a response to "'things we suffer unwillingly.'"[49] If we presuppose Augustine's definition then we cannot say that Christ experienced sorrow for, as Isaiah 53:7 states, "'he was offered because he himself willed it.'"[50] Aquinas's response to this objection hinges on the distinction between willing something as an end in itself and willing something merely as a means to an end. We can freely choose certain things as means which we would not choose as ends, such as "bitter medicine."[51] The bitterness of such medicine is "contrary to the will" considered in itself. But nonetheless a sick person may freely choose to take such bitter medicine "by reason of the end to which it is ordained," namely, "health."[52] For instance, a person will experience sorrow when their leg is amputated even though they freely willed to undergo this operation as a means to the end of saving their life. Similarly, Aquinas explains, "Christ's death and passion were of themselves involuntary, and caused sorrow, although they were voluntary as ordained to the end, which is the redemption of the human race."[53] Christ did not choose to experience the passion as an end in itself. Rather, the various forms of pain which constituted his passion were in and of themselves repugnant to his will and therefore sources of sorrow. Nonetheless, Christ freely willed to endure these pains and the sorrow which they caused for the sake of the end to which they were ordered: the salvation of the human race. So, the fact that Isaiah 53:7 testifies to the voluntary nature of Christ's passion does not mean that Christ was preserved from the experience of sorrow amidst his passion.

The tenth case of Isaiah 53 is in III, q. 18, a. 6, which asks "was there contrariety of wills in Christ?"[54] Drawing upon the terminology

---

49. *ST* III, q. 15, a. 6, obj. 4, quoting Augustine, *City of God* XIV.6.
50. Ibid., quoting Is 53:7.
51. *ST* III, q. 15, a. 6, ad 4.
52. Ibid.
53. Ibid.
54. *ST* III, q. 18, a. 6.

of Galatians 5:17, the second objection argues that the desires of Christ's "spirit" and "flesh" were in opposition to one another.[55] For, "in his flesh he shrank from the passion," yet "by the will of charity" which he possessed from the Holy Spirit Christ "willed the Passion."[56] Here the objection quotes Isaiah 53:7 as a biblical proof of the fact that Christ freely chose from charity to endure the passion: "'he was offered because he himself willed it.'"[57] In the body of the article, Aquinas establishes the basic points that inform his response to this objection. He first notes that it is normal for a person to desire "one thing with his rational appetite" even as he "wishes [for] another thing with his sensitive appetite."[58] This tension only becomes an opposition of contrariety if the sensitive appetite overpowers the rational, such that the person pursues their sensitive wish even though they know that doing so is contrary to reason. Aquinas says that Christ could have experienced tension between his sensitive and rational will, but never contrariety. As a man Christ rationally chose to endure the passion for the end of our salvation even though his sensitive appetite was naturally repulsed by the means needed for the acquisition of this end. Christ's natural and properly ordered appetite for sensory goods and the avoidance of sensory pain never frustrated his ability to choose, with his rational will, to do that which he knew to be the divine will.[59] Hence, Christ's rational choice to endure the passion, as spoken of by Isaiah 53:7, was not "impeded or retarded by the desires of [his] flesh."[60]

Cases 11–12: III, q. 22 (On the Priesthood of Christ)

Aquinas's eleventh reference to Isaiah 53 is in q. 22, a. 2. Granting that Christ is a priest, this article asks if "Christ himself was both priest and victim?"[61] The first objection sets up Aquinas's later reference to Isaiah 53. It argues in the form of a syllogism: a priest's job is to kill the sacrificial victim; Christ did not destroy himself; hence,

55. *ST* III, q. 18, a. 6, obj. 2.
56. Ibid.
57. Ibid., quoting Is 53:7.
58. *ST* III, q. 18, a. 6, co.
59. Ibid.
60. Ibid.
61. *ST* III, q. 22, a. 2.

"he was not both priest and victim."[62] In his response to this objection, Aquinas first grants the middle term of the above syllogism by acknowledging that "Christ did not slay himself."[63] The Son did not choose, through commission or omission, to actively cause his own death. He did not commit suicide. Yet there is a sense in which Christ "offered himself" just as a priest offers up a sacrificial victim to God.[64] For, as Aquinas explains, "of his own free will he exposed himself to death, according to Isaiah 53:7: 'he was offered because he himself willed it.'"[65] Aquinas uses Isaiah 53:7 here in order to supply a new, nuanced middle term to the syllogism regarding priests that was provided in the objection. He can now reason: priests slay sacrificial victims; Christ freely exposed himself to death; hence, in this way Christ is both priest and sacrificial victim. As Aquinas explains in the response to the second objection, Christ "freely offered himself to suffering," and so "in this respect he is a victim."[66]

Thus, in this article Aquinas helpfully clarifies what Isaiah 53:7 is (and is not) saying in regards to Christ's voluntary endurance of the passion. Christ freely chose to expose himself to suffering and death, but he did not actively attempt to bring about this suffering and death in a formal or material way. The nature of Christ's free offering of himself in the passion, of which Isaiah 53:7 speaks, can be further appreciated in light of the following comparison. Christ's free decision to expose himself to the passion is comparable to the free choice of a policeman who enters the house of a human trafficker in order to liberate the people who are held in slavery within. The police officer freely exposes himself to the danger of being in the criminal's house, but he does so for the sake of saving the captives; he does not actively will to encounter the violent criminal. Similarly, Christ freely chooses to expose himself to the danger of living and preaching and working miracles in the presence of his enemies, even though he knows that doing so will get him killed. Despite this knowledge, Christ risks himself in this way for the sake of saving

62. *ST* III, q. 22, a. 2, obj. 1.
63. *ST* III, q. 22, a. 2, ad 1.
64. Ibid.
65. Ibid., quoting Is 53:7.
66. *ST* III, q. 22, a. 2, ad 2.

humanity. He actively wills to live and preach and work miracles; he does not actively will to be arrested and killed. Yet, unlike the police officer, Christ has actively chosen with both his divine and rational human will to be capable of experiencing and feeling any harm and pain that does end up getting inflicted upon him. Whereas, if the police officer is caught by the trafficker, then he has no choice but to experience and feel the harm and pain that may be inflicted upon him.

The twelfth use of Isaiah 53 occurs in III, q. 22, a. 6. This article deals with the question of whether, as Psalm 110 indicates, Christ should be called "'a priest forever according to the order of Melchizedech.'"[67] The third objection argues that Christ should not be referred to as a priest of Melchizedech's order, but rather simply of his own order. For, Christ alone, and not Melchizedech, is without genealogy, father, or mother, and Christ alone lasts forever (per Heb 7:2).[68] In his response, Aquinas does not concede the conclusion of the objection, but he does grant the truth of the propositions used in support of that conclusion. He admits that Christ alone "had no earthly father, no heavenly mother, and no genealogy, according to Isaiah 53:8: 'who shall declare his generation?' and who in his divinity had neither beginning nor end of days."[69] Aquinas thus interprets Isaiah 53:8 here as referring to the virginal conception of Christ, the divine generation of the Son exclusively from the Father, and the eternity of the Son's divine being. While the Epistle to the Hebrews does say that Melchizedech lacked father, mother, and genealogy, and that he existed eternally, this is not to be taken literally; Hebrews says this only in the sense that "these details in his [Melchizedech's] regard are not supplied by Holy Scripture."[70] Conversely, Christ is actually, in fact, the eternal and divine Son of the Father who became human apart from the mediation of a human father.

<hr>

67. *ST* III, q. 22, a. 6, sc.
68. *ST* III, q. 22, a. 6, obj. 3.
69. *ST* III, q. 22, a. 6, ad 3, quoting Is 53:8.
70. Ibid.

Cases 13 to 16: III, qq. 31, 35–36, and 43
(On Christ's Genealogy, Birth, and Public Ministry)

Aquinas's thirteenth reference to Isaiah 53 once again concerns the issue of Christ's genealogy. In III, q. 31, a. 3, Aquinas considers whether the Gospels provide fitting records of Christ's genealogy. The first objection claims that "Christ's genealogy should not have been set down," since "it is written by Isaiah 53:8: 'who shall declare his generation?'"[71] In response Aquinas, drawing upon Jerome, claims that "Isaias speaks of the generation of Christ's divinity."[72] Conversely, the genealogy of Matthew is about "Christ's forefathers from whom he was descended according to the flesh." Hence, Matthew and Isaiah are speaking of different types of genealogies. Christ's divine generation from the Father cannot be spoken of adequately, nor, Aquinas says here, can "the manner of the incarnation."[73] But it is possible to speak about Christ's human ancestors.

The fourteenth case of Isaiah 53 is in III, q. 35, a. 6, which asks if Mary suffered in giving birth to Christ. In the body of this article, Aquinas claims that Christ was born in a miraculous manner: he "came forth from the closed womb of his mother" without "opening the passage from the womb."[74] Hence, Mary was a perpetual virgin in the sense that even birth did not open her womb.[75] But the second objection argues that Christ's birth should have involved pain, for "the end is proportionate to the beginning."[76] Since "Christ ended his life in pain," per "Isaiah 53:4: 'Surely he has carried our pains,'" then his birth should have also featured pain.[77] In response, Aquinas affirms the meaning of Isaiah 53:4, saying that Christ really did suffer "pains."[78] Yet, he argues that this is beside the point: the question is whether Mary suffered in giving birth, not whether Christ suffered

---

71. *ST* III, q. 31, a. 3, obj. 1, quoting Is 53:8. Aquinas also turns to Is 53:8 in order to deal with this objection in the *Super Matthaeum*, c. 1, l. 1, no. 15. See chapter 5, above.

72. *ST* III, q. 31, a. 3, ad 1.

73. Ibid.

74. *ST* III, q. 35, a. 6, co.

75. *ST* III, q. 28, a. 2.

76. *ST* III, q. 35, a. 6, obj. 2.

77. Ibid., quoting Is 53:4. I translate *dolores* here as "pains" rather than the given "sorrows."

78. *ST* III, q. 35, a. 6, ad 2. The word for "pains" here is *dolores*.

in being born. So the objection does properly interpret Isaiah 53:4 as a witness to the reality of Christ's pain, but this reality is not relevant to the question Aquinas seeks to answer in this context.

The fifteenth occurrence of Isaiah 53 is in III, q. 36, a. 1. This article asks if "Christ's birth should have been made known to all."[79] Aquinas begins to answer this question in the *sed contra* by quoting two biblical texts which speak of the "hidden" (*absconditus*) mystery of God, Isaiah 45:15 and 53:3.[80] The latter states: "'his look was, as it were, hidden [*absconditus*] and despised.'"[81] Aquinas thus takes it as a given of revelation that not everyone recognized the Messianic and divine identity of Jesus; the glory of his birth was not made known to all. Hence, Aquinas proceeds to give reasons why this was the case. The first reason that he gives in support of the revealed truth which Isaiah 45:15 and 53:3 testify to is a problematic one: "First, because this would have been a hindrance to the redemption of man, which was accomplished by means of the cross. For, as it is written in 1 Corinthians 2:8: 'If they had known it, they would never have crucified the Lord of glory.'"[82] Aquinas's argument here can be put into the form of a syllogism: (A) the redemption of the world was accomplished by the cross; (B) the cross happened because people did not recognize that Christ was the Lord of glory; (C) therefore, our redemption depended upon the concealment of Christ's glory from some individuals. On a purely literary level, Aquinas's words in this immediate context do appear to support this syllogism.

The theological problem with this syllogism is that it indicates that God actively willed to conceal the identity of Christ from some people precisely so that those people would be moved to crucify Christ. Concealing Christ's identity is the means to the end of getting people to misunderstand and kill Christ. God does something (hide Christ's identity) in order to move people to error (lack of faith in and understanding of Christ) so that they will sin (arrest, assault, and kill Christ). We thus have God actively willing error and

---

79. *ST* III, q. 36, a. 1.
80. *ST* III, q. 36, a. 1, sc.
81. Ibid., quoting Is 53:3.
82. *ST* III, q. 36, a. 1, co.

sin as a means and end, respectively. I do not think that Aquinas is committed to such a position.

As we have already seen in both the *Super Ioannem* and the *Super Matthaeum*, Aquinas argues two related points: first, those who killed Christ were guilty of the sin of murder; second, God could not have actively willed this sin.[83] Further, as we have seen, in *ST* III, q. 22, a. 2 (on whether Christ was both priest and victim), Aquinas makes it very clear that Christ did not kill himself but rather merely exposed himself to danger for our salvation.[84] The second objection of that article argues that Christ could not have been a sacrificial victim because human sacrifices were conducted by the gentiles, and God "reprehended" those sacrifices.[85] The objection supports this judgment with a quotation from Psalm 106:38: "'They shed innocent blood; the blood of their sons and of their daughters, which they sacrificed to the idols of Canaan.'"[86]

In his response to this objection, Aquinas distinguishes between the will of Christ and the will of the people who killed him. Christ freely willed to endure suffering for us, and this was a pleasing sacrifice to God. But those who freely willed to slay Christ "are not accounted as offering a sacrifice to God, but as guilty of a great crime. And a similitude of this sin was borne by the wicked sacrifices of the gentiles, in which they offered up men to idols."[87] So, here in III, q. 22, a. 2, Aquinas is clear: the slaying of Christ was an abominable crime that was foreshadowed by the horrific human sacrifices of the gentiles, and God was repulsed by all of these crimes. God did not actively will these crimes either as ends or as means. So, while the problematic nature of Aquinas's argument in III, q. 36, a. 1, remains, it would be a mistake to think that this argument encapsulates and adequately represents Aquinas's full understanding of the reasons for Christ's passion.

The sixteenth case of Isaiah 53 is in III, q. 43, a. 1, which considers

---

83. See Thomas Aquinas, *Lectura Super Ioannem*, c. 13, l. 5, 1815, and c. 18, l. 1, 2283; *Lectura Super Matthaeum*, c. 27, l. 1, 2336.

84. *ST* III, q. 22, a. 2.

85. *ST* III, q. 22, a. 2, obj. 2.

86. Ibid., quoting Ps 106:38.

87. *ST* III, q. 22, a. 2, ad 2.

"whether Christ should have worked miracles."[88] The second objection claims that Christ will come with works of "power and majesty" in his eschatological, second coming, and so it is fitting that in "his first coming he came in infirmity, according to Isaiah 53:3: 'a man of pains and acquainted with infirmity.'"[89] In response, Aquinas argues that the "infirmity" of which Isaiah 53:3 speaks was an "'infirmity' of the flesh, which is manifested in the passions."[90] The pain and infirmity which Christ suffered in his bodily passions does not render him incapable of working miracles or render such miraculous works unfitting. For, as Aquinas explains, in addition to coming in passible flesh Christ also "came 'in the power of God,' and this had to be made manifest by miracles."[91] Hence, Isaiah 53:3, while true, gives only half of the truth about Christ: he is both a man of pain and infirmity and a man of glory. His infirmity manifests his solidarity with sinners, and his miraculous works manifests his solidarity with God.[92]

Cases 17–24: III, qq. 46–47 and q. 49

(On the Passion of Christ)

This section of the *Tertia Pars* contains Aquinas's mature systematic exposition of the theological mystery of Christ's passion. He turns to Isaiah 53 in three out of these four questions: on the nature of the passion itself (q. 46), on the efficient cause of the passion (q. 47), and on the effects of the passion (q. 49). He does not refer to Isaiah 53 in q. 48, which deals with the efficiency of the passion, or, the "the manner in which" the salvific effects of the passion were "brought about."[93] Three cases of Isaiah 53 are in q. 46, four cases are in q. 47, and one case is in q. 49.

The first case of Isaiah 53 in this portion of the *Tertia Pars*, and the seventeenth total case in the *ST*, is found in III, q. 46, a. 1. In

88. *ST* III, q. 43, a. 1.

89. *ST* III, q. 43, a. 1, obj. 2, quoting Is 53:3. I translate *dolores* here as "pains" rather than the given "sorrows."

90. *ST* III, q. 43, a. 1, ad 2, quoting Is 53:3.

91. Ibid., quoting 2 Cor 13:4.

92. *ST* III, q. 43, a. 1, co. Aquinas says that Christ's miracles (1) confirm the truth of his divine teaching and (2) confirm the reality of the divine presence within him.

93. *ST* III, q. 48.

this article, Aquinas considers whether or not it was "necessary" for Christ to endure the passion for the salvation of the human race.[94] The second objection contains a syllogism: "what is necessary is opposed to what is voluntary"; "Christ suffered of his own free will"; therefore, "it was not necessary for him to suffer."[95] A quotation of Isaiah 53:7 supports the middle term by saying "'He was offered because he himself willed it.'"[96] Hence, the text of Isaiah 53:7 is used to support the argument that it was not necessary for Christ to suffer and die.

Aquinas's response to this objection builds upon a distinction between various kinds of 'necessity' that he makes in the body of the article. There is natural necessity, such as when a person suffers fatigue from hard manual labor. The reality of fatigue follows necessarily from the intrinsic, natural principles of the human body. There is also a necessity that is imposed from without, by some external efficient cause. For example, a man is necessarily bound in one spot when someone violently ties him up and prevents him from moving. Finally, a thing may be necessary in light of an end to be pursued. Such a necessity refers to a means that is strictly necessary, or at least fitting, in order to acquire the desired end. So, for instance, an athlete who desires the end of victory is necessarily bound to practice and condition in preparation for competition. Aquinas says that the nature of man and of God did not render Christ's suffering necessary. Further, there was no external necessity imposed upon Christ by God or even by himself to suffer, for Christ "suffered voluntarily."[97] Hence, Christ's passion was only necessary "from necessity of the end proposed," meaning that it was the most fitting means which Christ could employ to attain the end of our liberation from sin.[98]

Hence, in response to the second objection, Aquinas says that Christ's free decision to undergo the passion does rule out one form of necessity, namely, the kind that is imposed upon a person from an

---

94. *ST* III, q. 46, a. 1.

95. *ST* III, q. 46, a. 1, obj. 2.

96. Ibid., quoting Is 53:7.

97. *ST* III, q. 46, a. 1, co.

98. Ibid. On the distinction between a means that is strictly necessary and a means that is necessary in the sense of being most fitting, see *ST* III, q. 1, a. 2.

external efficient cause.[99] Since he is both God and man, no external power can force Christ to experience suffering against his will. In that sense, it is never 'necessary' for Christ to suffer. As Isaiah 53:7 testifies, Christ was not bound under necessity to suffer at the hands of his enemies in the same way that a helpless lamb is powerlessly led to the slaughter against its own will. Rather, Christ experienced suffering only because he freely chose to assume a passible human nature and to experience the various defects and pains that would be inflicted upon him in that nature. Christ's free decision to undergo suffering was 'necessary' only in terms of the end that he was pursuing, namely, our salvation from sin. When 'necessity' is understood in this sense then it does not contradict Isaiah 53:7's teaching that Christ freely chose to suffer.

The eighteenth case of Isaiah 53 in the *ST* is in III, q. 46, a. 6. This article asks a highly speculative question about a disturbing reality, namely, "whether the pain of Christ's Passion was greater than all other pains?"[100] Aquinas's answer begins by distinguishing between two different types of pain that Christ experienced as a man. First, Christ endured "sensible pain" which was "caused by something hurtful to the body."[101] So, Christ consciously felt the physical pain of scourging, crowning with thorns, and crucifixion. Second, Christ felt "internal pain," and this pain was "caused from the apprehension of something hurtful, and this is termed sadness (*tristitia*)."[102] Aquinas says that Christ experienced such sadness in response to his intellectual recognition of (1) "the sins of the human race," (2) especially in response to those sins which brought about his death, namely, the sins of his apostles and of his fellow Jews, and (3) in recognition of the impending "loss of his bodily life, which is naturally horrible to human nature."[103] Having distinguished between Christ's sensible and internal pain, Aquinas's conclusion in the body of the article is that "in Christ each of these [types of pain] was the greatest in this present life."[104]

---

99. *ST* III, q. 46, a. 1, ad 2.
100. *ST* III, q. 46, a. 6.
101. *ST* III, q. 46, a. 6, co.
102. Ibid.
103. Ibid.
104. Ibid.

But the fourth objection provides an interesting argument in defense of the conclusion that Christ could not have experienced as much of the internal pain of sadness as sinners do. It first establishes the principle that "the greater the good lost, the greater the pain" of sadness in response to that lost good.[105] Then, it states that Christ only lost his bodily life, whereas sinners lose the life of grace. Therefore, it concludes, sinners have far more to be sad about than Christ ever had.[106] In his response, Aquinas presumes the principle set forth in the objection, namely, that the pain of sadness is proportionate to the value of the good that is lost. He also accepts the statement that the life of grace is superior to bodily life.[107] Nonetheless, he still attempts to refute the objection's conclusion.

Aquinas's response to the fourth objection hinges upon three primary points, and he grounds the last point explicitly in the text of Isaiah 53. He explains:

Christ grieved not only over the loss of his own bodily life, but also over the sins of all others. And this grief in Christ surpassed all grief of every contrite heart, both because it flowed from a greater wisdom and charity, by which the pang of contrition is intensified, and because he grieved at the one time for all sins, according to Isaiah 53:4: "Surely he hath carried our sorrows [*dolores*]."[108]

So, first, it is true that Christ never lost the life of grace for himself, and thus never had that reason to grieve. But the objection falsely presumes that Christ never grieved over the sins of others. Aquinas rejects this presumption and states that Christ did in fact experience sadness or sorrows (*dolores*) over the sins of others. Second, the virtuous causes of Christ's sorrow made it more painful than the sorrow which any other person can experience. The internal pain of sorrow is caused by the intellectual recognition of evil and the revulsion of the will in response to that evil. Christ's infinite wisdom enabled him to recognize intellectually the true nature of evil more so than any other person, and his infinite charity caused his

---

105. *ST* III, q. 46, a. 6, obj. 4.

106. Ibid.

107. *ST* III, q. 46, a. 6, ad 4.

108. Ibid., quoting Is 53:4.

will to respond to the face of evil with an incomparable sadness and disgust.

Third, in his response to the objection Aquinas makes the intriguing claim that Christ experienced sorrow in response to each and every human sin ever committed. He explicitly quotes Isaiah 53:4 in support of this claim. Isaiah's text not only indicates that Christ bore our physical pains; it also shows that Christ entered into solidarity with us in our sorrows. For Aquinas, the Suffering Servant text supports the notion that Christ bore every sorrow in response to sin that every sinner has ever experienced, and therefore he experienced a far greater internal pain than any individual sinner ever could. Finite sinners are aware principally of those sins which they themselves commit and which are committed against them. They may also grieve in response to news of the sins committed by strangers. But they can never be aware in a precise way of every specific sin committed by every human being throughout the course of history. They could not acquire such awareness even over an entire lifetime. Yet Christ, as true God and true man, can have such an awareness, and Aquinas claims that Isaiah 53:4 is proof that he did in fact have such knowledge. Further, he experienced this comprehensive knowledge of sin "at one time [*simul*]," rather than little by little over a progressive period of time.[109] All at once, Christ endured "the pain of contrition" in response to every sin ever committed.[110] Simultaneously, he was contrite for "all the sins of the human race."[111] By enduring this unparalleled degree of the pain of contrition, Christ made satisfaction for the sins of humanity.[112] Hence, he is the exemplar cause for all contrite hearts and, as C. S. Lewis would say, the "perfect penitent."[113]

Aquinas's exegetical use of Isaiah 53:4 in this context is rather simple, but it has further logical implications. He claims that the reference in 53:4 to the Servant carrying our sorrows supports the notion that Christ knew what it was like to experience sorrow in

109. Ibid.

110. Ibid.

111. *ST* III, q. 46, a. 6, co.

112. *ST* III, q. 46, a. 6, co. and ad 2.

113. C. S. Lewis, *Mere Christianity*, in *The C. S. Lewis Signature Classics* (New York: HarperCollins, 2017), 52–56.

response to sin, and specifically that Christ grieved for all human sin at one time. On this basis, one could also read the text of Isaiah 53:4 in support of the notion that Christ experienced every other virtuous form of human sorrow as well, and not merely those forms of sorrow that are in direct response to sin. In this light, the text of Isaiah 53:4 can also speak of Christ's internal pain in response to the recognition of the ugliness of natural evils such as physical suffering and death. In the body of III, q. 46, a. 6, Aquinas makes it clear that Christ experienced sadness at the recognition that he was going to die, and he further adds that Christ "apprehended most vehemently *all* the causes of sadness."[114] That is, Christ was conscious of every evil and source of harm that there is, and so he endured the pain of sadness that accompanies the recognition of all of those tragedies.

While Aquinas does not explicitly draw out the logical implications of this notion, it seems to require the affirmation that Christ carried the sorrows not only of the penitent and the victim of sin, but also of the poor and widowed, of the laborer and the sick, of the person approaching death, and of all those who must righteously bear the internal pain that is caused by great harm and tragedy. Christ experienced radical solidarity with all those who virtuously recognize and endure the burden of suffering and who grieve for the sake of righteousness. This does not mean that Christ himself experienced all of the forms of sensible, bodily pain that people experience. For Christ did not endure the particular physical pain of cancer, for instance, or of blindness. But on an intellectual level he recognized the evil of such things, and on an emotional level he grieved with sadness for all those who endure such evils. Admittedly, Aquinas does not explicitly use Isaiah 53:4 in support of such a view, but the way he does exegete Isaiah's text lends itself to such an interpretation. So, it seems fitting to say that for Aquinas, Isaiah 53:4 testifies to the truth that Christ carried the sorrows of all penitents and of all those whose sadness is born of wisdom and charity.

The nineteenth occurrence of Isaiah 53 is in III, q. 46, a. 11. Here Aquinas asks a simple question: was it "fitting for Christ to be

---

114. *ST* III, q. 46, a. 6, co.; emphasis added.

crucified with thieves?"[115] Aquinas's answer to this question begins in the sed contra, where he quotes Isaiah 53:12: "'he was reputed with the wicked.'"[116] Isaiah's text "foretold" that Christ would be counted among evildoers, and so it provides a biblical testimony to the reality of the object which Aquinas will reflect upon in the remainder of the article. As the Gospels and Isaiah 53:12 indicate, Christ really was crucified alongside criminals, and in this article, Aquinas analyzes the various ways in which that historical event was fitting in accordance with the saving mission of the Son.

Aquinas's next four uses of Isaiah 53 are in q. 47, which concerns the efficient cause of Christ's passion. Cases 20–23 are all found in q. 47, a. 3, which deals with the complex question of "whether God the Father delivered up Christ to the Passion?"[117] Three of these cases are found in the body of the article. There, Aquinas begins by stating that Christ endured the passion freely "out of obedience to the Father."[118] Then, he affirms that the Father "did deliver up Christ to the Passion ... in three distinct respects."[119] He explains:

In the first way, because by his eternal will he preordained Christ's Passion for the deliverance of the human race, according to the words of Isaias (53:6): "the Lord has laid on him the iniquities of us all"; and again (53:10): "the Lord was pleased [*voluit*] to bruise him in infirmity." Secondly, inasmuch as, by the infusion of charity, he inspired him with the will to suffer for us; hence we read in the same passage (53:7): "He was offered because he himself willed it." Third, by not shielding him from the Passion, but abandoning him to his persecutors.[120]

Aquinas uses Isaiah 53 twice in support of the first explanation and once in support of the second. On their surface, Isaiah 53:6 and 10 appear to say that God actively willed and was even pleased by the suffering of Christ. But Aquinas interprets these verses as simply referring to the Father's eternal plan for Christ to undergo suffering. For Aquinas, God the Father bruised Christ and laid our iniquities on him simply in the sense that Christ's passion was in accord

---

115. *ST* III, q. 46, a. 11.
116. *ST* III, q. 46, a. 11, sc., quoting Is 53:12.
117. *ST* III, q. 47, a. 3.
118. Ibid.
119. *ST* III, q. 47, a. 3, co.
120. Ibid., quoting Is 53:6, 10, and 7 (respectively).

with the eternal providence of God. To say that God providentially willed the passion is not to say that he actively willed the contingent causes of Christ's suffering, namely, the unbelief, violence, and cowardice of Christ's enemies. In fact, the third explanation that Aquinas provides in the body of the article helps to support this reading of his uses of Isaiah 53:6 and 10. God the Father abandoned Christ into the hands of his enemies, which simply means that he did not actively intervene to save Christ. For from all eternity he had preordained to allow Christ to be handed over to his enemies, and it is to this that Isaiah 53:6 and 10 testify.

We can now turn to the second explanation that Aquinas provides in the body of III, q. 47, a. 3, regarding how the Father delivered up Christ to suffer. Aquinas uses Isaiah 53:7 in this context in order to provide a biblical witness to the freedom of Christ. Christ's free choice to undergo the passion, a choice about which Isaiah 53:7 speaks, was made possible because he possessed the moral virtue of charity. He received this supernatural virtue from the Father. Hence, the charity of Christ is the reason why he could freely choose to endure the passion, and it is also the reason why Aquinas can say that the Father delivered up Christ to suffer.[121]

Aquinas makes a similar point in his response to the second objection of III, q. 47, a. 3. This objection contains the fourth and final use of Isaiah 53 in this article. The objection argues that one should not say that the Father delivered Christ up to death in light of the fact that Christ freely "gave himself up for us, as it is written in Isaiah 53:12: "'he has delivered his soul unto death.'"[122] The presupposition here is that it is unlikely "that a man be given over to death by himself and by another also."[123] Aquinas responds simply by distinguishing between the divine will of God the Father and Son and the human will of the incarnate Son. As God, the Son and the Father both delivered Christ to death; and, as man, Christ also freely chose, from charity, to endure that which he and the Father divinely willed for

---

121. On Aquinas's treatment of the relationship between the will of the Father and Christ's charitable acceptance of the passion, see Joel Matthew Wallace, *"Inspiravit et voluntatem patiendi pro nobis, inundendo ei caritatem": Charity, the Source of Christ's Action Aaccording to Thomas Aquinas* (Siena: Cantagalli, 2013).

122. *ST* III, q. 47, a. 3, obj. 2, quoting Is 53:12.

123. Ibid.

him to endure from all eternity.[124] Thus, here Aquinas is saying that the text of Isaiah 53:12 should be interpreted as referring to the human will of Christ. As a man, Christ freely handed himself over to death in accord with the divine will of God.

Aquinas's twenty-fourth reference to Isaiah 53 is found in III, q. 49, a. 3. The entire question concerns the salvific effects of Christ's passion, and this specific article deals with the issue of whether Christ's passion released humanity from an obligation to endure punishment as a result of their sins. The *sed contra* consists exclusively of a quotation from Isaiah 53:4: "'Surely he has borne our iniquities and carried our sorrows.'"[125] Interestingly, in the remainder of the article Aquinas never explicitly explains how this verse from Isaiah relates to the question at hand or to the arguments that he offers in exposition of the answer to that question. Thus I will simply offer a brief explication of the primary points that are made in this article and then make some suggestions regarding how the text of Isaiah 53:4 relates to these points. In the body of the article, Aquinas makes two major points regarding what may be called the objective cause of humanity's liberation from punishment. First, Christ's passion "directly" freed humanity from "the debt of punishment" by providing a "sufficient and superabundant satisfaction" for the sins of humanity.[126] This means that in terms of strict justice, sinners no longer need to suffer punishment since Christ's passion was a more than suitable satisfaction in recompense for their sins. Second, the passion "indirectly" frees humans from the debt of punishment by liberating humanity from the sins which generate debts of punishment.[127]

In his replies to the three objections, Aquinas provides a rich and nuanced exposition of how Christians subjectively appropriate the objective deliverance from punishment that Christ won for them through his work of satisfaction. He makes three primary points. First, Christ's passion frees humans from the punishment of eternal damnation insofar as "it is applied, through faith and charity and the

---

124. *ST* III, q. 47, a. 3, ad 2.
125. *ST* III, q. 49, a. 3, sc., quoting Is 53:4.
126. *ST* III, q. 49, a. 3, co.
127. Ibid.

sacraments of faith."[128] These realities cause people to be "united to Christ" and thus to escape the spiritual death that is hell.[129] Second, baptism "configures" penitents to Christ and so frees them from any need to offer the "punishment of satisfaction" for their prebaptismal sins.[130] But those who sin after baptism are obligated to offer satisfaction for their sins, and these penitential works are forms of punishment. Through these free endurances of penitential suffering, they are "configured" to the suffering of Christ, and the satisfaction wrought by Christ's passion functions to lessen the degree of suffering that they need to endure in satisfaction for their sins.[131] Third, Christ's passion frees us from the punishment of spiritual death during this life, and it frees us from the punishment of bodily death at the eschaton. For "Christ's satisfaction works its effect in us inasmuch as we are incorporated with him, as the members with their head."[132] Hence, "as Christ first had grace in his soul with bodily passibility, and through the passion attained to the glory of immortality," so too the members of Christ's mystical body share in his charity, suffering, and death in this life, and then share in his resurrection in the next life.[133]

With this framework in mind, we can now discern how Aquinas may be interpreting and using the text of Isaiah 53:4 in III, q. 49, a. 3. One possibility is that the 'iniquity' that Christ carries on our behalf is the task of freeing us from the debt of punishment. So, Christ places upon his own shoulders the burden of offering a satisfaction that can free humanity from the iniquity of punishment. A similar interpretation would hold that, through his passion, Christ bears *away* the iniquities of our sins, temporal punishments, and eternal punishment. A third interpretation could unfold as follows: in the passion, Christ bore the iniquities of sensible and internal pain; we

---

128. *ST* III, q. 49, a. 3, ad 1.

129. Ibid.

130. *ST* III, q. 49, a. 3, ad 2.

131. Ibid.

132. *ST* III, q. 49, a. 3, ad 3.

133. Ibid. On the relationship between Christ's objective satisfaction on the cross and our subjective participation in it through grace and works of penance, see Daria Spezzano, "'Be Imitators of God (Eph 5:1)': Aquinas on Charity and Satisfaction," *Nova et Vetera* (English edition) 15, no. 2 (2017): 615–51.

are freed from the debt of punishment insofar as we are configured to Christ's passion; therefore, we are freed from the debt of punishment by bearing the iniquities of sensible and internal pain in union with the crucified Christ. Christ bore our iniquities and pains out of charity, and in doing so, he objectively satisfied for the sins of the human race. When we are united to Christ through charity and bear pain and sorrow out of love for God, then we subjectively appropriate the superabundant satisfaction that Christ offered to the Father. By doing so, we are freed from the punishments of damnation and permanent bodily death. These interpretations of Isaiah's text are consistent with the theological claims that Aquinas makes in this article as well as with the ways in which we have seen Aquinas interpret Isaiah 53:4 on earlier occasions.

Cases 25–26: III, qq. 51–52
(On Christ's Burial and Descent to the Dead)

The twenty-fifth case of Isaiah 53 occurs in Aquinas's treatment of the burial of Christ in III, q. 51, a. 1. The second objection argues that Christ's burial was not ordered toward our salvation, and therefore it was not fitting for him to be buried. In response, Aquinas claims that Christ's burial did bring about our salvation. Aquinas takes two steps to support this claim. First, he quotes Isaiah 53:9, "'he shall give the ungodly for his burial.'"[134] Second, he explains the meaning of this biblical verse by citing "a gloss" which states "'he shall give to God and the Father the gentiles who were without godliness, because he purchased them by his death and burial.'"[135] So, in order to support the salvific significance of Christ's burial, Aquinas turns to Isaiah 53:9 and interprets that verse with the aid of an authority. According to the gloss cited, Isaiah 53:9 testifies to the exchange that occurs as a result of Christ's burial: Christ goes down into the earth and the ungodly are raised up to the life of God.

The twenty-sixth instance of Isaiah 53 is found in III, q. 52, a. 1, which considers the question of "whether it was fitting for Christ to descend into hell."[136] In the body of the article Aquinas offers three

---

134. *ST* III, q. 51, a. 1, ad 2, quoting Is 53:9.
135. Ibid.
136. *ST* III, q. 52, a. 1.

reasons why it was fitting that Christ descended into hell, and he quotes Isaiah 53 in support of the first reason. Before we consider that explanation, though, it is necessary to clarify what Aquinas means by the terms 'hell' and 'descent.' He offers this clarification in q. 52, a. 2. There are three distinct levels of "hell" (*inferno*), namely, the hell of the lost, the hell of the just, and purgatory.[137] The inferno of the lost is a state of eternal damnation and is equivalent to the contemporary Catholic doctrine of hell. The inferno of the just refers to the state that was experienced by the righteous souls who died prior to the paschal mystery of Christ. Second, Aquinas distinguishes between two ways in which Christ was "in" these various "places."[138] In terms of "effect," Christ was in each level of hell: he shamed those in the hell of the lost, he gave hope to those in purgatory, and he gave the Beatific Vision to those in the inferno of the just.[139] Additionally, "a thing is said to be in place through its essence, and in this way" Christ's human soul "descended only into that part of hell wherein the just were detained."[140] In this realm of the righteous dead, the soul of Christ proclaimed the good news to the righteous souls detained there and lifted them up to the vision of God in his essence, a vision which they had been deprived of as a result of original sin.[141]

With these clarifications in mind, we can now examine how Aquinas interprets Isaiah 53 in support of the claim that it was fitting for Christ to descend into hell. He explains:

It was fitting for Christ to descend into hell. First of all, because he came to bear our penalty [*poenam*] in order to free us from penalty [*poena*], according to Isaiah 53:4: "Surely he has borne our infirmities and carried our sorrows." But through sin man had incurred not only the death of the body, but also descent into hell. Consequently since it was fitting for Christ to die in order to deliver us from death, so it was fitting for him to descend into hell in order to deliver us also from going down into hell.[142]

---

137. *ST* III, q. 52, a. 2, sc. and co.
138. *ST* III, q. 52, a. 2, co.
139. Ibid.
140. Ibid.
141. *ST* III, q. 52, a. 5, co.
142. *ST* III, q. 52, a. 1, co., quoting Is 53:4.

While the logic of this passage is fairly straightforward, the way in which Aquinas uses Isaiah 53:4 here raises complex theological questions. He draws two principal points from Isaiah's text: (1) Christ really experienced the same types of *poenas* that sinners experience, such as death, and (2) he did so precisely as a means of liberating sinners from permanent captivity to those *poenas*. Presupposing these two points, Aquinas then argues that it was fitting for Christ to endure the *poenam* of hell since he came to liberate sinners from hell. The context suggests that Aquinas is referring specifically and exclusively to the hell of the just, and so the logic is: Christ shared in the *poenae* that the souls of the just endure in the underworld, and he did so precisely in order to save souls from that *poenae*. Now, the primary *poenas* that the souls of the righteous dead endured were the privation of the Beatific Vision and the consequent pain of longing that that privation elicits. Could Christ really have shared in that type of *poenae*? In light of Aquinas's Christology, the answer is in a certain sense 'yes' and in another sense 'no.'

Christ could not have shared in the *poenae* of the righteous dead in a complete sense given that as a man he always possessed the Beatific Vision in his intellect. From the first moment of his conception in the womb of Mary, Christ knew the essence and will of God through a direct and immediate intellectual vision.[143] Nonetheless, during his temporal life he still experienced defects and pains of soul and body. His perfect intellectual knowledge of God did not prevent him from experiencing the internal pain of sorrow, fear, and anger, nor the sensory pain that comes from bodily harm.[144] Aquinas makes it clear that by his passion, Christ merited the full glorification of his soul and body, such that they would no longer be subject to such defects and pains.[145] Further, he claims that Christ received the fruits of this merit at the moment of his resurrection, for at that point his soul and body became completely impassible.[146]

---

143. See *ST* III, q. 9, a. 2, and the analysis of it by Joshua Lim, "The Necessity of Beatific Knowledge in Christ's Humanity: A Re-Reading of *Summa Theologiae* III, Q. 9," *The Thomist* 86, no. 4 (October 2022): 515–42.

144. *ST* III, q. 15, aa. 5, 6, 10.

145. *ST* III, q. 46, a. 6.

146. *ST* III, q. 54, a. 2.

But Aquinas does not clearly state whether Christ's soul experienced internal pain during the three days that he spent with the righteous dead in the inferno of the just. Hence, when Aquinas appeals to Isaiah 53:4 in order to support the idea that "Christ, in order to take our penalties [*poenas*] upon himself ... willed his soul to descend into hell," the exact nature of the *poenam* that Christ's soul endured in hell is vague.[147]

At most, Aquinas could mean the following: as Christ descended into the presence of the righteous dead and proclaimed the good news to them, his soul could still have been capable of experiencing the internal pain of sorrow. During his stay of "a day and two nights"[148] in the inferno of the just Christ could have grieved for (1) the absence of his body and all of the goods that are entailed in bodily life, (2) the pain of longing for his risen body, (3) the pain of longing for the full, unqualified enjoyment of his will at the intellectual vision of God, (4) the pain of longing for these gifts to be given to his fellow souls in the inferno of the just and for all souls, (5) or the pain of knowing all of the sins of humanity and the destinies of the damned. Especially in regard to ways 1–4, Christ could have experienced solidarity with the righteous dead in their suffering even as he prepared to take away their pains on the morning of the third day. In conclusion, this may be the sense in which Aquinas is interpreting Isaiah 53:4 in III, q. 52, a. 1: even in the netherworld, Christ shared in the pain and suffering of sinners; he knew what it was like to virtuously experience privation and to long for the fullness of glory. Yet he was able to liberate the righteous dead from their suffering precisely because he first shared in it—he came down to the souls of the just in the darkness of death and brought them up into the light of life.

Case 27: III, q. 68 (On the Relationship between Baptism and Satisfaction)

The twenty-seventh and final reference to Isaiah 53 in the *ST* is found in III, q. 68, a. 5, in which Aquinas inquires as to whether those who

147. *ST* III, q. 52, a. 4, co.
148. Ibid.

are baptized need to perform works of satisfaction. In the body of the article, he is emphatic that the newly baptized do not need to perform any works of satisfaction in reparation for their pre-baptismal sins. The reason for this is that "by baptism man is incorporated into the very death of Christ," and "Christ's death satisfied sufficiently" for the sins of the entire world.[149] But the first objection proposes an argument against this conclusion. It begins with the presupposition that "a man should be punished for every sin" that he commits, and then observes that "works of satisfaction are enjoined on sinners in punishment [*poenam*] of past sins."[150] Hence, the objection concludes, the newly baptized should also be "enjoined" to do works of satisfaction for their pre-baptismal sins.[151]

Aquinas's response to this objection begins by reaffirming the two foundational principles articulated in the body of the article. First, baptism unites the recipient to Christ by making them a member of Christ's mystical body.[152] Second, Christ's passion objectively satisfied for the sins of the whole world, and so the members of his body can share in that satisfaction. Aquinas explains this second point by saying, "the very pains [*poena*] of Christ were satisfactory for the sins of those who were to be baptized, just as the pain [*poena*] of one member can be satisfactory for the sin of another member."[153] He then quotes Isaiah 53:4, saying: "Hence it is written in Isaiah 53:4: 'Surely he has borne our infirmities and carried our pains.'"[154] With the help of Isaiah 53:4, Aquinas is saying that the baptized do not need to endure the *poenas* that are works of satisfaction precisely because Christ has already endured that *poenam* on their behalf. Since satisfaction was offered for sin, justice was not violated. That is, Christ has taken upon himself and completed the required task of performing a good work that satisfies for the sins of the entire human race. This objectively fulfills the demands of justice. Then, through the grace of baptism, the objective satisfaction

---

149. *ST* III, q. 68, a. 5, co.

150. *ST* III, q. 68, a. 5, obj. 1.

151. Ibid.

152. *ST* III, q. 68, a. 5, ad 1.

153. Ibid.

154. Ibid., quoting Is 53:4. I have translated *dolores* here as "pains" in place of the given "sorrows."

which Christ wrought in his passion is shared with and subjectively experienced by sinners. Hence, just as the head of the mystical body shared in the pains of the members, so now the members share in the satisfaction which was given by their head.[155]

CONCLUSION AND SYNTHESIS

We can now synthesize the various theological points that Aquinas draws from the text of Isaiah 53 in the *ST*. Just as he does in his earlier works, so too here in the *ST* Aquinas affirms the fundamental point that the text of Isaiah 53 is an explicit prophecy of the passion of Christ. The suffering and death of the Messiah are the realities that are immediately signified by the words of the prophecy. This prophecy reports the truth that was divinely revealed to the prophet by God, and hence those who deny or oppose this divine report are guilty of the sin of unbelief. In addition to making this fundamental point regarding the meaning of Isaiah 53, throughout the *ST*, Aquinas consistently turns to this biblical text in order to support his exposition of one or more of five theological themes. I will identify these themes below and then offer a synthetic explanation of the theological points that Aquinas makes with the help of Isaiah 53 in regards to those themes.

The first theme regards the divine generation of the Son and the extent to which his identity was revealed to humanity. "Who shall declare his generation?," asks Isaiah 53:8. According to Aquinas, this text refers primarily to the divine, eternal, incomprehensible generation of the Son from the Father. In a secondary sense, these biblical words also point to the fact that Christ had no divine mother, and that as man, he was conceived of a virgin and so lacked an earthly father. While the Gospel of Matthew can rightly trace Christ's human genealogy, no person can adequately describe Christ's generation in the womb of Mary or his eternal generation from the Father. Further, as Isaiah 53:3 indicates, the truth about Christ's divinity and Messianic identity was "hidden" from the knowledge of many of his contemporaries, and consequently they "despised" and rejected

---

155. On why works of satisfaction are needed for post-baptismal sins, see *ST* III, q. 49, a. 3.

the Lord of glory. Christ's Godhead was hidden from some by the bodily defects which he experienced as a man, defects about which Isaiah 53:2–3 speak. Nonetheless, by clearly testifying to the reality of Christ's humanity, these defects ultimately contributed to the revelation of Christ's divinity, and thus to the didactic end of the incarnation. This is seen most clearly in the case of Thomas the apostle, who came to profess the divinity of Christ precisely because he saw the risen, wounded body of the Lord.

The second theme is about the origin, nature, and saving significance of Christ's human defects and pain. Aquinas features Isaiah 53:3, 4, and 7 prominently in the service of this theme. Christ came in the power of God, which means that he worked miracles which testified to the reality of his divine nature. Yet, at the same time, Christ came in the frailty of human nature. He was one with God and one with sinners. He "bore our infirmities and carried our pains" (Is 53:4) in the sense that he assumed a passible human nature that was subject to real bodily defects and pain. Christ's body could be physically harmed, and his soul felt sensible pain in response to such harm. For the Son assumed not merely a material body but also a human soul. His experience of bodily defects and pain included the universal human burdens of hunger, thirst, and death. In addition, Christ experienced the internal pain of sadness (*tristitia*) and sorrow (*dolor*) whenever he was intellectually conscious of the reality of sin, evil, and harm. In this sense, he truly "carried our sorrows" (Is 53:4).

As God, Christ freely chose to assume a passible, fully human nature, and thus to be necessarily subject to the various defects and pains that would accompany the possession of such a nature. Additionally, as a man, he "was offered because he himself willed it" (Is 53:7), which means that with his rational human will he freely chose to endure these defects and pains. He made this free human choice despite the fact that his sensitive appetite naturally and properly reacted with repugnance, sorrow, and fear to the prospects of harm and pain. With his rational will, Christ chose to endure the passion as a means to the end of our salvation, but with his sensitive appetite he experienced revulsion at the prospect of the sensible pain which was innate to the passion. The significance of Christ's divine and human choice to undergo harm and pain is further revealed by the fact that the sensible and internal pain that he endured was greater in intensity than all other human experiences of pain. Despite being completely sinless, Christ experienced the pain of contrition for human sin in a way that surpassed the pain felt by every sincerely repentant human heart. He truly "carried our sorrows" (Is 53:4) in the sense that he grieved for every human sin ever committed, and he did so all at once. This pain of contrition that Christ experienced was also unsurpassed due to the fact that it proceeded from Christ's unsurpassed wisdom and charity. Further, Aquinas says that Christ grieved for "all the causes of sadness," implying that Christ shared in every virtuous form of sadness that righteous souls can experience.[156]

Aquinas refers to Christ's defects and pain on multiple occasions as forms of *poena*, or punishment. The immediate source of these *poenae* was the passible human nature that Christ possessed and which he inherited in union with all of the descendants of Adam. Since he was completely sinless, Christ did not deserve to endure these *poenae*, and the fact that he did endure them is exclusively due to the sins of humanity. That is, as both God and man, Christ freely chose to assume and experience a human nature that was subject to *poenae* exclusively for the sake of our salvation from sin. This is what Isaiah 53:5 means by saying that Christ "was wounded for our iniquities" and "bruised for our sins." Christ bore the *poena* of defects and pain so that he could help sinners to endure their defects and pain with charity. He "bore our infirmities" (Is 53:4), meaning that he bore the *poena* that we must bear, and by doing so he offered a superabundant satisfaction for the sins of the human race. Christ was truly "made sin" for us (2 Cor 5:21) and the Father "laid on him the iniquity of us all" (Is 53:6) in the sense that Christ freely offered himself as a sacrifice in reparation for our sins.

The third theme is about the relationship between the will of God and the human will of Christ in regards to the passion. As a man, Christ did not actively slay himself through commission or omission. But "he was offered because he himself willed it" (Is 53:7),

---

156. *ST* III, q. 46, a. 6, co.

which means that he did freely choose to expose himself to death. Hence, in that sense Christ is both the victim who was offered on the cross and the priest who offered up the victim. Christ's free choice to undergo the passion was necessary only in relation to the end to which it was ordered. Christ freely chose to endure the passion as a fitting means to the end of our salvation. From all eternity God foreknew and preordained that Christ should endure the passion for our salvation, and this is what Isaiah meant when he said that God "laid on him the iniquity of us all" (53:6) and that he "was pleased [*voluit*] to bruise him in infirmity" (53:10). The Father delivered up Christ to suffer in three ways: first, insofar as he eternally preordained the passion; second, because he did not rescue Christ from his enemies; third, by inspiring Christ's human will with the charity that he needed to make the free sacrificial offering of which Isaiah 53:7 speaks. Out of charity, Christ the man freely "delivered his soul unto death" (Is 53:12), but this does not mean that the Father did not also hand over Christ to his enemies in the senses specified above.

The fourth theme consists of the relation between Christ's passion and the deliverance of sinners from the debt of punishment. Every sin incurs punishments, and among those punishments includes the debt of satisfaction. When the debt of satisfaction is paid, then the sinner is freed from all of the punishments that they endure as a consequence for their sins. In this light, Isaiah 53:4 has at least two meanings: Christ "has borne our infirmities and carried our sorrows" in the sense that he (1) really experienced the various forms of *poena* that we suffer as descendants of Adam, such as defects of body and soul, and (2) by bearing these *poenas* of infirmity and sorrow with charity, he takes upon himself and completes the painful task of offering an objectively sufficient work of satisfaction for the sins of humanity.

Through baptism, the new members of Christ's mystical body receive a full share in the objective satisfaction that Christ enacted in his passion. As Christ shared in the infirmities and sorrows of sinners, so now newly baptized sinners share in the effects of his work. Baptism immediately delivers the soul from the punishment of spiritual death by infusing the life of grace, but full liberation from the *poena* of bodily passibility and death does not come until the eschaton. Christians who sin after baptism must subjectively appropriate the effects of Christ's objective work of satisfaction by performing their own penitential acts of satisfaction. These penitential acts are a form of *poena*, and when they are performed with charity they conform the penitent to the cross of Christ. As Christ bore *poena* with charity, and then entered into glory, so too penitents must bear their *poena* with charity in order to participate in the satisfaction wrought by Christ.

The fifth and final theme regards Christ's death among the wicked, his burial, and his descent to the dead. Christ was "reputed with the wicked" (Is 53:12), which means that he was condemned as and alongside dangerous criminals. "He shall give the ungodly for his burial" (Is 53:9) means that, as a result of his burial in the tomb, Christ was able to generate faith among the gentiles and thus give them to the Father. Christ's burial had saving significance. As his body laid in the tomb, Christ's soul descended to the inferno of the just. By doing so he "has borne our infirmities and carried our sorrows" (Is 53:4), meaning that he shared in the *poena* that the souls of the just experience in the underworld. Christ descended into the depths of righteous suffering in order to free the righteous dead from their suffering. Having shared in their pain for one day and two nights, Christ proceeded on Easter morning to give the righteous dead a share in his own heavenly glory.

In conclusion, the text of Isaiah 53 features prominently in the *ST* from both a quantitative and qualitative standpoint. Aquinas quotes Isaiah 53 more in the *Tertia Pars* alone than he does in any of his other major theological works. These quotations appear in each of the various structural parts which make up an *ST* article: the *sed contra*, the objections, the replies, and the body of the article. Regardless of where they are placed within an article, Aquinas almost always provides an explicit exposition of the meaning or meanings of these verses from Isaiah 53. He consistently interprets this biblical text in a way that serves to help clarify the mystery of Christ's human nature, will, and suffering. Two features of Aquinas's theological interpretations of Isaiah 53 in the *Tertia Pars* are particularly distinctive when compared to his earlier works. The first is the fact that he repeatedly draws upon this biblical text in order to explicate the causes, nature, extent, and salvific significance of the *poena* that Christ endured in solidarity with the descendants of Adam. The second is that he turns to Isaiah 53 over and over again in order to specify the relationship between the passion, the will of God, and the sensitive and rational human appetites of Christ. In sum, in the *Tertia Pars* Aquinas offers his most in-depth and nuanced exposition of Isaiah 53's teaching regarding the Servant's free embrace of suffering for the salvation of the world.

9

The Commentary on the Psalms

The previous chapter explored how Aquinas referenced Isaiah 53 a total of twenty-seven times in the *Summa Theologiae* in the service of his deeply analytical systematic theology. In this chapter, I examine the references to Isaiah 53 that Aquinas makes in his final biblical commentary, the *Super Psalmos*. This chapter consists of three parts. The first part examines the historical context of the *Super Psalmos* and gives a brief quantitative analysis of Aquinas's engagement with Isaiah 53 in that work. The second part presents a qualitative exposition of those cases of Isaiah 53. Finally, the third part concludes this chapter with a theological synthesis of the various Christological truths that Aquinas gleans from Isaiah 53 in his exegesis of the Psalms.

CONTEXT AND QUANTITATIVE ANALYSIS

Aquinas lectured on the Psalms in Naples during the 1272–73 academic year, and during that course he commented upon Psalms 1–54. The commentary that has come down to us is a *reportatio*, by Reginald of Piperno, of that course.[1] As we saw in the previous chapter, during this period in which he was lecturing on the Psalms, Aquinas was also busy writing the *Tertia Pars* of the *ST*.[2] Hence,

---

1. Torrell, *Saint Thomas Aquinas*, 403.
2. On the composition date, style, and theology of the *Super Psalmos* and its relation to

while the *Tertia Pars* contains the highest quantity of references to Isaiah 53 of any of Aquinas's works, the *Super Psalmos* definitely bears at least equal witness to the mature thought of Aquinas regarding the meanings of the text of Isaiah 53.

Despite having lectured on only about the first third of the Book of Psalms, Aquinas's *Super Psalmos* nevertheless contains an impressive twelve explicit references to the text of Isaiah 53.[3] We can only speculate regarding the number of times Aquinas would have referenced Isaiah 53 had he been able to comment upon all 150 Psalms. Regardless, the *Super Psalmos* that has come down to us today contains a significant quantitative engagement with Isaiah 53. Among Aquinas's biblical commentaries on individual books, only the *Super Matthaeum* and the *Super Ioannem* contain more cases of Isaiah 53 than the *Super Psalmos* does. Of the twelve references to Isaiah 53 that Aquinas makes in his commentary on the Psalms, he quotes Isaiah 53:7 the most, with a total of four cases. The remaining cases are as follows: 53 (without a specific verse) (x1), 53:1 (x1), 53:2 (x1), 53:2–3 (x2), 53:4 (x1), 53:6 (x1), and 53:9 (x1). In the qualitative analysis that follows, I explicate these cases according to the numerical order of verses in Isaiah 53, meaning that I first examine the case of Isaiah 53:1, and then that of Isaiah 53:2, and so on.

CASES OF ISAIAH 53 IN THE *SUPER PSALMOS*

Cases of Isaiah 53, vv. 1–4 and 6

The first case of Isaiah 53 in the *Super Psalmos* occurs in Aquinas's lecture on Psalm 27. In this lecture, Aquinas makes a general reference to Isaiah 53 but he does not quote a specific verse. Given that scripture identifies this Psalm as "'a Psalm for David himself,'" Aquinas says that this either means that the "literal sense" of the

---

the *Tertia Pars*, see James R. Ginther, "The Scholastic Psalms' Commentary as a Textbook for Theology: The Case of Thomas Aquinas," in *Omnia Disce: Medieval Studies in Memory of Leonard Boyle, O.P.*, ed. Anne J. Duggan (Aldershot: Ashgate, 2005), 211–29, and Ryan, *Thomas Aquinas as Reader of the Psalms*.

3. The Index Thomisticus actually identifies thirteen cases, but the first case is incorrect. The Index mistakenly identifies Aquinas's quotation of Is 52:1 in paragraph 78 of the sermon on Psalm 9 as a quotation of Is 53. The Latin and English texts provided by the Aquinas Institute correct this error.

Psalm is about David or that "he made this [Psalm] himself and he sang this and others."[4] Either way, Aquinas says that the "mystical sense" of this Psalm is about the "the prayer of Christ to the Father that he be freed from suffering evils."[5] This context establishes the foundation for Aquinas's Christological reading of Psalm 27:2, in which the Psalmist makes the following petition to God: "'Hand me not over together with the wicked, and with the workers of iniquity destroy me not.'"[6] Aquinas says that the content of this verse "can all be referred to Christ, who was considered to be among the criminals on the cross, as Isaiah 53 says."[7]

Hence, on the surface of Psalm 27:2, Christ appears to be asking the Father to deliver him from the fate that is described in Isaiah 53: the unjust condemnation and execution of the Servant as a criminal alongside of other criminals. Aquinas does not read the Psalm in this way, though. He does not say that in this Psalm Christ is praying for deliverance from the passion itself. Rather, Aquinas merely says that here Christ is praying that he will not be handed over to death for the same reason that the wicked are killed nor for the same "intention" of those who handed him over to death.[8] The wicked die as a result of their own sins, and the people who crucified Christ did so because they "intended the name of Christ to perish."[9] Conversely, Christ willed to endure death "because of our iniquity."[10] So, here Aquinas offers a somewhat counterintuitive interpretation of Psalm 27:2, but this interpretation serves to clarify the meaning of Isaiah 53. Isaiah 53's description of the Servant's death among the wicked does not mean that the Servant was actually a sinner who deserved that

4. Thomas Aquinas, *Super Psalmos*, Ps. 27, no. 247, quoting Ps 27:1. All references to the *Super Psalmos* will be to the Latin texts and the English translations available at aquinas.cc/la/en/~Psalm. The Latin text of Aquinas's commentary on Psalms 1–51 is based on the Parma edition of 1863, while the Latin text of his commentary on Pss 52–54 is based on the 1980 edition by Fr. Busa. Both editions have been transcribed and edited by the Aquinas Institute. The English translation of both of these Latin texts was done by Sr. Albert Marie Surmanski and Sr. Maria Veritas Marks.

5. *Super Psalmos*, Ps. 27, no. 247.

6. *Super Psalmos*, Ps. 27, no. 249, quoting Ps 27:2.

7. Ibid.

8. Ibid.

9. Ibid.

10. Ibid.

fate. Rather, unlike the criminals with whom he was crucified, Christ died for our sins and not for his own.

In our second case, Aquinas quotes Isaiah 53:1 in the course of his commentary on Psalm 44. In Psalm 44:11 the Psalmist says "'hear [*audi*], O daughter,'" and Aquinas identifies this daughter as the Church.[11] The Church, Aquinas says, must be "'swift to hear [*audiendum*]' . . . the Gospel or the word of Christ" and "the writings of the prophets, so that they might believe in Christ."[12] He then immediately quotes Isaiah 53:1, which states "'who has believed our report?'"[13] Aquinas presents the text of Isaiah 53:1 as an example of a prophetic writing that bears witness to Christ and which thus can generate faith in Christ. Hence, Psalm 44:11 exhorts the Church to hear and believe in those Christological reports that are contained in the Gospels as well as in prophetic writings such as Isaiah 53:1. While he does not use the phrase 'literal sense' in this context, Aquinas's analysis here once again indicates that he does identify Christ as the principal reality to which the words of Isaiah 53 refer.

Aquinas's third reference to Isaiah 53 is in the course of his analysis of Psalm 44. For Aquinas, this Psalm is about "the nuptials of Christ and the Church," and in v. 3 the Psalmist sings "the praise of the groom," namely, Christ.[14] The Psalmist says that Christ is "'beautiful above the sons of men,'" and Aquinas interprets this as referring to "a fourfold beauty in Christ."[15] Christ possessed unsurpassable beauty in terms of his divinity, his "justice and truth," his "honorable and virtuous" life, and finally in his "beauty of body."[16] In regards to Christ's physical beauty, Aquinas fields an objection that is based on a paraphrase of the text of Isaiah 53:2: it seems that Christ was not physically beautiful, the objection claims, since "'we have

---

11. *Super Psalmos*, Ps. 44, no. 458, quoting Ps 44:11.

12. Ibid., quoting Jas 1:19.

13. Ibid., quoting Is 53:1.

14. *Super Psalmos*, Ps. 44, no. 451. As many have pointed out, Aquinas thinks that the Psalms speak about Christ through both the literal and the spiritual senses. See, for instance, Martin Morard's analysis in "Sacerdoce du Christ et sacerdoce des chrétiens dans le Commentaire des Psaumes de saint Thomas d'Aquin," *Revue Thomiste* 99 (1999): 119–42, esp. 125–56.

15. *Super Psalmos*, Ps. 44, no. 452, quoting Ps 44:3.

16. Ibid.

seen that there is in him no beauty or comeliness.'"[17] In response to this objection, Aquinas insists that Isaiah is not speaking about the general appearance of Christ's body but rather about the way that he appeared "in his Passion, in which his body's form was deformed by the multitude of his afflictions."[18] Isaiah 53:2 depicts the "contempt" that Christ's enemies had toward him during the course of his physical suffering. Thus, for Aquinas there is no contradiction between the beauty of which Psalm 44:3 speaks and the lack of beauty to which Isaiah 53:2 testifies. Both biblical texts speak the truth about Christ's physical appearance. As a man Christ possessed the physical beauty that "was appropriate to his state" and his "nature," but that beauty was marred during the course of his passion.[19]

The fourth case occurs in Aquinas's commentary on Psalm 33. While analyzing Psalm 33:1, Aquinas makes a reference to the fact that there were contemporaries of Jesus who "did not know him."[20] Aquinas then offers a quotation from Isaiah 53:2–3 in order to provide a biblical description of their ignorance: "'we have seen him, and there was no sightliness [in him]'; and they despised him: 'whereupon we esteemed him not.'"[21] For Aquinas, Isaiah 53:2–3 describes the view of unbelievers toward Christ and it clarifies why they did not believe. The agony and misery that Christ endured in his passion clouded the vision of some of his contemporaries and led them to see Christ as a mere man who was unworthy of their faith and esteem.

The fifth case is a reference to Isaiah 53:2–3 that Aquinas makes while commenting on Psalm 49. This Psalm opens with a declaration that God will reveal himself and "'come manifestly'" to his people "out of Zion, the loveliness of his beauty.'"[22] Aquinas interprets these lines as a reference to the pouring out of the Holy Spirit upon the apostles in Jerusalem at Pentecost. From that historical

---

17. Ibid., paraphrasing Is 53:2. The paraphrase states: "'vidimus et non erat in eo species neque decor.'"

18. Ibid.

19. Ibid.

20. *Super Psalmos*, Ps. 33, no. 324.

21. Ibid., quoting Is 53:2 and 53:3, respectively. Author's translation of "'vidimus eum, et non erat aspectus': et contempserunt eum: 'unde nec reputavimus eum.'"

22. *Super Psalmos*, Ps. 49, no. 490–91, quoting Ps 49:3 and 49:2, respectively.

moment in Jerusalem, God's "beauty began to be diffused" to the whole world.[23] Aquinas interprets God's 'beauty' here specifically as God's "calling" of the world to faith in Christ.[24] He then acknowledges that even prior to Pentecost "Christ himself certainly began this diffusion" of God's beauty or calling to humanity.[25] Nonetheless, Aquinas claims that Christ's beauty "was not seen, since he was encompassed by weakness."[26] He then offers a quotation from Isaiah 53 which combines parts of vv. 2–3: "'we have seen him [v. 2] the most abject of men, a man of sorrows [v. 3].'"[27] For Aquinas, Isaiah 53:2–3 testifies to the fact that the passion of Christ hid his beauty from many of his peers. God's call to sinners, a calling which he began through Christ and continues through the apostles, was initially rejected by some on account of the humiliation and misery of God's messenger. The sorrow and degradation of Christ masked his divinity and garbled his divine message. Yet, Aquinas concludes, "after his Passion, his strength and power appeared."[28] Hence, during the historical event of the passion, the beauty of God was hidden to the eyes of many, but the resurrection which followed that passion provided the ultimate diffusion of God's loveliness to the world.

The sixth case is a quotation from Isaiah 53:4 which occurs amidst Aquinas's comments on Psalm 18. The Psalmist says that God "'has set his tabernacle in the sun,'" and Aquinas interprets this verse as a figurative reference to "the reality" that is Christ.[29] He presents several different Christological readings of this verse, but the one that is relevant for our purposes is as follows: the tabernacle of God is the "body" of Christ, and this body is in the sun in the sense that it is "passible," for it suffers "in the heat" of the sun.[30] Aquinas supports this interpretation with the words of Isaiah 53:4: "'Surely he has borne our infirmities and carried our sorrows.'"[31] Christ's human

---

23. *Super Psalmos*, Ps. 49, no. 490.

24. Ibid.

25. Ibid.

26. Ibid.

27. Ibid., quoting parts of Is 53:2 and 53:3. Author's translation of "'vidimus eum novissimum virorum, virum dolorum.'"

28. Ibid.

29. *Super Psalmos*, Ps. 18, no. 152, quoting Ps 18:6.

30. Ibid.

31. Ibid., quoting Is 53:4.

flesh is the tabernacle of God, the locus of divinity and sanctity in the cosmos. Nonetheless, Christ has shared in the pain and sorrow of all of Adam's descendants. Christ suffered with us in toil and labor and under the heat of the sun. Christ, the creator of all things, is nonetheless subject to the environmental afflictions that all humans experience.

The seventh case is found in Aquinas's analysis of Psalm 52. This Psalm decries the widespread sin and unbelief of humanity, saying: "'All have gone aside, they have become unprofitable together; there is none who does good.'"[32] Commenting on this verse, Aquinas says: "All have fallen away from the understanding of and search for God."[33] He then quotes Isaiah 53:6, which states "'Every one has turned aside into his own way.'"[34] Hence, both Psalm 52:4 and Isaiah 53:6 speak of the same reality: humanity's mass turning away from God. This abandonment of God involves a loss of "true faith" and "love of God," and this absence of faith and charity renders a person's works "unprofitable for him in relation to the prize of eternal life."[35] Isaiah 53:6, then, describes the malady and problem for which the Suffering Servant is the cure. Christ came to offer himself as a sacrifice in order to draw humanity out of the darkness of sin and error into which they had thrown themselves and into the light of faith and charity.

Cases of Isaiah 53:7 and 53:9

The eighth case of Isaiah 53 in the *Super Psalmos* that we will examine takes place in Aquinas's exegesis of Psalm 34. "This psalm," Aquinas explains, "is either written in the person of David, or of Christ, or of both."[36] If the Christological character of this Psalm is granted, then Aquinas specifies that the text can be interpreted as speaking "mystically" and "at length" upon "the Passion of Christ."[37] One such example of this Psalm's mystical references to Christ's passion is found in v. 15, in which the Psalmist laments that "'they

32. *Super Psalmos*, Ps. 52, no. 519, quoting Ps 52:4.
33. Ibid.
34. Ibid., quoting Is 53:6.
35. Ibid.
36. *Super Psalmos*, Ps. 34, no. 345.
37. Ibid.

rejoiced against me, and came together. Scourges were gathered together upon me, and I knew not.'"[38] For Aquinas, this text refers to the fact that Christ's pagan and Jewish enemies, among both the leaders and the people, worked together to bring about his death. And yet, amidst his affliction at their hands, Christ "'knew not,'" meaning that he "acted as though ignorant" by "remaining silent and not speaking."[39] To provide further biblical support for this interpretation, Aquinas quotes three scriptural texts, among which is Isaiah 53:7: "'he shall be led as a sheep to the slaughter.'"[40] Aquinas turned to the direct and clear Christological meaning of Isaiah 53:7 in order to help him exegete the ambiguous final words of Psalm 34:15. In sum, both Psalm 34:15 and Isaiah 53:7 testify to the "patience of Christ" amidst his passion.[41] Christ endured hatred, insults, and persecution from his enemies with silence; he refused to even offer a verbal, intellectual defense of his innocence and teaching, and in this his supreme patience is revealed.

The ninth case of Isaiah 53 occurs in the context of Aquinas's comments on Psalm 37. In Psalm 37:14 the Psalmist states: "'But I, as a deaf man, heard not and as a dumb man not opening his mouth.'"[42] Aquinas interprets this verse as a depiction of the "patience" of a just man, and especially of the patience of Christ. He says that those who lack patience will be "disturbed in soul" when they are "afflicted," and this interior pain will result in a verbal expression of disturbance.[43] In order to avoid being disturbed in soul and consequently in words, the afflicted person should strive "to be like a deaf man who does not hear the evil words" that are spoken about them and to them.[44] When the just person refuses to hear the evil that is uttered against them, then they are able to "be like one mute," for they will "not utter disturbed words."[45] Aquinas says that "Christ particularly did this, as is said" in Matthew 27:14, Psalm 38:2, and

<hr>

38. *Super Psalmos*, Ps. 34, no. 355, quoting Ps 34:15.
39. Ibid., quoting Ps 34:15.
40. Ibid., quoting Is 53:7. The other texts that Aquinas quotes here are Ps 37:14 and Jer 11:19.
41. Ibid.
42. *Super Psalmos*, Ps. 37, no. 402, quoting Ps 37:14.
43. Ibid.
44. Ibid.
45. Ibid.

Isaiah 53:7: "'He shall be led as a sheep to the slaughter.'"[46] Aquinas argues that the just behavior of the afflicted man, as depicted in Psalm 37:14, is fulfilled to a supereminent degree by Christ in his passion, as testified to by Isaiah 53:7. As his enemies afflicted him and led him to death, Christ acted like one who was deaf and mute. In his soul, he did not dwell upon the evils that were enacted against him, and with his words, he did not lash out against the perpetrators of those evils.

Our tenth case of Isaiah 53 is in Aquinas's lecture on Psalm 38. In Psalm 38:9–10 the Psalmist laments that he has become "'a reproach to the fool,'" for he was "'dumb, and I opened not my mouth.'"[47] Just as he did with Psalm 37:14, so too here Aquinas interprets this verse as a reference to the patience of the Psalmist. He explains: "It is a sign of patience that a man does not render evil for evil when words of rebuke are brought against him."[48] In particular, this passage from the Psalm speaks of "continuing patience," as opposed to the patience of someone who may "remain silent for an hour, [but] afterward he sometimes becomes impatient and begins to speak a lot."[49] In order to illustrate such continuing patience, Aquinas quotes Isaiah 53:7, saying: "'He shall be led as a sheep to the slaughter and shall be dumb as a lamb before its shearer, and he shall open not his mouth.'"[50] Both Psalm 38:10 and Isaiah 53:7 speak of one who was "dumb" (*obmutui* in Ps 38, *obmutescet* in Is 53) and who did not open his mouth (*et non aperui os meum* in Ps 38, *et non aperiet os suum* in Is 53). For Aquinas, the thematic connection between these two biblical passages is supported by their nearly identical Latin renderings. Both biblical texts can be applied to Christ, who in his patience never uttered "reproaches" against God or his neighbor even as the latter afflicted him.[51] Christ thus persevered in perfect patience throughout the trial of his passion.

The fourth and final case of Isaiah 53:7 and the eleventh total case

46. Ibid., quoting Is 53:7.
47. *Super Psalmos*, Ps. 38, no. 413, quoting Ps 38:9–10.
48. Ibid.
49. Ibid.
50. Ibid., quoting Is 53:7.
51. Ibid.

of Isaiah 53 in the *Super Psalmos* is found in the context of Aquinas's exegesis of Psalm 49:3, which states "'God shall come manifestly.'"[52] Aquinas takes this passage as an opportunity to reflect upon the differences between Christ's first and second comings. During his incarnate life on earth "God came hidden in human weakness," but "at the second coming he will be manifest."[53] Aquinas then offers a paraphrase of Isaiah 53:7 in order to illustrate how "in his first coming" Christ "showed meekness," for "'as a lamb before the shearer he was led.'"[54] During his incarnate life Christ exercised silence and patience as he was "judged" by his enemies and when he "bore with evil men."[55] Conversely, when he comes in glory Christ "shall speak" and "will cry out like one in labor."[56] Thus, just as he did with his three earlier references to Isaiah 53:7 in the *Super Psalmos*, here Aquinas interprets this biblical text as a reference to the virtuous and patient silence of Christ in the face of his enemies. Like a lamb who does not object as he is led before his shearer, so too Christ does not defend himself or lash out when his enemies lash out against him.

The twelfth and last case of Isaiah 53 in the *Super Psalmos* is in Aquinas's lecture on Psalm 16. Aquinas interprets this Psalm as "a prayer in which he [David] asks to be heard for the sake of justice."[57] The Psalmist begins his prayer by begging God to hear and answer him, and he does so by assuring God that he prays "'not from deceitful [*dolosis*] lips' but from straightforward ones."[58] Following this interpretation Aquinas quotes Isaiah 53:9, which states: "'There was no deceit [*dolus*] in his mouth.'"[59] Aquinas then proceeds to identify two ways of being "deceitful," namely, with one's words and with one's actions.[60] The latter form of deceit occurs when one's actions are inconsistent with one's words. Aquinas concludes his engagement with Psalm 16:1 by quoting a "gloss" which states: "deceitful

---

52. *Super Psalmos*, Ps. 49, no. 491, quoting Ps 49:3.

53. Ibid.

54. Ibid., paraphrasing Is 53:7. Author's translation of "'tamquam agnus coram tondente ductus est.'"

55. Ibid.

56. Ibid.

57. *Super Psalmos*, Ps. 16, no. 115.

58. Ibid., quoting Ps 16:1.

59. Ibid., paraphrasing Is 53:9. Author's translation of "'dolus non fuit in ore ejus.'"

60. Ibid.

lips are those that say, 'Lord, Lord,' and do not do the will of my Father.'"[61] By citing Isaiah 53:9 in the context of this analysis of the nature of deceit, Aquinas sheds light on the integrity of Christ. Christ never speaks falsehoods, only truths. Further, his actions are always consistent with his words and prayers. Christ not only prays to and praises the Father, but he also actively does the will of the Father. For these reasons, Christ's prayers surpass all other human prayers in terms of their worthiness to be heard by the Father.

CONCLUSION AND SYNTHESIS

In the *Super Psalmos*, Aquinas turns to Isaiah 53:1 ("who has believed our report?") in order to indicate that the entirety of Isaiah 53 is an example of a prophecy that testifies to the Christian faith that has been proclaimed by the apostles. Hence, the divine report that is contained in Isaiah 53 can and should generate Christian faith in those who read it and hear it. Yet, despite the clear Christological teaching of Isaiah 53, Aquinas says that Isaiah 53:2–3 indicates that many would reject and despise Christ during his agony. The pain that Christ's enemies inflicted upon him veiled his divine glory from the eyes of many of his contemporaries. Through Christ, God was calling sinners to himself, and yet the suffering of the incarnate Son prevented some people from accurately hearing and faithfully embracing the beauty of Christ's divine call to them. Nonetheless, Christ revealed his supreme glory and beauty in a dramatic and unsurpassed way through his resurrection from the dead and pouring forth of the Holy Spirit at Pentecost. By his conquest of death and giving of the Spirit, Christ diffused the beauty of his truth and love throughout the world for all to see.

Aquinas reads Isaiah 53:6 ("Every one has turned aside into his own way") as a description of the universal fall of humanity away from faith and charity and into unbelief and sin. Sinners suffer death as a punishment for their sins, but Christ did not experience death due to any sin of his own, for he was completely without sin. Rather, Christ was violently killed by sinners who sought to rid his name

61. Ibid.

from the earth, and so for this reason he was crucified and "reputed with the wicked" (Is 53:12). Yet Christ himself freely chose to endure this suffering in order to save humanity from their wickedness. Christ, whose flesh was the very tabernacle of God upon earth, bore "our infirmities and carried our sorrows" (Is 53:4) in order to bring humanity back to the way of faith and charity. He assumed a passible human nature and was crucified with the wicked under the burning sun in order to lead the wicked into the light of glory.

Aquinas consistently interprets Isaiah 53:7 ("He shall be led as a sheep to the slaughter," etc.) as a revelation of the virtuous manner in which Christ treated his enemies. Throughout his passion, Christ acted like a deaf and mute person. He refused to pay attention to the insults and slanders that were uttered against him. He refused to verbally lash out at his enemies or even simply argue in his own defense. At no point did he utter a reproach toward God or his neighbors. Similarly, Aquinas reads Isaiah 53:9 ("There was no deceit in his mouth") as a testimony to the moral integrity of Christ. Christ spoke only the truth and never falsehoods. Further, he acted in accord with the truth that he spoke, and he not only prayed to the Father but also actively carried out the will of the Father for him. Thus, even amidst his passion, Christ's words and actions toward his neighbors and toward God were completely free of all deceit. Consequently, the prayers of Christ are of greater merit than all other human prayers.

Conclusion

Synthesizing Aquinas's Christological
Exegesis of Isaiah 53

This book has provided a quantitative and qualitative analysis of every reference to the text of Isaiah 53 that Aquinas made throughout the course of his career in his major theological works. This analysis included Aquinas's lecture on Isaiah 53 in the *Super Isaiam* as well as the 115 additional references to Isaiah 53 that he made in his biblical commentaries, *SS*, and *ST*. Having completed this direct investigation of the number, place, and function of Isaiah 53 in Aquinas's works, we can now synthesize our findings.

In this concluding chapter I do two things. First, I provide a quantitative synthesis that identifies how often and where Aquinas quoted each particular part of the twelve verses in Isaiah 53. This quantitative synthesis enables us to see which verses and subsections of Isaiah 53 featured most prominently in Aquinas's works. Second, I present a synthetic exposition of the major Christological points that Aquinas drew out from the text of Isaiah 53 throughout his major theological works.

QUANTITATIVE SYNTHESIS

In order to more precisely identify how many times and when Aquinas quoted particular passages from Isaiah 53, I have divided each verse of his version of Isaiah 53 into 'a' and 'b' sections, as follows:

TABLE 10-1. SUBSECTIONS OF ISAIAH 53:1–12

53:1: [a] Who has believed our report? [b] and to whom is the arm of the Lord revealed?
53:2: [a] And he shall rise up as a tender plant before him, and as a root out of a thirsty ground: [b] there is no form in him, nor comeliness: and we have seen him, and there was no sightliness, that we should be desirous of him:
53:3: [a] Despised, and the most abject of men, a man of sorrows, and acquainted with infirmity: [b] and his look was as it were hidden and despised, whereupon we esteemed him not.
53:4: [a] Truly he has borne our infirmities and carried our sorrows: [b] and we have thought him as it were a leper, and as one struck by God and afflicted.
53:5: [a] But he was wounded for our iniquities, he was bruised for our sins: [b] the chastisement of our peace was upon him, and by his bruises we are healed.
53:6: [a] All we like sheep have gone astray, every one has turned aside into his own way: [b] and the Lord has laid on him the iniquity of us all.
53:7: [a] He was offered because he himself willed it, [b] and he opened not his mouth: he shall be led as a sheep to the slaughter, and shall be dumb as a lamb before his shearer, and he shall not open his mouth.
53:8: [a] He was taken away from distress, and from judgment: who shall declare his generation? [b] because he is cut off out of the land of the living: for the wickedness of my people have I struck him.
53:9: [a] And he shall give the ungodly for his burial, and the rich for his death: [b] because he has done no iniquity, neither was there deceit in his mouth.
53:10: [a] And the Lord was pleased to bruise him in infirmity: [b] if he shall lay down his life for sin, he shall see a long-lived seed, and the will of the Lord shall be directed in his hand.
53:11: [a] Because his soul has labored, he shall see and be filled: [b] by his knowledge shall this my just servant justify many, and he shall bear their iniquities.
53:12: [a] Therefore will I distribute to him very many, and he shall divide the spoils of the strong, because he has delivered his soul unto death, and was reputed with the wicked: [b] and he has borne the sins of many, and has prayed for the transgressors.[1]

1. This version of Is 53:1–12, along with all references to this text throughout the remainder of this chapter, is the Aquinas Institute's English translation of Thomas's Latin version of Is 53. The one exception is Is 53:7a, which is my own translation of "oblatus est quia ipse voluit."

Presupposing the above subdivisions of each verse of Isaiah 53, the table on the following pages details how many times and in what works Aquinas quoted each of those subdivisions.

The table below enables us to make several significant observations regarding the number and place of Aquinas's references to Isaiah 53 throughout the course of his life. The far-left column lists each subsection of each of the twelve verses of Isaiah 53. It also contains a row for generic ("gen") references to Isaiah 53 and a row for

TABLE 10-2. CASES OF SPECIFIC PARTS OF ISAIAH 53:1–12 IN AQUINAS'S MAJOR THEOLOGICAL WORKS

Is 53	Is	Jer	Lm	SS	Mt	Jn	Rom	1 Cor	2 Cor	Gal	Eph	2 Thes	2 Tm	Heb	ST	Pss	TOTAL
General				x1											x1	x1	3
v. 1						x2		x1			x1	x1			x1	x1	7
v. 2a																	0
v. 2b																x1	1
vv. 2–3	x1 2b/3a			x1 2b/3b	x1 2b/3a			X1 2b/3a								x1 2b/3b	X2 2b/3b; 2b/3a	7
v. 3a					x1										x1		2
v. 3b						x1									x1		2
v. 4a		x1		x2	x2	x1				x1					x7	x1	15
v. 4b					x2												2
v. 5a			x1		x1									x1	x1		4
v. 5b																	0
v. 6a															x1	x1	2
v. 6b	x1			x1											x1		3
v. 7a				x1	x5	x5		x1			x1			x1	x6		20
v. 7b	x2	x1			x7	x3	x1	x1						x1		x4	20
v. 8a					x2	x2								x1	x2		7
v. 8b		x1		x1	x1			x1									4
v. 9a								x1							x1		2
v. 9b																x1	1
v. 10a															x1		1
v. 10b																	0
v. 11																	0
v. 12a	x1				x1	x2			x1		x2		x1		x2		10
v. 12b					x1									x1			2
TOTAL	5	3	1	7	24	15	2	6	1	1	4	1	1	5	27	12	115

references which combine words and phrases from both v. 2 and v. 3. The bottom row of the table specifies the total number of cases of Isaiah 53 in each of Aquinas's works. This row shows that the overwhelming majority of Aquinas's references to Isaiah 53 in his biblical commentaries and major systematic works came during the final four years of his life. Beginning with the *Super Matthaeum* (ca. 1269) and concluding with the *Super Psalmos* (1273), Aquinas made ninety-nine explicit references to Isaiah 53. Of those, sixty-six total references are contained in his two Gospel commentaries and in the *Summa*.

Hence, Aquinas turned to the text of Isaiah 53 most frequently toward the end of his life when he was commenting upon the New Testament and when he was setting forth his mature, systematic account of Christ's suffering in the *Tertia Pars* of the *ST*. This makes sense when one thinks, as Aquinas did, that the content of Isaiah 53 is inherently Christological. A Christological reading of Isaiah 53 renders that text conducive to the interpretation of New Testament references to Christ's suffering and death as well as to a systematic exposition of the causes, nature, and purpose of Christ's suffering. Yet it is also worth noting that the *Super Psalmos* contains twelve cases of Isaiah 53. This is despite the fact that Aquinas only commented upon about one-third of the Book of Psalms. Hence, it may also have simply been the case that in his later years Aquinas was more conscious and appreciative of the text of Isaiah 53 than he had been throughout the majority of his scholarly life, or perhaps it is because he also viewed the Psalms as being full of Christological content. In any event, from a purely numerical standpoint, the overwhelming majority of Aquinas's references to Isaiah 53 in our sample of his writings occurs in works produced near the end of his life.

In terms of specific verses of Isaiah 53, Aquinas quoted v. 7 far more than any other verse. He referenced v. 7 a total of forty times; twenty of those references were to v. 7a, which depicts the Servant's free decision to undergo suffering and death. The other twenty referred to v. 7b, which depicts the Servant as a peaceful and silent lamb. Aquinas quoted each subsection of v. 7 more than he quoted any other part (subsection or complete verse) of Isaiah 53. The closest competitor was v. 4a, which Aquinas quoted fifteen times. These three texts (7a, 7b, and 4a) thus comprise nearly half of Aquinas's total number of references to Isaiah 53. Aquinas used these three texts in order to emphasize the reality of Christ's pain and suffering (v. 4a), the divine and human freedom with which he endured that suffering (v. 7a), and the patient, passive, and gentle manner with which he suffered (v. 7b).

Aquinas's fourth most quoted portion of Isaiah 53 is v. 12a. He quoted this text ten times, and most of those cases refer to Christ's death among the wicked. Aquinas also uses this text, like Isaiah 53:7a, in order to describe how Christ freely hands himself over to death. He interprets 53:12a as a witness to the errant and unjust condemnation of Christ and Christ's consequent solidarity with those who are persecuted. Isaiah 53:8a is Aquinas's fifth most cited portion of Isaiah 53. All seven of his quotations from this text concern the "generation" of the Suffering Servant. The remaining number of Aquinas's references to complete verses or subsections of verses in Isaiah 53 are spread out fairly evenly. The only verse that does not receive any mention at all is v. 11. Similarly, there are no individual cases of vv. 2a, 5b, or 10b. Consequently, in our sample of Aquinas's works, his only engagement with vv. 11, 2a, 5b, and 10b are in his lecture on Isaiah 53 in the *Super Isaiam*.

Aquinas rarely quoted those portions of Isaiah 53 that seem to depict God as actively inflicting pain upon the Servant. Apart from his lecture on Isaiah 53 in the *Super Isaiam*, he only referenced Isaiah 53:6b ("the Lord has laid on him the iniquity of us all") three times. While he quotes v. 8b four times, only three of those references are to that portion of 8b that states "for the wickedness of my people have I struck him." Aquinas quotes v. 10a ("And the Lord was pleased to bruise him in infirmity") only one time. Hence, while many contemporary readers may find these passages of Isaiah 53 to be dramatic, challenging, and consequently worthy of sustained attention, Aquinas himself only very rarely turned to them. Further, as I will detail in the qualitative section below, his readings of these challenging verses are not straightforward. Rather, he interprets these passages as testifying to a highly nuanced account of the relationship between God's will and Christ's suffering.

Having established these quantitative and historical observations regarding the number and place of Aquinas's references to Isaiah 53, we can now proceed to a qualitative synthesis of his engagement with this biblical text.

QUALITATIVE SYNTHESIS:
AQUINAS'S CHRISTOLOGICAL
READING OF ISAIAH 53

In this section I provide a synthetic exposition of Aquinas's theological exegesis of Isaiah 53. I detail how Aquinas interprets Isaiah 53 as a prophecy of the incarnation and paschal mystery of Christ. I explicate the various Christological and soteriological points that Aquinas draws out from the text of Isaiah 53 in his 115 references to that text as well as in his lecture on Isaiah 53 in the *Super Isaiam.*

In his first scholarly work of theology, the *Super Isaiam,* Aquinas identified Christ as the primary referent of Isaiah 53. He states this in the preface, following Jerome, and he is faithful to this initial interpretation throughout the remainder of his scholarly career. In his lecture on and references to Isaiah 53 in the *Super Isaiam,* as well as in all of his ensuing biblical commentaries and systematic works, Aquinas consistently and exclusively identifies the Suffering Servant of Isaiah 53 as Christ. This is the fundamental characteristic of Aquinas's reading of Isaiah 53. The *verba* of Isaiah 53 focus upon only one *res,* Christ. No other historical figure is the referent of this Suffering Servant text. Despite being generally open to the possibility of a pluriform literal sense of scripture, Aquinas identifies no such pluriform meaning regarding the identity of the Suffering Servant in Isaiah 53. While numerous passages of scripture, such as the Psalms, possess a Christological spiritual sense, Isaiah 53 does not refer to Christ in this secondary way. Rather, the literal sense of Isaiah 53 is about Christ, and Christ only. Christ is the first and exclusive *res* that God willed the *verba* to signify.

The *Super Ioannem* is the only place where Aquinas appeals to external evidence outside of the text of Isaiah 53 in order to support his claim that Christ is the literal sense of that passage. Commenting on John 12:37–41, Aquinas observes that the evangelist quotes Isaiah 53:1 ("Lord, who has believed our report? and to whom has the arm of the Lord been revealed?") as a prophecy of the fact that many would not believe in Christ. Aquinas then focuses upon the evangelist's claim in John 12:41: "These things said Isaias, when he saw his glory, and spoke of him." For Aquinas, these words show that no less an authority than John the evangelist is claiming that Isaiah himself had seen Christ. That is, Isaiah could predict that many would not believe in Christ precisely because he had received a divine revelation about the future incarnation and paschal mystery of Christ. In Isaiah 53:1–12, Isaiah wrote down the content of that Christological revelation that he had received. So, both God and Isaiah intended the *verba* of Isaiah 53 to refer to the *res* that is Christ. In sum, Aquinas is confident that the literal sense of Isaiah 53 is about Christ not only because of the nature of that text itself and the authority of Jerome, but also because the fourth Gospel claims that Isaiah saw and wrote about Christ. Hence, Aquinas's reading of Isaiah 53 is informed in a fundamental way by his reading of John 12.

Given that the literal sense of Isaiah 53 is about Christ, Aquinas thinks that this biblical text can lead readers to the Christian faith. In the *Super Ioannem,* Aquinas says that even the contemporaries of Jesus who refused to believe in him still knew that Isaiah 53 was an explicit prophecy about the death of the Messiah. Given that this is clearly about the Messiah, and given that its descriptions of the Messiah's humiliation and exaltation correspond precisely to Christ's passion and resurrection, those who read Isaiah 53 should be led by it to explicit faith in Jesus as the Christ. Aquinas states this firmly in the *ST,* and in the *Super Psalmos* he equates the evangelical force of Isaiah 53 to that of the Gospels. That is, those who read the *verba* of Isaiah 53, like those who read the Gospels, should come to believe in and contemplate the historical and divine *res* that is the paschal mystery of Christ.

In the *Super Isaiam,* Aquinas provided a detailed *divisio textus* of Isaiah 53:1–12. He claimed that the primary theme of this biblical passage is the passion of Christ. But the text also speaks of the exaltation that Christ will experience as a result of his passion. The text can be divided into four major parts. The first part (v. 1) establishes that the Christological content which will unfold throughout the remainder of the chapter is a great mystery that will be difficult for many to believe. The second part (v. 2a) is a similitude of the exaltation that Christ will receive. The third part (vv. 2b–7) focuses upon what Aquinas calls Christ's "humiliation," that is, his passion. The fourth part (vv. 8–12) centers upon the exaltation of Christ and the saving fruits of his passion. Within these four major parts, Aquinas identifies various subdivisions which detail the passion and exaltation of Christ in their own ways. For our purposes, perhaps the most significant aspect of Aquinas's *divisio* of Isaiah 53 is that it shows once again how committed he is to a Christological exegesis of this passage. Every major and minor part of Isaiah 53 is about the passion and exaltation of Christ.

Having established these fundamental aspects of Aquinas's interpretation of Isaiah 53, I can now explicate the speculative theological insights that Aquinas draws out from the various verses of this biblical passage. Isaiah's text contains numerous Christological themes.

The first theme involves the origin and identity of Christ. Aquinas consistently interprets Isaiah 53:8a ("who shall declare his generation?") as a reference to the eternal, incomprehensible generation of the Son from the Father. Isaiah's words indicate that many will not believe in the divine filiation of Christ. The Suffering Servant is the son of David in time and yet, from all eternity, he is the only begotten and consubstantial Son of the Father. Even those who do believe in this sublime mystery will never be able to fully understand it or perfectly express it. At times Aquinas also claims that Isaiah's words regarding the mysterious generation of the Son can also apply to Christ's miraculous conception within the womb of the virgin Mary. Christ's generation from Mary is a miraculous mystery in its own right. Many do not believe in it, and even those who do cannot fully comprehend it. Just as he was born from a Father alone in eternity, so now in time Christ is born of a mother alone. He has no human father, just as he had no divine mother. Yet as Son of God and Son of Mary, Christ is fully God and fully human. The dual natures of Christ enable him to act as the "arm of the Lord" (Is 53:1b). Christ is the instrument through which the Father accomplishes his saving work on behalf of the world.

The second theme is the reality, nature, and origin of Christ's suffering. Christ was "a man of sorrows [*dolores*], and acquainted with infirmity" (Is 53:3a). "Truly," Isaiah says, "he has borne our illnesses and carried our sorrows [*dolores*]" (Is 53:4a). Aquinas interprets these words of Isaiah in an anti-Docetic fashion. They are biblical proof that Christ "truly" (*vere*) experienced suffering, and Christ's suffering was proof of his real humanity. Christ's body could be harmed and his soul could feel sensible and internal pain. In the *Super Isaiam*, the *SS*, and the *ST* Aquinas repeatedly calls the harm and pain that Christ experienced a "punishment" (*poena*). Christ bore these *poena* in union with all of the descendants of Adam. That is, Christ experienced *poena* of body and soul because he possessed a real, passible human nature in solidarity with all of the children of Adam. Christ endured the *poena* of infirmity that all those who live in a postlapsarian world must bear: hunger, thirst, weariness, bodily pain, sorrow, fear, and death. In his passion, especially, Christ's body was "wounded" (*vulneratus*) and "bruised" (*attritus*) (Is 53:5a). For Aquinas, the scarlet cloak which the soldiers draped upon Jesus (Mt 27:28) reflects the scarlet, wounded, and bruised body of the suffering Lord.

Depending upon the context, Aquinas interprets the Servant's *dolores* (Is 53:3a, 4a) as either 'pain' or 'sorrow.' Yet the two interpretations are not mutually exclusive. For sorrow is simply a particular type of pain. Christ's human soul felt sensible pain when his body was harmed and when he experienced corporeal passions such as hunger. But his soul also felt purely internal pain, which Aquinas calls sorrow or sadness (*tristitia*). For instance, in Gethsemane Christ experienced the emotional pain of sorrow and fear at the prospect of his impending arrest, physical torture, and death. As a true man, Christ's sensitive appetite was naturally and properly saddened and repulsed at the prospect of the various forms of sensible pain and social rejection that his passion would involve. This is the case even though, as Isaiah 53:7a and 53:12a indicate, Christ freely chose with his rational will to endure the passion.

And, for Aquinas, Christ did not only experience sadness at the thought of his own impending sensible pains and bodily death. Further, Aquinas reads Isaiah 53:4a ("truly he has … carried our sorrows") as indicating that Christ grieved with the internal pain of sorrow in response to the sins of humanity. And the pain of Christ's sorrow was unsurpassed because, as Isaiah 53:4a states, Christ bore the pain of *our* sorrows. That is, all at once he recognized and grieved over every sin that ever had been and ever would be committed by humanity. In this sense, Christ was the ultimate penitent; his unsurpassed contrition, born of infinite wisdom and charity, was a pleasing sacrifice of repentance that he offered to the Father in satisfaction for all of the sins of humanity. Further, while he does not explicitly link this claim to the text of Isaiah 53:4a, in *ST* III, q. 46, a. 6, Aquinas claims that Christ's soul "apprehended most vehemently all the causes of sadness." Hence, Christ not only bore our sorrow over sin (moral evil) itself, but he also bore *all* the sadness that we experience as a result of the various consequences of sin: the sadness that is caused by loneliness, failure, ignorance, loss of loved ones, poverty, fear, physical and mental handicaps, injustice and oppression, and the prospect of death, to name but a few. Christ grieved with all those who experience the internal pain of sadness in the face of the reality of sin and its moral, social, physical, and eternal consequences.

The third Christological theme that Aquinas draws from Isaiah 53 concerns the unjust rejection and persecution of Christ. Christ was "despised, and the most abject of men" (Is 53:3a). He was "reputed with the wicked" (Is 53:12a). Aquinas interprets these passages as prophecies of the fact that Christ's enemies would errantly condemn him as a grave criminal. Members of the Roman and Jewish powers in Jerusalem unjustly identified Christ as an evildoer who needed to be removed from society. They handed over Christ to abuse and death. Christ's violent punishment alongside violent criminals shrouded his divine and Messianic identity from the eyes of many. In his passion, Christ's glory "was as it were hidden and despised, whereupon we esteemed him not" (53:3b). As he hung upon the cross, there was "no form in him, nor comeliness: and we have seen him, and there was no sightliness, that we should be desirous of him" (Is 53:2b). Consequently, many of Christ's peers "thought him as it were a leper, and as one struck by God and afflicted" (Is 53:4b). Aquinas does not interpret Isaiah 53:2b–3 and 4b as statements regarding any natural spiritual or physical deformity or imperfection of Christ. Rather, all of these verses concern the fact of Christ's unjust punishment upon the cross and the consequent scandal that this punishment caused. Christ, true God and true man, the exemplar of all virtue, was treated as a criminal and as one who has been rejected by God. In this way, Isaiah 53 testifies to Christ's solidarity with all those who suffer injustice at the hands of men, and in particular to Christ's solidarity with those who are persecuted for their obedience and witness to God. Christ is the ultimate martyr. Further, Isaiah 53 testifies to a great mystery: Christ's passion, despite its salvific value, was a stumbling block to many of his peers. The passion caused many to turn away in revulsion from the face of God incarnate.

Aquinas's fourth theme is that Christ endured the agony and injustice of his passion like a perfectly innocent and peaceful lamb. Christ was put to death despite the fact that he had "done no iniquity, neither was there deceit in his mouth" (Is 53:9b). Apart from the lecture on Isaiah 53 in the *Super Isaiam*, the *Super Psalmos* is the only place where Aquinas quotes Isaiah 53:9b. There, he interprets this text as indicating the perfect moral integrity of Christ. Christ exclusively spoke the truth, and he always acted in accord with the truth. He obeyed and carried out the will of the Father in every circumstance. The perfect moral virtue with which Christ endured the cross is an example to all Christians to remain steadfast in faith and righteousness even during the agony of life in the world. Aquinas interprets Isaiah 53 as testifying in a particularly clear way to the virtuous manner in which Christ treated his enemies amidst his passion. Christ "prayed for the transgressors" (Is 53:12b), saying "Father, forgive them, for they know not what they do" (Lk 23:34). Christ's prayer for those who crucified him manifests the breadth of his love, for he wills the good for both his friends and his enemies.

Christ's love for sinners is the reason why he "opened not his mouth" and was "led as a sheep to the slaughter" (Is 53:7b). As he was arrested, tried, forced to carry his cross, and crucified, Christ was "dumb as a lamb before his shearer" (Is 53:7b). As indicated in the above quantitative analysis, Aquinas quotes these words of Isaiah 53:7b as much as any other text from Isaiah 53. He consistently interprets this verse as referring to Christ's patience, benevolence, and gentleness amidst his passion. Christ never uttered or did evil toward his enemies even as they persecuted him. He did not seek revenge but rather turned the other cheek. He remained verbally and physically passive throughout his suffering. While at times he answered the questions of those who interrogated him, for the most part he acted like a silent and deaf man amidst his persecution. He did not offer lengthy, passionate, and detailed defenses of his innocence. Rather, Christ focused upon simply enduring his suffering with righteousness. Aquinas says that Christ exercised this passive, patient, and gentle silence out of love for his enemies, in order to bring about their conversion and correction. Aquinas thus points to Isaiah 53:7b, 9b, and 12b as examples for those who are undergoing persecution and assault. Like Christ, Christians must love even their enemies. They must strive to counter verbal and physical violence with consistent patience, prayer, and gentleness.

The fifth Christological theme involves the relationship between the will of God, the will of Christ, and the passion. Isaiah 53:8b states: "for the wickedness of my people have I struck him." As early as the *Super Isaiam*, Aquinas interprets this text as indicating that God merely allowed (*permisi*) Christ's enemies to harm him. God did not actively will that Christ would be rejected and put to death. Likewise, in the *Super Matthaeum* Aquinas adds that both the Father and the Son, as God, chose to permit Christ's enemies to harm him. In the *Super Ioannem*, Aquinas specifies that Christ, as God, had the ontological power to actively prevent his enemies from harming him. Yet he freely chose as God and man to endure the harm that would be inflicted upon him. This is the meaning of Isaiah 53:7a: "He was offered because he himself willed it." Christ did not actively seek to be betrayed, arrested, and put to death. He did not command or counsel these actions. But he did freely permit them and endure them.

Isaiah 53:10a states, "and the Lord was pleased [*voluit*] to bruise him in infirmity." This text could be interpreted as implying that God actively wills and delights in the pain of Christ in and of itself. Yet Aquinas does not read it in this way. Rather, in the *Super Isaiam*, Aquinas interprets this text as signifying merely the Father's command to Christ to endure the passion and Christ's consequent, free obedience to that command. Aquinas supports this interpretation by linking Isaiah 53:10a to the text of Philippians 2:8, which states that Christ was "obedient unto death, even death on a cross." For Aquinas, both Isaiah 53:10a and Philippians 2:8 show that Christ's passion was pleasing to God and thus meritorious precisely because Christ endured it out of obedience. Yet this does not mean that the Father actively willed for Christ to be rejected, persecuted and put to death by his enemies. In fact, the Father merely permitted Christ's enemies to afflict him with harm and pain. But given that Christ was in fact rejected and attacked by some of his contemporaries, the Father consequently did actively will for Christ as a man to endure that rejection and violence. That is, the Father commanded Christ to abstain from using his divine power to escape the hands of his enemies, and he was "pleased" (*voluit*) by Christ's free choice to obey that command, as well as by Christ's free choices to obey God in all things even throughout the pain of his passion.

Aquinas uses Isaiah 53:10a and 53:7a in a similar way in *ST* III, q. 47, a. 3. There he says that God "was pleased [*voluit*] to bruise" (Is 53:10a) Christ simply in the sense that he eternally preordained for Christ to endure the passion for the salvation of sinners. God eternally willed to command Christ to endure the pain that would be inflicted upon him by his enemies. God also eternally planned to abstain from actively intervening to save Christ from his enemies. In addition, by the charity that Christ had from the Father and for the Father, he freely chose as a man to obey the Father's command to endure the violence of the passion. This is what it means to say that Christ "was offered because he himself willed it" (Is 53:7a).

Further, Aquinas frequently turns to the text of Isaiah 53:7a in order to emphasize the intentional manner with which Christ approached his passion. Christ knew that he had enemies who sought to kill him, and yet he did not try to avoid their attacks. He freely exposed himself to the threat of death by engaging in preaching and works which he knew would elicit the ire of some of his contemporaries. Further, unlike the paschal lambs who were led in ignorance to the Jerusalem Temple to be slaughtered, Christ is the paschal lamb who knew what awaited him in Jerusalem and yet who chose to go there anyway. On the night he was betrayed, he knew that Judas and members of the Sanhedrin plotted against him. Yet he did not seek to flee from Jerusalem. Rather, he "took" the bread and "broke it" (1 Cor 11:23, Mt 26:26) as a sign of his intention to hand his body over to be broken upon the cross. In Gethsemane, Christ had the power to repel the soldiers with merely his words, and yet he permitted them to seize him (Jn 18:6). In all of these ways, says Aquinas, Christ "was offered because he himself willed it" (Is 53:7a).

Aquinas even insists that Christ, as he hung upon the cross, had the power to freely determine the exact moment in which he would die. This does not mean that he actively brought about his death through commission or omission. But it does mean that he had the ontological power to deter the violent effects of the attacks that were levelled against him. Just as in Gethsemane Christ had the divine power to repel the soldiers, so too upon the cross he had the power to prolong his bodily life indefinitely. Mere humans, obviously, do not have this power. Consequently, when Christ did die, he did so only because he freely allowed himself to die. He freely permitted his soul to depart from his body. This is what it means to say that he "has delivered his soul unto death" (Is 53:12a). No one took Christ's life from him apart from his permission. He laid down his life of his own accord (Jn 10:18).

The sixth Christological theme that Aquinas derives from Isaiah 53 is that human sin was the reason for Christ's passion. This means two things. First, Christ's suffering and death were not a punishment for his own sins. He was sinless. Hence, he "was wounded *for our* iniquities" and "was bruised *for our* sins" (Is 53:5, emphasis added). This means that the sins of humanity were the fundamental cause of Christ's passion. He suffered and died as a result of "the wickedness of my people" (Is 53:8b). Second, Christ underwent the passion precisely in order to save humanity from their sins. "By his bruises we are healed" (Is 53:5b). Christ suffered and died as a means of saving sinners. This is the sense in which Christ "has borne the sins of many" (Is 53:12b). He "has borne our infirmities and carried our sorrows" (Is 53:4a) in the sense that he took away our sins and maladies, and he did so precisely by sharing in our pain and sorrow.

How did Christ's passion take away human sin? For Aquinas,

Isaiah 53 depicts the cross as a salvific act of satisfaction, merit, and priestly sacrifice. All of humanity is infected with sin, for "all we like sheep have gone astray" (Is 53:6a). Humanity needs to perform a work of satisfaction that will heal them of their sinfulness and repair the various damages caused by their sins. Christ's passion is that work of satisfaction. "The Lord has laid on him the iniquity of us all" (Is 53:6b). This passage signifies that Christ has taken upon himself the burdensome and painful task of offering satisfaction for the sins of the human race. Christ has "borne the sins of many" (Is 53:12b) in the sense that he undertook the harrowing task of repairing the damages caused by human sin and giving to God something more pleasing than all of human sin is displeasing.

In the *SS* and the *Tertia Pars* of the *ST*, Aquinas frequently draws upon Isaiah 53 in order to explain how Christ's passion satisfies for human sin. The passion of Christ was objectively sufficient to satisfy for the sins of the entire world precisely because of the charity and obedience with which Christ endured the cross. In his passion Christ "has borne our infirmities and carried our sorrows" (Is 53:4a) out of love for God and neighbor. His heroic acts of charity and obedience even amidst pain and death were infinitely pleasing to God and so they overshadowed the injustice of all human sin. Yet Christ's passion, understood merely as a historical event of the distant past, does not in and of itself liberate people from their sins or wipe away the numerous consequences of sin. Rather, sinners in every age, before and after Christ, must personally and actively participate in the objective satisfaction that Christ enacted upon the cross. Sinners do this through the grace of faith, repentance, baptism, and the life of charity. By suffering with Christ and for Christ out of charity and obedience, sinners are conformed to Christ and so share in the satisfaction that he wrought upon the cross. According to Aquinas, Christ carried our sorrows in order to empower us to help him carry his cross.

Christ also saved sinners through merit. Christ merited from both his teaching ministry and his passion. As a teacher, Christ "labored" for the conversion of sinners, and consequently "he shall see" the gentiles brought to faith and thus "be filled" (Is 53:11a). And "by his knowledge," that is, his teaching, Christ merited grace which will "justify many" (Is 53:11b). Christ also merited for sinners by the way in which he endured the humiliation of his passion. As Isaiah 53:7a and 12a testify, Christ freely chose to suffer: "he was offered because he himself willed it" and "he has delivered his soul unto death." Christ freely endured the passion precisely out of love for sinners and loving obedience to God. Further, amidst his agony Christ exercised perfect patience, gentleness, and mercy toward his enemies, "like a lamb led to the slaughter" (Is 53:7b). Christ even "prayed for the transgressors" (Is 53:12b) who killed him. And the perfectly innocent, merciful lamb who freely chose to suffer out of love and obedience was also the eternal Son of God: "who shall declare his generation?" (Is 53:8a). So, the divine dignity of the one who suffered, and the freedom and love with which he suffered, made Christ's passion meritorious for sinners. As a result of Christ's passion sinners are reborn in grace and become "a long-lived seed" (Is 53:10b). Justified and sanctified sinners are the "spoils" (Is 53:12a) that Christ won by his passion, and God "distributes to him very many" of these reborn children of Eve. These spiritually regenerated sinners are empowered to do God's will through, with, and in Christ: "the will of the Lord shall be directed in his hand (Is 53:10b). And Christ entrusts the care of his newly acquired treasures to the Church: "he shall divide the spoils of the strong" (Is 53:12a).

Christ's passion was also a priestly sacrifice. Christ was not merely a sacrificial victim. He is also the priest who offered up the sacrificial victim. This is what it means to say that "he was offered because he himself willed it" (Is 53:7a). Christ "has delivered his soul unto death" (Is 53:12a), and thus he is simultaneously both priest and victim. As already indicated, this does not mean that Christ actively killed himself through commission or omission. Rather, it simply means that as God he freely assumed a passible human nature, and as man he freely chose out of love to obey the Father's command to endure the passion in that passible nature. As a man, Christ freely chose to abstain from using his power to escape the violence that was inflicted upon him. Further, Christ freely chose the passion insofar as he knowingly exposed himself to danger by accomplishing the works that he was sent to do: teaching, performing miracles, establishing a Church, and ultimately making his final journey to Jerusalem. In all of these ways, Christ freely offered himself to the Father as a perfect sacrifice of thanksgiving, supplication, and atonement on behalf of sinful humanity. And unlike all other priests, who have to offer sacrifices in atonement for their own sins as well as the people's, Christ the innocent lamb offered himself in sacrifice purely for the sins of others: "he was wounded for our iniquities, he was bruised for our sins" (Is 53:5a).

On the basis of Isaiah 53, Aquinas also includes Christ's burial among his saving works. Isaiah 53:9a states, "he shall give the ungodly for his burial, and the rich for his death." Aquinas only comments upon this passage three times. In the *Super Isaiam*, he interprets this text as referring to Christ's burial by ungodly people, namely, the Judean and Roman authorities who crucified him. In his commentary on 1 Corinthians, Aquinas simply quotes Isaiah 53:9a in support of Paul's statement that Christ "was buried" (1 Cor 15:4). Only in the *ST* does Aquinas comment on the saving significance of Christ's burial. There he appeals to a gloss and interprets Isaiah 53:9a in a different way than he had done in his two earlier references to this text. In the *ST* Aquinas says that Christ is the one who gives the ungodly, namely, the gentiles, to the Father as a result of his death and burial. That is, Christ's death and burial are the reason why he is able to justify the gentiles and present them in holiness to the Father.

Aquinas also turns to Isaiah 53 in order to explain the saving value of Christ's descent to the dead. Christ "has borne our infirmities and carried our sorrows" (Is 53:4a) even in the realm of the dead. Christ descended to the inferno of the just in order to proclaim the good news to them, yet in doing so he shared in their *poena*. Aquinas does not specify the exact nature of the *poena* that Christ endured in the underworld. Nonetheless, he states that Christ bore the *poena* of the righteous dead precisely in order to free them from that *poena*. Having shared in their *poena*, Christ then rose from the dead and gave the souls of the just a share in his own eternal life.

The seventh and final Christological theme that Aquinas draws out from Isaiah 53 is the personal exaltation and glorification of Christ following his passion. In Aquinas's *divisio textus* of Isaiah 53 in the *Super Isaiam*, he identifies the two major themes of Isaiah 53:1–12 as the humiliation and exaltation of Christ, respectively. And while Aquinas's theological exegesis of Isaiah 53 typically focuses upon the Servant's humiliation, he nonetheless also acknowledges that the Servant's humiliation was inseparably linked to his exaltation. The freedom and love with which Christ entered into and endured his passion not only merited grace for sinners. Even more fundamentally, Christ's obedient and merciful offering of self in the passion merited his own exaltation: "he was taken away from distress, and from judgment" (Is 53:8a). In the *Super Isaiam*, Aquinas says that these words of Isaiah 53:8a are about Christ's resurrection from the dead, which was the reward for his passion. And he interprets Isaiah's words alongside Philippians 2:9, which states "for which cause, God also has exalted him." Philippians 2:8–9 states that God raised Jesus from the dead due to his obedience unto death, even death on a cross. Hence, for Aquinas, the *verba* of Isaiah 53 and Philippians 2 refer to the same *res*, albeit from different historical vantage points: the Suffering Servant's story does not end in humiliation and death; rather, "because his soul has labored" in loving obedience and service even unto death, he merited to "see and be filled" (Is 53:11a) for all eternity. Precisely because he laid down his life for sinners, Christ was able to rise again and give sinners a share in his own risen, glorified life: "if he shall lay down his life for sin, he shall see a long-lived seed" (Is 53:10b). And so now, through grace, all those who share in the Servant's obedience, patience, and gentleness unto death will also share in his conquest of death.

CONCLUSION

This work shows that Aquinas's engagement with the text of Isaiah 53 increased significantly in the final four years of his life. The vast majority of his references to this text are contained in four theological works from those years, namely, the *Super Matthaeum, Super Ioannem, Summa Theologiae,* and *Super Psalmos.* For whatever reason, Aquinas thought it fitting to turn to the text of Isaiah 53 far more in these works than he had done in earlier, comparable works such as his commentaries on the epistles of Paul and his commentary on Peter Lombard's *Sentences*.

Yet Aquinas's interpretations of Isaiah 53 remained substantially consistent throughout the course of his life. Aquinas's cursory *Super Isaiam* was his first scholarly work of theology. His lecture on Isaiah 53, and five additional references to Isaiah 53 in that commentary, proved to be foundational for the ensuing 110 explicit references to that biblical text that he would make throughout the remainder of his life. It is true that at times in his later works the depth of Aquinas's theological engagement with Isaiah 53 increased dramatically in relation to the level of engagement that was present in the *Super Isaiam*. Most notably, in the *SS* and *ST*, Aquinas's theological exegesis of Isaiah 53 is far more sophisticated than it is in his earlier, cursory commentaries. A similar thing can be said regarding his reading of Isaiah 53 in the commentaries on Matthew and John. There he uses Isaiah 53 in the service of his thorough theological expositions of the mysteries of Christ's life and death. Yet despite the increased theological sophistication of Aquinas's engagement with Isaiah 53 in his later years, at no point does he offer a reading of Isaiah 53 that departs in any serious way from the initial interpretations that he provided in the *Super Isaiam*. Rather, Aquinas's numerous theological interpretations of Isaiah 53 in the *Super Isaiam* and in all of his ensuing works build upon and complement one another.

Aquinas consistently and exclusively interpreted Isaiah 53 as a prophecy of Christ. When he turned to this text in his biblical commentaries and systematic works, he typically did so in order to emphasize one of three Christological themes. Those themes are the voluntary nature of Christ's passion, the gentleness and patience with which Christ endured the passion, and the source and nature of Christ's various sufferings. These and all of the numerous Christological insights that Aquinas drew out from Isaiah 53 combine to produce a robust and compelling portrait of the nature and saving value of Christ's cross. While Aquinas's exegetical and systematic account of the cross is not reducible to his interpretations of Isaiah 53, nonetheless his engagement with Isaiah 53 in and of itself provides a speculatively rich and moving theology of Christ's passion.

Appendix

Cases of Isaiah 53 in the *Opuscula*

In addition to the 115 cases of Isaiah 53 that are found in Aquinas's biblical commentaries, *SS*, and the *ST*, Aquinas also makes six explicit references to the text of Isaiah 53 across five of his shorter theological works. These shorter works are typically referred to as the *Opuscula,* or "little" works.[1] In these relatively smaller theological works, Aquinas's six references to Isaiah 53 are brief and his interpretations mirror the type of interpretations that we have seen throughout this book. Hence, the purpose of this appendix is not to advance radically new conclusions regarding Aquinas's understanding of the meaning of Isaiah 53. Rather, my purpose here is simply to complete the exhaustive quantitative and qualitative analysis of Aquinas's reception of Isaiah 53 that this book sets out to accomplish. Consequently, in this appendix I will identify the place of these last six cases of Isaiah 53 in Aquinas's corpus and then briefly analyze the meaning of Aquinas's interpretations of Isaiah 53 in those places.

There are three cases of Isaiah 53 in Aquinas's sermons. The first and second cases are found in the sermon entitled *Veniet Desideratus.* The first case occurs in the context of a discussion regarding God's justice and mercy. Aquinas points out that justice required sinners to suffer the condemnation of death. Yet God, in his mercy, desires peace and reconciliation between sinners and himself. Hence, the

---

1. Torrell, *Saint Thomas Aquinas,* 144.

demands of both justice and mercy need to be fulfilled. This is accomplished, Aquinas explains, through Christ:

Thus the Lord has sent someone to settle: not a human being, not an angel, but God's Son, who satisfied [*satisfaceret*] through mercy so that it did not fall short of justice in anything. And so it happened that there was in the same [man] justice to the full and infinite mercy, and so *mercy and truth have met one another; justice and peace have kissed one another* (Ps 85:11). It was justice to the full in this respect, that he punished very harshly [*durissime punivit*], but infinite mercy because he bore the punishment in himself [*in se ipso poenam sustinuit*], as we read in Isaiah 53:4: "truly, our infirmities he took away himself and our pains he bore himself."[2]

In this passage Aquinas says that God both punished and was punished. Isaiah 53 shows that God, as Christ, endured the punishment of suffering and death, and yet he did so precisely out of mercy for sinners. For by becoming human and dying on the cross, Christ saved humanity from sin and its punishments. Aquinas expands upon this theme in the lines which immediately follow his reference to Isaiah 53. He says that Christ "came to battle against the devil, like a strong soldier"; he "came to take away the contamination of sin, like a doctor"; and finally, Christ "came to be in our company, like a friend."[3] As a soldier, doctor, and friend, Christ suffered in order to deliver sinners from their enemies and in order to heal them from their pains.

The second case of Isaiah 53 in *Veniet Desideratus* is used to highlight the desire of humanity to be saved from their sins. Describing the plight of sinful humanity, Aquinas remarks, "man was weak through an incurable wound, since it had corrupted the whole human nature."[4] Weighed down by their sinfulness and weakness, sinners "had a strong desire for the remedy of salvation. Isaiah 53:2 reads: 'We have seen him,' and it continues: 'we have desired him, a despised man, the last of men, a sorrowful man who knew

---

2. Thomas Aquinas, "*Veniet Desideratus*," in *The Academic Sermons*, trans. Mark-Robin Hoogland (Washington, D.C.: The Catholic University of America Press, 2010), 29–30. The Latin text cited is the 2014 Leonine edition, edited by the Aquinas Institute and available at aquinas.cc/la/en/~Veniet.S1-1. All references to Aquinas's sermons will include the title of the sermon and the page number from the English translation by Hoogland.

3. Aquinas, *Veniet Desideratus*, 30.

4. Ibid.

weakness.'"[5] In an effort to biblically ground the notion of sinful humanity's desire for salvation, Aquinas paraphrases and combines Isaiah 53:2–3. These passages are meant to show that sinful humanity, the sorrowful and despised man, desires salvation from the Lord.

The third case of Isaiah 53 in Aquinas's sermons occurs in the homily *Germinet Terra*. This sermon is about the birth of Mary, the mother of Christ. At the beginning of the sermon, Aquinas quotes Isaiah 53:8, saying: "Isaiah says about Christ: 'Who will tell of his generations?'"[6] He then explains, "The generation of Christ rests in a way on the generation of Mary—I speak here of Christ's generation in time."[7] Just as we saw in his major theological works, in this homily Aquinas interprets Isaiah 53:8 as a reference to the generation of Christ. Specifically, in this context Aquinas is referring to the generation of Christ's humanity in the womb of Mary.

The fourth case of Isaiah 53 is found in I.227 of the *Compendium of Theology*. In this chapter Aquinas sets out to explain "why Christ willed to die."[8] He says that Christ endured the passion in order to offer satisfaction for sins and to be an example of perfect charity, fortitude, obedience, and patience. He employs Isaiah 53 in regards to the patience of Christ, saying:

Further, he gave an example of patience, a virtue that prevents sorrow from overwhelming man in time of adversity; the greater the trials, the more splendidly does the virtue of patience shine forth in them. Therefore, an example of perfect patience is afforded in the greatest of evils, which is death, if it is borne without mental turbulence. Such tranquility the prophet foretold of Christ: "He shall be like a lamb that before its shearers is dumb, and shall not open his mouth" (Is 53:7).[9]

Isaiah 53 shows that Christ endured the greatest evil, death, without being overwhelmed by sorrow. Christ remained silent and passive as he was violently led to death, and in doing so he provided a supreme example of patience.

5. Ibid., 31.

6. Thomas Aquinas, "Germinet Terra," in *The Academic Sermons*, 259.

7. Aquinas, "Germinet Terra," 259.

8. Thomas Aquinas, *Compendium of Theology*, I.227. Here I cite the 1979 Leonine edition and the English translation by Cyril Vollert, both of which have been edited by the Aquinas Institute and are available at aquinas.cc/la/en/~CT.

9. Aquinas, *Compendium of Theology*, I.227.

The fifth case of Isaiah 53 is in Aquinas's treatment of the passion of Christ in his *De Articulis Fidei et Ecclesiae Sacramentis*. Commenting upon Christ's prediction of his passion in Matthew 20:18–19, Aquinas points out that the Manicheans errantly taught that Christ did not possess a real human body and nor did he really experience bodily death. Rather, his seeming humanity and death were mere fantasies. Aquinas points out that the Manicheans' teaching is "contrary to what is said in Isaiah 53:4, 'Truly he has borne our infirmities,' and 'he was led like a sheep to the slaughter,' which is also said in Acts 8:32."[10] Aquinas quotes Isaiah 53:4 and 53:7 (the latter by way of Acts 8) for the simple purpose of affirming that Christ really did suffer an authentic, bodily death, just like all other humans experience. Hence, the Manichean denial of the incarnation and passion is contrary to the teaching of both the Old and New Testaments.

Our sixth and final case of Isaiah 53 in Aquinas's theological *Opuscula* is found in the *Expositio in Symbolum Apostolorum*. Here Aquinas once again links Christ's passion with the virtue of patience. He says that "great patience is exemplified" when someone remains patient despite suffering "intensely."[11] He then specifies that Christ "suffered greatly upon the cross," and he did so "with all patience, because, 'when he suffered, he did not threaten' (1 Pt 2:23). And again: 'he shall be led as a sheep to the slaughter and shall be dumb before his shearer, and shall not open his mouth' (Is 53:7)."[12] Isaiah 53 depicts Christ's silence amidst his passion, and Aquinas points to this silence as a concrete example of what it looks like to endure intense suffering with great patience. And, given the additional fact that Christ freely chose to endure the passion when he could have avoided it "if he so wished," Aquinas concludes that the patience that Christ practiced upon the cross "was of the highest degree."[13]

---

10. Thomas Aquinas, *De Articulis Fidei et Ecclesiae Sacramentis* II, a. 2. I cite the 1979 Leonine edition that was edited by the Aquinas Institute and which is available at aquinas.cc/la/en/~DeArticuli.I.Pt1.A2.T. The translation is my own.

11. Thomas Aquinas, *Expositio in Symbolum Apostolorum*, a. 4. I cite the 1954 Taurini Latin edition and the 1939 translation by Joseph B. Collins, both of which were edited by the Aquinas Institute and are available at aquinas.cc/la/en/~Credo.

12. Aquinas, *Expositio in symbolum Apostolorum*, a. 4.

13. Ibid.

In conclusion, Aquinas's references to Isaiah 53 in the *Opuscula* are largely Christological. With the exception of the paraphrase of Isaiah 53:2–3 found in the sermon *Veniet Desideratus,* Aquinas uses Isaiah 53 in the remaining five cases as a biblical text that speaks about the humanity and passion of Christ. His interpretations of Isaiah 53 in the *Opuscula* are thus completely consistent with the interpretations that he offered in his biblical commentaries, *SS,* and the *ST.* In the *Opuscula,* Aquinas reads Isaiah 53 as a testimony to Christ's human generation in the womb of Mary, to the reality of Christ's human nature and bodily death, to the penal yet salvific nature of Christ's suffering and death, and to the exemplary patience that Christ exercised throughout his passion.

Bibliography

In this bibliography I list every primary and secondary source that I have cited in this book. I also list a few among the many texts which may be of interest to those who seek to learn more about Thomistic theology, atonement theory, or the Suffering Servant of Isaiah 53.

THE WORKS OF THOMAS AQUINAS

In this book I located each of Aquinas's references to the text of Isaiah 53 using the following online index of his works: Corpus Thomisticum, "Index Thomisticus," available at corpusthomisticum.org/it/index.age. With the exception of his sermons, all of my references to specific works of Aquinas relied upon the Latin and English editions of those texts that are published by the Aquinas Institute in Lander, Wyoming. These texts are available online at aquinas.cc/.

Aquinas, Thomas. *The Academic Sermons.* Translated by Mark-Robin Hoogland. Washington, D.C.: The Catholic University of America Press, 2010.
———. *Commentary on 1 Corinthians.* 1953 Marietti Latin edition. Translated by Fabian Larcher and Daniel Keating.
———. *Commentary on 2 Corinthians.* 1953 Marietti Latin edition. Translated by Fabian Larcher, revised and edited by the Aquinas Institute.
———. *Commentary on 2 Thessalonians.* 1953 Marietti Latin edition. Translated by Fabian R. Larcher.
———. *Commentary on 2 Timothy.* 1953 Marietti Latin edition. Translated by Fabian R. Larcher.
———. *Commentary on Ephesians.* 1953 Marietti Latin edition. Translated by Matthew L. Lamb.
———. *Commentary on Galatians.* 1953 Marietti Latin edition. Translated by Fabian Larcher.
———. *Commentary on Hebrews.* 1953 Marietti Latin edition. Translated by Fabian R. Larcher.

———. *Commentary on Jeremiah.* 1863 Parma Latin edition. Translated by Ben Martin and the Aquinas Institute.

———. *Commentary on Job.* 1965 Leonine Latin edition. Translated by Brian Becket Mullady and revised by the Aquinas Institute.

———. *Commentary on John.* 1972 Marietti Latin edition. Translated by Fabian Larcher, revised and edited by the Aquinas Institute.

———. *Commentary on the Lamentations of Jeremiah.* 1863 Parma Latin edition. Translated by Mark Foudy and the Aquinas Institute.

———. *Commentary on Matthew.* 1951 Marietti Latin edition, supplemented with Latin texts from the Leonine Commission. Translated by Beth Mortenson and Jeremy Holmes.

———. *Commentary on the Psalms.* 1863 Parma Latin edition (Pss 1–51) and 1980 Busa Latin edition (Pss 52–54). Translated by Albert Marie Surmanski and Maria Veritas Marks.

———. *Commentary on Romans.* 1953 Marietti Latin edition. Translated by Fabian Larcher.

———. *Commentary on the Sentences.*
Book II, d. 21–44. 1858 Parma Latin edition. Translated by the Aquinas Institute.
Book III, d. 1–22. 1947 M. F. Moos Latin edition and Provisional Leonine edition. Translated by the Aquinas Institute.
Book IV, d. 1–13. 1947 M. F. Moos Latin edition and Provisional Leonine edition. Translated by Beth Mortenson. Edited and annotated by Michael Bolin, Jeremy Holmes, and Peter Kwasniewski.

———. *Compendium of Theology.* 1979 Leonine Latin edition. Translation by Cyril Vollert, edited by the Aquinas Institute.

———. *De Articulis Fidei et Ecclesiae Sacramentis.* 1979 Leonine edition, edited by the Aquinas Institute.

———. *De Potentia Dei.* 1953 Marietti Latin edition. Translated by the English Dominican Fathers, revised by the Aquinas Institute.

———. *Expositio in Symbolum Apostolorum.* 1954 Taurini Latin edition. Translation by Joseph B. Collins, edited by the Aquinas Institute.

———. *Literal Commentary on the Prophet Isaiah.* 1974 Latin Leonine edition. Translated by Louis St. Hilaire.

———. *Summa Theologiae.* Leonine Latin edition. Translated by Fabian Larcher, revised and edited by the Aquinas Institute.

OVERVIEWS OF AQUINAS'S LIFE AND THOUGHT

Chenu, M. D., OP. *Toward Understanding of Saint Thomas.* Translated by A. M. Landry, OP and D. Hughes, OP. Chicago: Henry Regnery, 1964.

Davies, Brian. *The Thought of Thomas Aquinas.* Oxford: Oxford University Press, 1992.

Farrell, Walter. *A Companion to the "Summa."* 4 vols. New York: Sheed and Ward, 1945–48.

O'Meara, Thomas Franklin. *Thomas Aquinas: Theologian*. Notre Dame, Ind.: University of Notre Dame Press, 1997.

Porro, Pasquale. *Thomas Aquinas: A Historical and Philosophical Profile*. Translated by Joseph G. Trabbic and Roger W. Nutt. Washington, D.C.: The Catholic University of America Press, 2016.

Stump, Eleonore. "Biblical Commentary and Philosophy." In *The Cambridge Companion to Aquinas*, edited by Norman Kretzmann and Eleonore Stump, 252–68. Cambridge: Cambridge University Press, 1993.

Torrell, Jean-Pierre. *Aquinas' Summa: Background, Structure, and Reception*. Translated by Benedict M. Guevin, OSB. Washington, D.C.: The Catholic University of America Press, 2005.

———. *Saint Thomas Aquinas, vol. 1: The Person and His Work*. Third edition. Translated by Robert Royal and Matthew K. Minerd. Washington, D.C.: The Catholic University of America Press, 2023.

Tugwell, Simon. "Thomas Aquinas: Introduction." In *Albert and Thomas: Selected Writings*, translated and edited by Simon Tugwell, 201–352. New York: Paulist Press, 1988.

Weisheipl, James A. *Friar Thomas D'Aquino: His Life, Thought, and Work*. Garden City, N.Y.: Doubleday, 1974.

FUNDAMENTAL PRINCIPLES OF AQUINAS'S BIBLICAL THEOLOGY

Baglow, Christopher. "Rediscovering St. Thomas Aquinas as Biblical Theologian." *Letter and Spirit* 1 (2005): 137–46.

Dauphinais, Michael, and Roger Nutt, eds. *Thomas Aquinas: Biblical Theologian*. Steubenville, Ohio: Emmaus Academic, 2021.

Johnson, Mark. "Another Look at the Plurality of the Literal Sense." *Medieval Philosophy and Theology* 2 (1992): 117–41.

Levering, Matthew. *Participatory Biblical Exegesis: A Theology of Biblical Interpretation*. Notre Dame, Ind.: University of Notre Dame Press, 2008.

Marshall, Bruce. "Absorbing the Word: Christianity and the Universe of Truths." In *Theology and Dialogue: Essays in Conversation with George Lindbeck*, edited by Bruce Marshall, 69–104. Notre Dame, Ind.: University of Notre Dame Press, 1990.

Martin, Francis. *Sacred Scripture: The Disclosure of the Word*. Naples, Fla.: Sapientia Press of Ave Maria University, 2006.

Martin, Francis, and William Wright IV. *Encountering the Living God in Scripture: Theological and Philosophical Principles for Interpretation*. Grand Rapids, Mich.: Baker Academic, 2019.

Prugl, Thomas. "Thomas Aquinas as Interpreter of Scripture." In *The Theology of Thomas Aquinas*, edited by Rik Van Nieuwenhove and Joseph Wawrykow, 386–415. Notre Dame, Ind.: University of Notre Dame Press, 2005.

Roszak, Piotr. "Revelation and Scripture: Exploring the Scriptural Foundation of *sacra doctrina* in Aquinas." *Angelicum* 93 (2016): 191–218.

Roszak, Piotr, and Jorgen Vijgen, eds. *Reading Sacred Scripture with Thomas Aquinas: Hermeneutical Tools, Theological Questions and New Perspectives.* Turnhout: Brepols, 2015.

Smalley, Beryl. *The Study of the Bible in the Middle Ages.* Notre Dame, Ind.: University of Notre Dame Press, 1989.

Synave, Paul. "La Doctrine de saint Thomas d'Aquin sue le sens littéral des Ecritures." *Revue Biblique* 35, no. 1 (1926): 40–65.

Synave, Paul, and Pierre Benoit. *Prophecy and Inspiration: A Commentary on the "Summa Theologica" II-II, Questions 171–78.* Translated by Avery R. Dulles and Thomas L. Sheridan. New York: Desclee, 1961.

Waldstein, Michael M. "On Scripture in the *Summa Theologiae.*" *Aquinas Review* I (1994): 73–94.

Zarb, M. Seraphinus. "Utrum S. Thomas unitatem an vero pluralitatem sensus litteralis in sacra Scriptura docuerit?" *Divus Thomas* 33 (1930): 337–59.

AQUINAS'S BIBLICAL COMMENTARIES AND INTERPRETATIONS OF SPECIFIC BIBLICAL PASSAGES

Bonino, Serge-Thomas. *Reading the Song of Songs with St. Thomas Aquinas.* Translated by Andrew Levering. Washington, D.C.: The Catholic University of America Press, 2023.

Guggenheim, Antoine. *Jésus-Christ, Grand Prêtre de l'Ancienne et de la Nouvelle Alliance: Étude du commentaire de saint Thomas d'Aquin sur l'Épître aux Hébreux.* Langres: Parole et Silence, 2004.

Levering, Matthew. *Christ's Fulfillment of Torah and Temple: Salvation According to Thomas Aquinas.* Notre Dame, Ind.: University of Notre Dame Press, 2002.

———. *Paul in the "Summa Theologiae."* Washington, D.C.: The Catholic University of America Press, 2014.

Levering, Matthew, and Michael Dauphinais, ed. *Reading John with St. Thomas Aquinas: Theological Exegesis and Speculative Theology.* Washington, D.C.: The Catholic University of America Press, 2005.

———. *Reading Romans with St. Thomas Aquinas.* Washington, D.C.: The Catholic University of America Press, 2012.

Levering, Matthew, Piotr Roszak, and Jorgen Vijgen, eds. *Reading Job with St. Thomas Aquinas.* Washington, D.C.: The Catholic University of America Press, 2020.

Morard, Martin. "Sacerdoce du Christ et sacerdoce des chrétiens dans le Commentaire des Psaumes de saint Thomas d'Aquin." *Revue Thomiste* 99 (1999): 119–42.

O'Reilly, Kevin E. "'The Light of Thy Countenance, O Lord, is signed Upon Us': Psalm 4:7 and the Christological Foundations of the Natural Law." *The Thomist* 86, no. 3 (July 2022): 335–72.

Paretzky, A. "The Influence of Thomas the Exegete on Thomas the Theologian: The Tract on Law (I-II qq. 90–108) as a Test Case." *Angelicum* 71 (1994): 549–77.

Ryan, Thomas F. *Thomas Aquinas as Reader of the Psalms.* Notre Dame, Ind.: University of Notre Dame Press, 2020.

Sirilla, Michael G. *The Ideal Bishop: Aquinas's Commentaries on the Pastoral Epistles.* Washington, D.C.: The Catholic University of America Press, 2017.

Torrell, Jean-Pierre, and Denise Bouthillier. "Quand saint Thomas méditait sur le prophète Isaïe." *Revue Thomiste* 90 (1990): 5–47.

Valkenberg, Wilhelmus G. B. M. *Words of the Living God: Place and Function of Holy Scripture in the Theology of St. Thomas Aquinas.* Leuven: Peeters, 2000.

Weinandy, Thomas G., Daniel A. Keating, and John P. Yocum, eds. *Aquinas on Scripture: An Introduction to His Biblical Commentaries.* London: T&T Clark International, 2005.

AQUINAS'S MORAL THEOLOGY

Austen, Nicholas. *Aquinas on Virtue: A Causal Reading.* Washington, D.C.: Georgetown University Press, 2017.

Berquist, Richard. *From Human Dignity to Natural Law: An Introduction.* Washington, D.C.: The Catholic University of America Press, 2019.

Decosimo, David. *Ethics as a Work of Charity: Thomas Aquinas and Pagan Virtue.* Stanford, Calif.: Stanford University Press, 2019.

Di Noia, J. A. "Not 'Born Bad': The Catholic Truth about Original Sin in a Thomistic Perspective." *The Thomist* 81, no. 3 (July 2017): 345–59.

Gardner, Elinor. "Punishment as Medicine in the Thought of St. Thomas Aquinas." *The Thomist* 87, no. 1 (January 2023): 1–42.

Garrigou-Lagrange, Reginald. *Reality: A Synthesis of Thomistic Thought.* Translated by Patrick Cummins. Jackson, Mich.: Ex Fontibus Co., 2006.

Koritansky, Peter Karl. *Thomas Aquinas and the Philosophy of Punishment.* Washington, D.C.: The Catholic University of America Press, 2012.

Long, Steven A. *The Teleological Grammar of the Moral Act.* Second edition. Ave Maria, Fla.: Sapientia Press, 2015.

McCabe, Herbert. *God and Evil in The Theology of St. Thomas Aquinas.* Edited by Brian Davies. London: Continuum, 2010.

McInerny, Ralph. *Ethica Thomistica: The Moral Philosophy of Thomas Aquinas.* Revised edition. Washington, D.C.: The Catholic University of America Press, 1997.

Stump, Eleonore. "Providence and the Problem of Evil." In *The Oxford Handbook of Aquinas,* edited by Brian Davies and Eleonore Stump, 401–17. Oxford: Oxford University Press, 2012.

Sweeney, Eileen. "Vice and Sin." In *The Ethics of Aquinas,* edited by Stephen J. Pope, 151–68. Washington, D.C.: The Catholic University of America Press, 2002.

Titus, Craig Steven. "Passions in Christ: Spontaneity, Development, and Virtue." *The Thomist* 73 (2009).

AQUINAS ON THE TRINITY, CHRISTOLOGY, AND ATONEMENT

Berger, David. *Thomas Aquinas and the Liturgy.* Translated by Christopher Grosz. Naples, Fla.: Sapientia Press of Ave Maria University, 2005.

Cessario, Romanus. *The Godly Image: Christian Satisfaction in Aquinas.* Washington, D.C.: The Catholic University of America Press, 2020.

Emery, Gilles. *The Trinity: An Introduction to Catholic Doctrine on the Triune God.* Translated by Matthew Levering. Washington, D.C.: The Catholic University of America Press, 2011.

Garrigou-Lagrange, Reginald. *The Love of God and the Cross of Jesus.* 2 vols. Translated by Sister Jeanne Marie. London: Herder, 1948.

Gondreau, Paul. *The Passions of Christ's Soul in the Theology of St. Thomas Aquinas.* Providence, R.I.: Cluny Media, 2018.

Legge, Dominic. *The Trinitarian Christology of St. Thomas Aquinas.* Oxford: Oxford University Press, 2017.

Lim, Joshua. "The Necessity of Beatific Knowledge in Christ's Humanity: A Re-Reading of *Summa Theologiae* III, Q. 9." *The Thomist* 86, no. 4 (October 2022): 515–42.

Mansini, Guy. "Obedience Religious, Christological, and Trinitarian." *Nova et Vetera* (English edition) 12, no. 2 (2014): 395–413.

Margerie, Bertrand de. "Mort sacrificielle du Christ et peine de mort chez Thomas d'Aquin, commentateur de Saint Paul." *Revue Thomiste* 83 (1983): 396–97.

Nieuwenhove, Rik Van Nieuwenhove. "'Bearing the Marks of Christ's Passion': Aquinas' Soteriology." In *The Theology of Thomas Aquinas*, edited by Rik Van Nieuwenhove and Joseph Wawrykow, 277–302. South Bend, Ind.: University of Notre Dame Press, 2010.

———. "St. Thomas Aquinas on Salvation, Making Satisfaction, and Restoration of Friendship with God." *The Thomist* 83, no. 4 (2019): 521–45.

Peterson, Brandon. "Paving the Way? Penalty and Atonement in Thomas Aquinas' Soteriology." *International Journal of Systematic Theology* 15, no. 3 (2013).

———. "Would a Forgiving God Demand Satisfaction? An Examination of Mercy and Atonement." *Angelicum* 93, no. 4 (2016): 875–94.

Spezzano, Daria. "'Be Imitators of God' (Eph 5:1): Aquinas on Charity and Satisfaction." *Nova et Vetera* (English edition) 15 (2017): 615–51.

Stump, Eleonore. *Atonement.* Oxford: Oxford University Press, 2018.

Waldow, Daniel. "Aquinas on the Nature of Christ's Punishment and its Role in His Work of Satisfaction." *New Blackfriars* 103, no. 1103 (January 2022): 7–28.

Wallace, Joel Matthew. "*Inspiravit et voluntatem patiendi pro nobis, inundendo ei caritatem"*: *Charity, the Source of Christ's Action According to Thomas Aquinas.* Siena: Cantagalli, 2013.

White, Thomas Joseph. *The Incarnate Lord: A Thomistic Study in Christology.* Washington, D.C.: The Catholic University of America Press, 2015.

THEORIES OF ATONEMENT

Aulen, Gustaf. *Christus Victor: An Historical Study of the Three Main Types of the Idea of the Atonement.* Translated by A. G. Hebert. Eugene, Ore.: Wipf and Stock, 2003.

Balthasar, Hans Urs von. *Mysterium Paschale.* Translation and introduction by Aidan Nichols. San Francisco, Calif.: Ignatius Press, 2000.

Craig, William Lane. *The Atonement.* Cambridge: Cambridge University Press, 2018.

————. *Atonement and the Death of Christ: An Exegetical, Historical, and Philosophical Exploration.* Waco, Tex.: Baylor University Press, 2020.

Farrow, Douglas. *Theological Negotiations: Proposals in Soteriology and Anthropology.* Grand Rapids, Mich.: Baker Academic, 2018.

Gathercole, Simon. *Defending Substitution: An Essay on Atonement in Paul.* Grand Rapids, Mich.: Baker Academic, 2015.

Jeffery, Steve, Michael Overy, and Andrew Sach, eds. *Pierced for Our Transgressions: Rediscovering the Glory of Penal Substitution.* Wheaton, Ill.: Crossway Books, 2007.

John Paul II, Pope. *A Catechesis on The Creed, Volume Two: Jesus, Son, and Savior.* Translation from *L'Osservatore Romano* (English edition). Boston: Pauline Books and Media, 1996.

Loewe, William. *Lex Crucis: Soteriology and the Stages of Meaning.* Minneapolis, Minn.: Fortress, 2016.

O'Collins, Gerald. *Jesus Our Redeemer.* Oxford: Oxford University Press, 2007.

Rutledge, Fleming. *The Crucifixion: Understanding the Death of Jesus Christ.* Grand Rapids, Mich.: Eerdmans, 2017.

Waldow, Daniel. "From Whom Was Humanity Saved? The Ransom Soteriology of Origen's Commentary on the Epistle to the Romans." *International Journal of Systematic Theology* 21, no. 3 (July 2019): 265–89.

————. "A Love Greater Than Which Cannot Be Imagined: Divine Goodness and Mercy in Anselm's *Cur Deus homo.*" *The Heythrop Journal* 62, no. 4 (July 2021): 703–18.

OLD TESTAMENT THEOLOGY, THE BOOK OF ISAIAH, AND THE SUFFERING SERVANT

Balthasar, Hans Urs von. *The Glory of the Lord: A Theological Aesthetics, vol. 6: Theology: The Old Covenant.* Translated by Brian McNeil and Erasmo Leiva-Merikakis. San Francisco, Calif.: Ignatius Press, 1991.

Bergsma, John, and Brant Pitre. *A Catholic Introduction to the Bible, vol. 1: The Old Testament*. San Francisco, Calif.: Ignatius Press, 2018.

Blenkinsopp, Joseph. *Isaiah*. 3 vols. Anchor Yale Bible 19–19b. New York: Doubleday, 2000–2003.

———. *The Anchor Bible: Isaiah 40–55: A New Translation with Introduction and Commentary*. New York: Doubleday, 2002.

Childs, Brevard S. *Isaiah*. Old Testament Library. Louisville, Ky.: Westminster John Knox Press, 2000.

———. *The Struggle to Understand Isaiah as Christian Scripture*. Grand Rapids, Mich.: Eerdmans, 2004.

Clifford, Richard J. "Second Isaiah." In *The Anchor Bible Dictionary, vol. 3: H–J*, edited by David Noel Freedman. New York: Doubleday, 1992.

Janowski, Bernd, and Peter Stuhlmacher, eds. *The Suffering Servant: Isaiah 53 in Jewish and Christian Sources*, translated by Daniel P. Bailey. Grand Rapids, Mich.: Eerdmans, 2004.

Jerome. *Commentary on Isaiah: Including St. Jerome's Translation of Origen's Homilies 1–9 On Isaiah*. Translation and introduction by Thomas P. Scheck. Mahwah, N.J.: Newman Press, 2015.

McKenzie, John L. *The Anchor Bible: Second Isaiah: Introduction, Translation, and Notes*. Garden City, N.Y.: Doubleday, 1968.

Ramage, Matthew. *Dark Passages of the Bible: Engaging Scripture with Benedict XVI and Thomas Aquinas*. Washington, D.C.: The Catholic University of America Press, 2013.

Shepherd, Charles E. *Theological Interpretation and Isaiah 53: A Critical Comparison of Bernhard Duhm, Brevard Childs, and Alec Motyer*. London: Bloomsbury, 2014.

Stuhlmueller, Carroll. "Deutero-Isaiah and Trito-Isaiah." In *The New Jerome Biblical Commentary*, edited by Raymond E. Brown, Joseph A. Fitzmyer, and Roland E. Murphy, 329–48. Englewood Cliffs, N.J.: Prentice Hall, 1990.

Biblical Index